NOISES AFTER DARK

Ruth

Hope you enjoy
the book

John T

NOISES AFTER DARK

(MEMOIRS OF A DOCTOR IN EAST AFRICA)

JOHN TOMLINSON

Matador
Unit E2 Airfield Business Park,
Harrison Road, Market Harborough,
Leicestershire. LE16 7UL
Tel: 0116 2792299
Email: books@troubador.co.uk
Web: www.troubador.co.uk/matador
Twitter: @matadorbooks

ISBN 978 1803137 070

British Library Cataloguing in Publication Data.
A catalogue record for this book is available from the British Library.

Printed and bound by CPI Group (UK) Ltd, Croydon, CR0 4YY
Typeset in 9.8 Minion Pro by Troubador Publishing Ltd, Leicester, UK

Matador is an imprint of Troubador Publishing Ltd

This book is dedicated to those who volunteer for humanitarian work around the world, and importantly to all the local unsung heroes who, despite many adversities, try to help their communities.

HOW TO LEAVE A REVIEW

Thank you so much for taking the time to read *Noises After Dark* and I hope you enjoyed it. If you have any time and wouldn't mind leaving a review so that more people can find and read my book, that would be greatly appreciated.

You can do this by leaving a review on the following link to the Troubador website (https://bit.ly/3U6DaaG).

In addition you can always leave a review on the website of the organisation from where you purchased the book.

FOREWORD

John Tomlinson's story is extraordinary. It may be one of many stories from the Horn of Africa, yet others are not half as unbelievably dramatic or brave as his.

Things operate on whole other principles, structures and logics in that chaotic part of the world. Whilst John was impelled by the simple human virtue of wanting to help and heal vulnerable humans, in Somalia he found entirely different societies stretched to madness, and he himself caught up in a vortex of competing factions: war, horror, arrest, torture and often hopelessness. But like others of his extraordinary kind he ploughed on bringing succour and hope to those people who were discounted victims of bandits and thugs or just the unforgiving environment of ancient enmities or brutal climate conditions.

It is the story of a survivor trying to help others do the same. How many owe their lives to John and his fellow workers we'll never know, but I have met many of these extraordinary individuals all over the world and one is left embarrassed by how less we are in comparison to them, and just how magnificent others than ourselves can be.

This is the fascinating and gripping story of one such magnificent man.

Bob Geldof

INTRODUCTION

(Please note that this story is based on the author's memoirs and true events. All characters, except for the author, have been anonymised. It is the author's choice to donate the majority of the profits from this book to the Save the Children Fund (SCF) charity.)

Moved by the increased media coverage of the humanitarian crisis in Ethiopia in 1985, I decided to pack my bags and volunteer for the Save the Children Fund (SCF). My post was intended to help rebuild, and run, a small sustainable hospital in a remote part of northern Somalia. The hospital would serve the local and surrounding population, which included refugees, who were largely ethnic Somalis from Ethiopia. However, faced with diminishing supplies, poorly trained staff, and murmurs of civil unrest, the enormity of the task soon became clear.

Recounting both the harrowing and humorous aspects of living in Somalia, *Noises After Dark* depicts the full spectrum of a community in peril. Throughout the book, you will discover the risks and sacrifices that affect volunteers working overseas and discover the unsung heroes and humanity behind the stories. In the context of a country that is increasingly not at peace with itself, this book offers first-hand experience, and emotional understanding, of historical events. The book hopes to pay tribute to the unsung heroes working in conflict zones today.

The story starts, where else, but at the beginning. It takes you with me, a young doctor, to another country and another culture. I need to settle in quickly, and become accepted, despite a very different health system and cultural attitudes.

Initially the situation in Somalia was relatively peaceful, but it was a remote existence. It was a time before the Internet and mobile phones. The only contact with the outside world was through BBC World Service radio broadcasts, visits made by the national SCF officer, and morale-boosting letters from family and friends. These letters were collected approximately every one to two months, as part of a supply trip, from a PO Box in neighbouring Djibouti.

The first half of the book immerses you in some of the difficulties I confronted, including poor women and children's health and the secretive nature of some aspects of Somali society. The latter was largely due to the secret police, which monitored everything.

However, the drums of civil unrest were beating. In the second half of the book I take you into a more dangerous time, and you join me in a war zone with all the ramifications.

Importantly, throughout the book there are always Noises After Dark.

1.

IT STARTED WITH LIVE AID

"Let me through, let me through, I'm a doctor," he shouted. The crowd parted as if Moses had arrived.

It was the 23rd of October 1984. It was late evening. I had finished work earlier than usual, and I was sitting in a bar near the hospital with work colleagues. Outside, we heard a car make a sudden screech, followed by a thud. "Good God. What was that?" asked one of my colleagues. Our table of junior doctors had run out into the street to find a crowd gathered around a motorcyclist. He was slumped across the road. The most senior colleague amongst us volunteered to take charge of the situation.

After quickly checking the motorcyclist, the senior doctor was just about to start resuscitation, but then stopped. "I can feel a faint pulse, and his breathing is back. Call an ambulance!" he ordered. I tapped the senior doctor on the shoulder to attract his attention. "Not now, not now," he declared, while focusing on the pulse and breathing of his latest patient.

A bystander had already called for an ambulance, and after a very short time it arrived. The senior doctor was still focused on the pulse and breathing. He remained kneeling, whilst waiting

1

for the ambulance team to place the motorcyclist onto the trolley. I tapped on his shoulder again. "I've already said not now," he repeated.

The ambulance crew squeezed through the crowd. Scanning the patient's body, they quickly noticed that only one foot was protruding out of the motorcyclist's trousers. One trouser leg seemed hollow. My senior colleague was both mortified that he had missed this and puzzled, as there was no obvious bleeding. I tapped on his shoulder again, but harder this time. He turned, and I handed him a false leg that I had found under the motorbike.

"I think this might be his," I hinted, with a smile. "Perhaps it should go with him in the ambulance."

"The moral of the story is that's why you don't get a slightly inebriated Samaritan cardiologist to sort out a trauma case in the dark!" laughed another colleague. "They never look below the waist."

That night, our senior colleague was the brunt of everyone's jokes, even when we arrived back at the flat. It was when we were preparing a late meal that a flatmate yelled, "Hey, come and see this. Come now, straightaway." He was already sitting in the living room, watching the TV. Holding our plates of food, we all meandered through to see what all the fuss was about.

Our banter stopped immediately.

On the TV, there was a report by Michael Buerk, a BBC reporter. The shocking and tragic scenes of the biblical famine in Ethiopia were like nothing that we had ever seen before. The scenes gripped us all. Slowly, one by one, we sat. As the report continued, we looked down at the food we were holding, knots in our stomachs. This news report certainly placed the Ethiopian crisis centre stage, as it was shared around the world, galvanising public support. On a personal note, the report haunted me for days after. A week later colleagues at work were collecting money for UK charities, including Oxfam and Save the Children Fund. Like many I made a donation, and I carried on with life and my busy job.

On Saturday the 13th of July 1985 at twelve noon (UK time), I sat with my partner, and friends, to watch the Live Aid concert. This was a concert like no other, having been pulled together by Bob Geldof, the Boomtown Rats front man, and Midge Ure, lead vocalist for Ultravox. The concert was beamed live and simultaneously from the Wembley arena in London and the JFK Stadium in New York. More than 75 top artists had agreed to take part, and it became one of the largest live TV broadcasts ever held by satellite link-up. It was beamed across more than 150 countries, and it drew a global audience of around 1.5 billion. The initiative had also inspired concerts to be held in a number of other countries.

The UK show ended around ten at night (UK time) with all performers singing a live version of the Band Aid song 'Do They Know It's Christmas?'. This had been recorded in November 1984, and it had topped the charts for five weeks over the Christmas period. The American concert ended at four in the morning (UK time) with the USA for Africa song 'We Are the World', which had been recorded in January 1985. The concert therefore lasted around 16 hours.

At that time, I was still a junior doctor going through training, but the Live Aid experience had a great influence on me. "I think I should do more than just donate," I proudly declared to everyone present. "Being a doctor, I could actually volunteer and contribute in some way." Without giving it much thought, and being a little jaded after a 16-hour concert, they all nodded in agreement. A medical friend, who was sitting nearby, was deep in thought, ruminating on the issue.

"What about you?" I asked him.

"I don't think there'll be much demand for a urologist in a children's feeding centre," he replied. Point taken I thought.

Over the next few weeks, I gave the issue more attention. A colleague who had worked abroad advised me that I should have a broader medical education to enable me to be more proficient in a third-world setting. I finally concluded that I would be of more use if I finished my post-graduate medical training before volunteering. This decision was fully supported by my partner and friends at the time.

My training was completed in 1986. News reports at that time suggested that almost 160 million people were still being affected by famine in East Africa. I was not completely sure what to do. In the interim, my own life had dramatically changed. My partner had left me, and I was a complete wreck. Was it something about me? Was it my job, and the hours I had to work? Was there someone else? I didn't know. I couldn't sleep, had no appetite, and lost weight. Concerned about the way things were going, my friends reminded me about the pledge that I had made whilst watching the Live Aid concert.

It was something that I really wanted to do. Going somewhere I believed that I could make a contribution would occupy me, as well as being useful to others.

I applied to a number of organisations, and received a very prompt reply from Save the Children Fund (SCF), who invited me for an interview. Ahead of the meeting I was informed that there were two posts on offer. One was in the Sudan, and the other in Somalia. Although I had Ethiopia in mind, I was informed that both countries had large numbers of Ethiopian refugees due to the ongoing crisis in Ethiopia. I'd heard of Sudan, and I knew where it was on the map. I was less sure about Somalia, and I decided to explore further.

In the early to mid-1980s, Somalia was rarely in the news. My world atlas, and other books at home, only had certain sections of Somalia on different pages. I couldn't find any map of the whole of the country. Was this perhaps a reflection of its importance, I wondered?

On my way to the interview, I stayed over with a friend in Cambridge. Whilst there, I decided to visit the University library, supposedly one of the best in the world. Surely this esteemed organisation could help me? Apparently not, as even they were unable to offer a complete map of Somalia. The only claim to fame for the country seemed to be that in 1977 it was the last place in the world to have had a case of smallpox before the disease's eradication. I decided that Sudan might be a safer bet, and I headed to London.

On entering the SCF office to commence my job interview, I was greeted by a senior SCF Officer. He was standing in front of a large map on the wall. It was the continent of Africa, and there was a red circle around the north of Somalia with an arrow pointing to somewhere called Borama. I presumed, before starting the interview, that this was where I would be going. I was correct. Sudan was never mentioned.

The interview was relatively brief. "I can see from your curriculum vitae that you already have some overseas experience," commented the Officer.

5

"Yes. I've worked in both Jamaica and Australia."

"And your time in Jamaica was at the university hospital in Kingston?"

"Err, yes. For 12 months," I replied. "I'd like to point out that since being back in the UK I've tried to get broad experience, and this year I've recently completed my GP royal college exams," I added.

"Yes. You also have obstetric and paediatric experience, which is excellent," said the Officer, whilst nodding approvingly. He seemed more than satisfied.

I was given some information about the post, including that it would be in a hospital, which served the local population and any referred refugees. The SCF officer pointed to the map. He then mentioned a few other issues, including that the project was partly funded through Live Aid. It seemed they were desperate for someone to go to Borama. I agreed to think about it, and I would get back to them within 48 hours. I consulted friends and family. The unanimous view was that I should go where I was most needed, and if that was Somalia, then so be it. Anyway, it would only be for six months.

I accepted the post, and from then things happened fast. This was good for me, as I had no time to change my mind. After seeking advice on what to take, I had my vaccinations against anything and everything, packed my suitcase and I was raring to go. I wasn't absolutely sure what fully lay ahead, but I'd been reassured I would be briefed along the way. The urgency to get me there seemed paramount.

My parents were anxious both about my health, and that they wouldn't be able to see me for many months. But they appreciated that I had finally developed a sense of purpose. They stood proudly in airport departures to see off their son, the doctor. As the Live Aid Charity through SCF was supporting my post and project, their son could rightly describe himself as an SCF or Live Aid doctor. The whole Live Aid programme had such a huge profile, and this resonated with my parents. It was also easy for them to explain to others.

"Take care of yourself," said my father, as he held out his hand to shake mine.

"Remember we love you very much. Come home safely," added my mother, dabbing her eyes with her handkerchief.

I shook my father's hand, and I gave my mother a hug.

"I'll be home before you know it," I reassured them. As I passed through the departure gate, I was feeling quite tense, but I had made my decision, and I needed to see this through. I took a deep breath, and I continued to the departure gate.

2.

JOURNEY TO
THE NORTH OF SOMALIA

My outbound journey took me via Nairobi in Kenya, where the Regional Director briefed me. I then went onto Mogadishu. Here, I was instantly hit by the dense heat and humidity. The Somali officials in the airport all looked like very serious characters. They were standing in a line, dressed in their blue uniforms. Their main concern seemed to be finding the appropriate visa in my passport. There was a thorough examination of my personal suitcase, but once they saw the SCF stickers on the boxes I was waved through.

Waiting outside was Brad, the SCF Director for Somalia. He was a tall, well-built guy with dark brown hair, wearing black thick-rimmed spectacles, a white short-sleeved shirt, and jeans. "Welcome, welcome, hope you had a good journey," he said with a smile. He had a well-spoken voice, almost like a TV newsreader. Amidst the usual conversational pleasantries, I was led to a white vehicle in the car park. We set off for the local SCF office.

There I was, sitting in a Land Rover riding around the streets of Mogadishu, my first taste of Somalia. I rested my elbow on the edge of the open-door window, the breeze wafting over my shoulder. "You'll be staying here for three nights before we head north," explained Brad, in a raised voice. I could just hear him over the roar of the engine, and the wind that was gushing through the window.

In comparison to my brief experience in Nairobi, the streets looked very dirty and more poverty-stricken. Most buildings had corrugated iron sheet roofing and peeling whitewashed walls. We stopped at a lookout point along the coast. Brad invited me to get out of the vehicle. There was a pale sandy beach below. Waves were lapping the coast, and a handful of boys were diving into the blue inviting sea. "The sea looks lovely, doesn't it?" said Brad. "But it's infested with sharks. Along the coast is an abattoir, and sewage goes untreated straight into the sea. Perfect for a shark smorgasbord!" We returned to the Land Rover, and we continued on our journey.

That evening, in the SCF office, Brad gave me a short report to read on Borama, whilst he poured drinks. I read that it was the capital of the Awdal region, sits in a mountainous extension of the Great Rift Valley in North Somalia, and, at an altitude of around 4,500 feet, is close to the Ethiopian border. It had a population of about 60,000, although the exact figure was unknown. Wonderful, I thought. I like mountains and fresh air.

I was to work in a Somali government hospital, and I would lead on the care for women and children. A basic hospital had been in Borama for numerous years. It served the whole of Awdal region, which covers over 21,000 square kilometres (8,200 square miles), making it slightly larger than the country of Wales. The total population was unknown but could be around 400,000. The aim of the project was to make it sustainable so that it could be handed over to the local health service after a few years. It would contribute towards the World Health Organisation (WHO) programme called 'Health for All by the Year 2000'. Perhaps a bigger task than I had expected, but fourteen years gave the project plenty of time.

Brad explained there might be a tendency for the townsfolk to ask me to expand my role in the hospital once in post. However, I was not to be encouraged to run the whole hospital, as a Somali medical counterpart, employed by the government, would look after the male wards. There would also be two SCF nurses working with me. Good, people I can share the work with, and I would not be alone.

I was not to do any home visits, but to offer everything from the hospital. I was not sure about this one, but I presumed there must be a reason. I would also be taking over from another SCF doctor, who has been there helping to start up the project for a few weeks. Great, I get some form of handover, and previous wisdom.

When I had finished, I put the report on the table. "Oh, and by the way, this is probably our most difficult post at this time," said Brad quietly. What? Not so great. More to the point, this fact was not mentioned in either London or Nairobi.

My role had become more complicated with each briefing session, less appealing, and seemingly more difficult.

Brad also explained the rationale for the three-day wait. He wanted us to travel on a more reliable Boeing 707 plane that only flew to the port of Berbera on the northern coast. The other option was an unreliable old Fokker propeller plane that went directly to the town of Hargeisa. Not dying en route sounded good to me.

Three days later, we were at Mogadishu airport. The Somali Airlines Boeing 707 flight to Berbera was the only flight on the departure board. There was no formal queue for the plane, and no seat numbers that could be reserved. So, it was a complete free for all. There was a large crowd of people with their luggage, pushing and shoving, trying to get through the departure gate, and on to the plane.

Once on the plane, we managed to get seats on the right-hand side looking out over the wing. I had the window seat, Brad was in the middle and another European man sat on the aisle seat, quietly reading his book. As the plane started, I saw flames shoot out from the back of the engine outside my window.

"My God!" I shouted, leaping from my seat. I thought this plane was supposed to be the more reliable option. I was ready to get off immediately. I looked at Brad. His face seemed unnerved, but I could see his hands were gripping his seat.

The man in the aisle seat was unruffled. He placed his book down on his lap, and he turned to us. "Stay calm, that happens every time," he said with a German accent. "I thought the same on my first flight. My faith is in that guy over there on the tarmac. He's a Lufthansa engineer, and services all these Somali Airline planes. We won't be going anywhere without his say so."

I sat back down. Clenching the arms of my own seat, I looked back outside the window. There was a wave from the engineer. The plane lurched and moved forwards for take-off. I leaned back in my seat. I looked at Brad who had beads of sweat running down his forehead.

"Are you OK?" I asked.

"Sort of. Well not really," said Brad. "I don't actually like flying. Though travelling around by plane is part of the territory with my work. I sometimes wonder if I'm in the right job."

After landing in Berbera, I looked down the runway on leaving the plane. It was enormous.

"One of the longest in the world," commented Brad. "Apparently, this is one of the emergency landing sites for the NASA Space Shuttle if you can't make it back to the USA. It's right on the Horn of Africa, and really easy to see from outer space. The Americans have an interest here in ensuring it's operational."

An SCF Land Rover was waiting alongside the airport runway. I was introduced to Mahdi the driver, as we waited for the luggage to be unloaded. With no real terminal, all the bags and boxes were placed out in the sun on the hot tarmac for each passenger to identify. Once the luggage was loaded, we promptly left, and sped along the tarmac road.

The road was mostly straight, and the scenery quite barren. Brad explained that we had to drive about 160km (100 miles) uphill to Hargeisa, and then on to Borama. We entered through the Hargeisa city gates about two hours later. I was struck by the sudden transformation from empty roads to bustling streets, which were full of vehicles, and people heading in every direction. Not unlike Mogadishu, the buildings were all single storey with corrugated iron roofing, and their whitewashed exteriors peeling in the strong sunlight. Many had high walls built around their compounds, which made it difficult to see inside. Brad informed me that Hargeisa was the capital of the North, and it was where the vast majority of UN and Non-Governmental Organisations (NGOs) based themselves.

The first task was to go to a police station in Hargeisa. Apparently, my UK driving licence was not acceptable, and I needed to take the Somali driving test. I found this strange, as I was informed that in the UK you could use a Somali licence to obtain a British one. As I'd been given little explanation, I was not sure what the process would involve. A police officer looked at my UK licence, and asked me for a spare passport photo. He took me out the back of the station into a car park. I was asked to read a number plate on a vehicle a few metres away, which I did. That was it, and twenty minutes later, after this complex process, I had a Somali driving licence.

After lunch, we set off on the 120km (75 mile) journey to Borama. It would take about two and a half hours, and it was important to get there before sunset. We left the gates of Hargeisa, and we travelled along a tarmac road. This fizzled out halfway through the journey to be replaced by a rocky, bone-shaking and stomach-churning dirt track. The track intermittently split into a number of paths to avoid flat-topped acacia trees, thorny bushes and large boulders, but always remerged. The Land Rover created a swirling cloud of dust as we sped along. The potholes were both numerous and enormous. You didn't drive over them, but simply went in one side, and at some point came out the other.

On the way we passed small villages, and the occasional military checkpoint. Most people seemed to live in aqals (small, transportable domes made of wooden sticks, and a sort of thatched matted roof). At each checkpoint we had to slow down, but once the soldiers saw the SCF logo they waved us through. After two and a half hours, we reached Borama. I could see that the town was set amongst a series of small hills. One large hill sat like a giant Mexican hat, with houses cascading down the sides. As we entered through the gates into the town, small children, herding their sheep and goats, stared at us as we passed them by.

We arrived shortly after at the SCF compound. Two older men jumped to their feet, and they opened the solid blue iron gates, which were about chest height. A third man continued to sit, whilst trying to light a charcoal fire in an old cut-off oil drum.

We stepped out of the vehicle, and I admired the breath-taking sunset taking place on the imposing mountains in the distance.

"That's Ethiopia," said Brad. "It's less than nine kilometres away, but somewhere you can't go. It's a closed border due to all the troubles between the two countries."

Troubles, I thought, what troubles? Something else no one has told me about.

3.

A TOUR OF BORAMA

The single-storey SCF house was made of grey stone bricks, corrugated iron sheet roofing, and glazed windows, framed with green metal. Covered with red bougainvillea, it looked quite pretty. The large compound had lots of plants and bushes, including orange trees. I was introduced to the three guards. Jama, Malik and One-eyed Hussein. Jama looked very old, and he had a visible cataract in one eye. He wore a traditional koofi hat, plain blue cotton shirt, patterned sarong, and walked with a stick. Malik and Hussein were dressed similarly but without a hat. One-eyed Hussein, as indicated in the name, had one eye on the right, and didn't wear a patch over the empty socket on the left. I said hello and shook their hands.

Before we could say anything more the door of the house burst open, and out came the SCF team. Brad did the honours of introducing Cathy (a midwife) and Gina (a children's nurse). I was given a quick tour of the house. First, we went to the kitchen to meet Deeqa, the cook and cleaner. I noticed she had a serious face with a small scar on the left-hand side near her eye. Her hair was tied up inside her headscarf. She then continued to get dinner ready, and she was obviously anxious to get it prepared on time. The kitchen was cramped but had a gas camping oven, a chopping area, and lots of coloured plastic containers on the shelves.

The house itself was sparsely furnished. Each of the four bedrooms had a metal-framed bed with a mattress and a mosquito net. The main living and dining room had a red Formica dining table, and matching chairs. The table was already set for dinner. There were small wooden stools around the room, with mattresses on the floor acting as low-level sofas. Back in the hallway there was a large filter tank for drinking water and a gas-operated fridge. The shower room had two washing options. There was a bucket on the floor with a mug, or a plastic bucket with holes in, which was hanging from the ceiling.

We went back outside the house. Next to the front door, there was a large metal cover on the floor, which Cathy lifted up to show the underground water tank for the house. Nearby was a bucket on a rope, which needed to be lowered into the tank, in a similar manner to taking water from a well. However, the highlight was a small room, which had a 'sit down' toilet. So far, all the toilets I had used in Somalia had been the 'bend down' version, where you stood on footplates and squatted over a pit latrine. This toilet also sat over a smelly pit latrine, and did not have a conventional toilet seat, but it was still the height of luxury. Apparently, it was fitted for Princess Anne a number of years before when she made a visit. Who would have thought I would be sitting on Princess Anne's throne in the middle of Africa? My parents would be impressed.

Deeqa had prepared dinner, spaghetti bolognese followed by papaya for dessert. Not what I was expecting, but of course there had been a time when much of Somalia was an Italian territory. After dinner I noticed I was the odd one out, as everyone else started to smoke. Brad opened a small bottle of whiskey.

"I thought this was a dry country?" I asked.

"True," said Brad, "but you're allowed to bring in small quantities of alcohol for your own consumption. You're just not allowed to share any with local people, as this would be frowned on." He poured a small amount for everyone.

I put my hand over my glass. "Not for me thanks, I don't touch the stuff." This caused a few raised eyebrows.

"We'll see how long that lasts," said Gina. "You'll find there's not much to do here in your spare time."

It was great chatting to everyone, but I was now exhausted, and really needed to sleep. I asked which room was mine, and I went to bed early. I wasn't used to sleeping under a mosquito net, so initially it felt a little claustrophobic.

I lay there staring at the ceiling. The journey alone had made me realise how remote the town was. It had taken six days to get here from London. Even if you removed extra days for briefing and catching the right plane, it would still take at least three days. I could hear the deafening noise of the crickets chirping outside my bedroom window, and the chatter of the guards, as they sat around their fire. I thought about my family and friends. I was already missing them, and wondered what they were all doing back home.

After a short time, I heard weird loud growling noises. They were seemingly coming from just outside the compound, and getting closer. I got out of bed to peer out of my bedroom window, but it was very dark. The guards were now nestled in their blankets around the fading fire. Surely if they were sleeping the noise couldn't be anything dangerous. I checked that my windows were firmly shut, tucked myself under my blankets, and tried to get to sleep.

I was awoken by a knock on the bedroom door. I looked at my watch. It was already seven in the morning.

"Wakey-wakey, time to get up. We need to take you around the hospital," announced Brad as he walked in. With no time to shower, I went straight to the dining room. On the table there was hard bread and jam for breakfast, with mugs of tea.

"Today we're not working as such, unless there's an emergency, so it's a good day to take you around the sights," said Cathy. She seemed a gentle soul, and was always smiling. She had a pretty face, a small stature of about five feet two inches, and mousy coloured hair in a short pixie style. She was wearing a tie-dyed purple and white dress, with blue plastic flip-flops.

I asked Gina how we were to get to the hospital.

"Well, today we have a lot to do, so probably best we go in the Land Rover. It's about 15 minutes on foot. So close enough to walk if you want, but it depends on the heat really."

Gina seemed to be a more serious character, and perhaps a little anxious in nature. She had a more medium height of about five feet six inches, with a slender build, and shoulder-length straight, black hair. Wearing grey hiking shoes, she always seemed to be walking in a determined fashion to wherever she was going. Both Gina and Cathy had been here for a number of weeks prior to my arrival. From the previous night's conversation, it was obvious that they were both very passionate about, and committed to, their work.

We all bundled into the vehicle, and drove slowly out of the SCF compound, along a dirt track. A small number of people, who were walking along the road, stared at the vehicle as we passed by. We entered through the compound's green metal gates, and we pulled up in front of the hospital. The five ruined, green and white single-storey buildings were in poorer condition than I was expecting.

Brad informed me that there had been a health facility of sorts since the British were in Borama during World War II. SCF had been here before, in 1982, and they left in 1984 with the hospital in a reasonable condition. Following earthquakes and damage from the fighting with Ethiopia, just over two years later, it was even worse than when they started.

Sitting in the sun of the hospital forecourt, like old shipwrecks, were two dust-covered Land Rovers. No wheels, no seats or steering wheel, no lights, nothing. Everything had been stripped for parts. The remaining frames were partly propped up on bricks, leaning to one side on the rocky floor.

We were met by a small handful of people. They looked like a motley crew. A guy called Abdi Aposto seemed to lead the introductions. He was a very short, thin man, probably in his sixties, or even early seventies. He was wearing a trilby-style brown hat. Somewhat unusual, I thought, for the middle of Africa. He had kind eyes, and he spoke very good English. He quickly introduced me to the other staff. One member of the team was very small, less than five feet, and had a badly bent and twisted back. I presumed he had developed scoliosis of the spine when young.

Before I could introduce myself to everyone, Abdi Aposto proudly led a procession around the hospital buildings in the compound. There were two male wards in slight disrepair, and one women and children's ward in greater need of repair. The twenty or so patients in each of the wards were lying on either blankets, or old mattresses, on the floor. There were no curtains, or privacy, between patients. There was also another empty children's ward, which was in complete ruin and in need of a rebuild. On the women's ward, I was introduced to two local nurses, Asha and Saynab.

From here, I was taken to the pharmacy, where there was virtually no medication, and then to a dark and dusty old X-ray room. Inside, there was an ancient looking X-ray machine, which had wires protruding from the rear. We then visited a kitchen with enormous old pots to make porridge, and other food, for the patients. Outside, there was a food store, with no food. Lastly, I was taken to an old operating theatre. At this point, one of the hospital team introduced himself to me as Axmed Theatre. He seemed to wear a constant smile, and he took the lead to show me inside. A layer of dirt indicated that it had obviously been unused for some time.

Abdi Aposto looked at me with a little sadness in his eyes. "Dr John, you can see there is much to do."

"Yes, much to do Abdi, I can see," I said despondently.

"Abdi, where are all the Somali nurses?"

"Mostly gone, Dr John. There's nothing really to keep them here. But we do have a few good people left, like Asha and Saynab."

I could see another compound next door, where the buildings looked in slightly better condition. "What's that over there, Abdi?" I asked.

Another member of the team replied, "That's my Tuberculosis (TB) hospital." He suddenly came to life telling me all about his work. I discovered that the World Health Organisation (WHO) funded the treatment for TB across Somalia, including this facility. The staff were all local, but a team of Finnish staff from

WHO visited every three months or so with supplies. I wondered how well this actually worked in practice.

We walked across and went inside. It wasn't much better than what I had just witnessed in the main hospital. The patients did have mats on the floor, and they were eating, although I later discovered that relatives had supplied the food. At least the pharmacy was well stocked with TB medication.

"What's your name again?" I asked my guide.

"My name is Aaden TB." He turned to his colleague with the twisted spine. "This is my assistant. You are welcome any time, Dr John." I now pondered if his assistant had suffered from TB in his spine when younger.

We went back to the vehicle. I noticed goats wandering all over the hospital compound, eating whatever they found, and feral cats seemed to be everywhere.

I turned to Abdi Aposto. "Do I call you Abdi Aposto or Abdi?" I enquired.

"Abdi is just fine," replied Abdi.

"Well Abdi, thank you. This has been very enlightening. Will I see you here tomorrow?"

"Of course," said Abdi. "This is my hospital. I'm always here." I could tell he meant it. This was his hospital, and this was someone who seemed very genuine.

Where were we to start? The SCF team had been working in this environment awaiting supplies, and an engineer, to help rebuild. I turned to Brad who had been quiet the whole tour. He looked at me. "Remember your brief. We have to renovate, yes, but we have to train up local staff. Ultimately, they can't be totally reliant on us. It's the only way for this place to be sustainable." I nodded politely, but I wondered what I had let myself in for.

21

Next, we set off for Tug Wajali refugee camp, where there was a separate SCF team posted. Following the crisis in Ethiopia, and problems between the Ethiopian and Somali governments, many ethnic Somalis had crossed over the Ethiopian border back into Somalia. This was just one of many refugee camps in the area. The journey to the camp was partly back down the road towards Hargeisa. I was told that the camp had been here for some time and was semi-permanent. The SCF team lived in tents, slept on camp beds, and ate a limited diet from camping tables. They were a very dedicated bunch, but I noticed they didn't seem to smile much. Presumably, the workload had taken its toll.

We had a quick wander into one section of the camp. It was a fairly windswept terrain, with constant swirling dust storms. Most of the refugees were living in tents, but some had the domed aqals, similar to those we had seen earlier in the countryside. However, here, there were none with the traditional thatched matted roof. They were covered with whatever the owner had. This included small sections of tin sheeting, tent tarpaulin, plastic sheets, plastic bags, and even bits of cardboard. My heart went out to these poor people. What must it be like living like this, with no sense of anything better in the immediate or medium-term future?

I noticed a group of dust-covered children, all playing happily. One boy ran nearby. He had a long stick with a nail on the end, which punctured a tin can, creating a sort of wheel. He was racing his creation against his friends. Their world was perhaps different to the adults. No responsibilities, they had been born or brought up here. This place was home to them, and they knew nothing else. The visit had made me feel very lucky to be working, and living, in Borama. Not everyone had a Princess Anne toilet.

I looked at Brad. "Can I ask a question?"

"Sure, fire away."

"You've mentioned troubles at the border yesterday, and today we have a camp which is semi-permanent. Could you explain the background a little more for me, please?"

"Well, it's all a bit complex. Ethiopia and Somalia have a love, but mostly, hate relationship. The Europeans drew up the borderlines with Ethiopia a long time back. This gave a large chunk of land to Ethiopia, which is the main source of conflict. They've been fighting over it, ever since."

"But when was the last time?" I enquired.

"The most recent major event would have been the Ogaden war back in the 1970s. I think it was 1977-78."

"So, what happened?"

"Initially, the Somalis were winning. However, the twist in the story is that the Russians were initially backing both sides, but in the middle of the war they decided to only back Ethiopia."

"Support in what way?" I asked.

"They sent in crack Cuban troops and Russian advisers, and the Somali army had to retreat. Since then, there are intermittent skirmishes along the border, so you need to be careful sometimes."

I thought for a moment. "So, the Russians, are they still around here?"

"Russia has been courting African countries throughout the Cold War, just like the USA. Somalia was first formed in 1960 from the previous Italian and British Somalilands. They both became independent that year, and then merged. The current President has been in power since 1969, following a military coup. Soon after, they became a socialist state with Russian help in 1970."

"Are they still involved?"

"No not here in Somalia, but they still have a heavy presence over the border, supporting the Ethiopian president, Mengistu."

Absorbing all this new information, we walked back to our vehicle to head home. Parked nearby there was another Land Rover, which had arrived from Hargeisa. I was introduced to Donald, the current SCF doctor in Borama, who I was to replace. He was returning from an arranged break. Brad announced he had to return to Mogadishu via Hargeisa. Cathy and Gina were to travel with him, as it was now their turn for a short break in Hargeisa.

"I'll be back soon to see how you're getting on," said Brad. "Meanwhile, I'll leave you in the capable hands of Donald." All three then sped away.

Donald was about five feet seven inches tall, with a broad Glaswegian accent. His dark, wavy hair was dusty and windswept from the journey. He brushed it back with one hand. "Glad to meet you," said Donald. "Let's crack on and get back to Borama before sundown." That evening I noted Deeqa had made spaghetti bolognese, with papaya for dessert. Over dinner Donald talked about the poor facilities, and lack of supplies and staff in the hospital. He was somewhat frustrated by the lack of progress, but accepted he was 'holding the fort' for the next doctor.

Later, I lay in my bed, listening to the crickets outside my window, and the guards chatting around their fire. Tonight, there were no weird growls, which I had discovered were hyenas. Apparently, they would often come into the edges of the town at night, looking for food amongst the rubbish. My head was spinning with the scenes from the refugee camp, and thoughts of how to tackle the enormous problems in the hospital.

4.

IN AT THE DEEP END

The next day, I was more organised. My alarm woke me at seven in the morning. Despite my mosquito net, I noticed a number of mosquito bites on my arms, and one right on the end of my nose. I was first into the shower. The water had been chilled by the night air, and was what you might describe as refreshing. I did my best to shave in the cold water, and then went to the dining room for breakfast.

My bright red nose did not go unnoticed. "Morning Rudolf," quipped Donald. "You'll learn that you have to carefully tuck your mosquito net right under your mattress, and all the way round. If not, the little blighters manage to get in somewhere for their midnight feast."

That morning, in the hospital, there was a small line of patients who were waiting to be seen. Donald suggested that first we should go to see my Somali doctor counterpart, as he was back at work today. Dr Khalif stood in the shade of the veranda, at the front of the hospital. He was outside his office with Abdi by his side. He waved to me, so I walked across. He shook my hand, and he invited me into his office. Inside there was reasonable furniture, including a desk and a chair. In fact, it looked much better than any other room in the hospital.

Dr Khalif seemed very pleasant. About my height (five feet ten inches/1.78 metres), neat hair, well-dressed in shirt and trousers, with polished brown shoes. No dust to be seen. "Would you like to look around the hospital?" he asked.

"I had a quick tour yesterday," I said, "but I would appreciate a second look with yourself." Donald nodded, and agreed to see the line of patients outside the women's ward, whilst I became acquainted with Dr Khalif.

We slowly ambled around the hospital compound, whilst Dr Khalif listed all the things that needed improving. His English was excellent. His expectation seemed to be a total rebuild, urgently reopening the operating theatre, paying salaries for new staff, and all to be funded by SCF. He clearly wanted the hospital to flourish, but these requests were not in line with my briefings or our budget. He then explained that he was from the south of Somalia, close to the Kenyan border. "I've been posted here, and I will do what I can, but the truth is that I'd really like to be posted closer to home." I could understand this, but now wondered how long he would actually be here. At this point, Dr Khalif excused himself, and with Abdi, he set off to the male wards to start work.

I returned to the women's ward, where Donald was sitting waiting for me. "Did he give you his full list?"

"More or less," I replied.

"I need to tell you something," said Donald. "I realise you've only just arrived, but the real reason I wasn't here yesterday is that I had an interview for my next post with UNICEF in Hargeisa. How can I put this? They want me to start like yesterday." He quickly continued. "Before you say anything, you need to know

26

I've already been hanging on here for a few weeks for someone to be appointed full time. Cathy and Gina are very good, and I'm only just down the road, sort of."

I was getting used to surprises. What was I to say? I had expected a handover, but no one had said for how long.

That evening, Deeqa had once more prepared spaghetti bolognese and papaya for dinner.

"Do you eat this every night?" I asked jokingly.

"Actually, yes," replied Donald. "I've had this every night for two months since arriving. It seems to be the only thing on the menu." Donald pulled a small bottle of whisky from a bag. "I can't complain. The way I see the world is that eating is a necessity, but drinking, well that's enjoyable," and with that he poured himself a drink, and offered me one.

"Thanks, but not for me," I replied.

"Well, we'll see how long that lasts. There's not a lot to do around here. I'm pleased to be off to Hargeisa, where there's more of a social life."

That evening, we both sat on the steps outside the house. I looked up at the night sky. "Such a beautiful night. I don't think I've ever seen so many stars."

"True, but instead of a candlelit dinner, and a beautiful woman, I'm stuck with you." Donald laughed and poured himself another whisky.

I couldn't remember how many whiskies Donald had drunk, but the small bottle was virtually empty, and I was sure it had been full when the evening started. I guess it can be lonely with just yourself, and a plate of spaghetti bolognese.

That night, I lay on my bed, listening to my new bedtime music of crickets and the chatter of the guards sitting around their fire. I suddenly remembered. I sat up on the bed, and I tucked my mosquito net tightly under, and all the way around, my mattress. I lay back on the mattress to sleep.

I could hear a faint buzz go past my left ear. In the dark, I patted around the top of my bed to find my torch. I shone the beam around the inside of the net, but couldn't see a mosquito. I lay back and waited. Within a few minutes, there was another faint buzz in the air. This time, I lay very still, and gently switched on the torch. There, on my left arm, was a very large mosquito, settling down like a North Sea oil rig. With my right hand, I slapped really hard, as quick as I could. The mosquito was no more. Importantly, there was no bloodstain, so it hadn't yet bitten. With a sense of satisfaction, I lay back, and went to sleep.

A UNICEF vehicle arrived early the next morning to collect Donald. Even he was not prepared for this sudden departure, and he quickly packed his belongings. He climbed into the vehicle, and he opened the window. "By the way, a bit of advice. One of my mistakes has been doing too many home visits. You get asked to do them all the time, and usually by those who don't need them, or think they're too important to come to the hospital. My advice is to get them to come to the hospital. Good luck, and see you around." He closed the window, and he set off for Hargeisa.

With Cathy and Gina still away, I was by myself. I spent the whole day in the hospital. A line of patients was already waiting. Today, I met one of the interpreters, a local guy called Idris. He seemed very gentle and softly spoken. He had short afro-hair, and a small gap between his two upper front teeth. Dressed in shirt and trousers, he only had old blue plastic flip-flops for shoes. I noticed he had two buttons missing from his shirt. He was good with the patients, very attentive to my every word, and seemed to be explaining everything I said in great detail. Today was mostly a long line of chest infections and diarrhoea. Dr Khalif was not evident, and Abdi seemed very busy sorting out old storerooms.

That evening, after dinner, I went outside to sit with the guards. They seemed a little surprised but welcomed me, and I pulled up another rock for me to sit on. Jama was in full flow, chatting away. His English was not fluent, but he could speak enough for a conversation.

I discovered that he was not sure how old he was, but by his own admission he was old. If I were to believe his likely date of birth, I calculated he would be 106. He told me stories of when he was in the army. In World War Two, he had been in the King's African Rifles Regiment, 71st Battalion, fighting the Japanese in Burma. He described how he had never seen the sea before joining up. However, his first journey was by boat to Ceylon and then India. What he had encountered in Burma had obviously affected him, as he occasionally stopped to compose himself. At the end of his tale, he suddenly stood up, smiled a toothy grin, stamped his foot, and showed me his best military salute. The other guards seemed very amused by his antics.

The night air was beginning to get chilly. Jama was wrapped in an old blanket. He took it off and offered it to me. It was a nice gesture, but I politely declined. I did not want him to be cold. I said goodnight and went to bed. That night, I listened to the crickets, and the guards, who were still laughing at Jama. I decided I had to do something about Deeqa, and her daily menu. I drifted off to sleep.

In the middle of the night, I was awoken by the sounds of whispering and chattering. At first, I thought I was dreaming, or

29

it was the guards. I opened one eye, my vision a little blurred, to see what looked like a ring of men standing around my bed. They were all holding oil lamps. I quickly sat up in bed, and I rubbed my eyes. They began to argue and shout in Somali, waving their lamps at each other, and then me.

"Dr John, Dr John." Seeing Abdi Aposto, I was slightly more relaxed.

"Abdi, what's all this about? What's going on?"

"Everything is OK, but we have a sort of emergency. You must come." Despite this 'sort of emergency', Abdi seemed quite relaxed.

I learned that they wanted me to go to someone's house, but exactly for what, I was not sure. I remembered the mantra from SCF and the advice from Donald. No home visits. "Abdi, can they bring the patient to the hospital? I will be able to examine them much better there," I asked drowsily, still not thinking clearly.

Abdi shrugged his shoulders but he agreed, and explained to the group of men. This made the arguing and shouting worse. One man began to wave his walking stick in the air. Eventually, Abdi managed to file them out of the bedroom, and they set off into the town.

I swiftly dressed, and Abdi, with oil lamp in hand, led me to the hospital. It was difficult walking on the rocky ground in the dark. At one point, we suddenly stopped. Abdi yelled something in Somali, and he swung his lamp from left to right. A voice called back from the blackness. "Everything is OK, we can walk on," instructed Abdi. We then passed a soldier armed with an AK47 assault rifle, who acknowledged Abdi as we walked past. It was a military checkpoint. This was something I hadn't spotted in the day. I was suddenly glad that Abdi was with me.

In the hospital, we went into a pitch-black room. With the oil lamp, I could just see a mattress on the floor, and a plastic chair. A large group of men all holding oil lamps, moments later, brought in an elderly gentleman. He was sweating, coughing, and seemed quite listless.

I was now more awake, and, at this point, I realised I had a dilemma. Was I supposed to be seeing him at all, as he was a man? My SCF remit was to deal with women and children. I had specifically been told not to get involved in the male side of the hospital. Why had Dr Khalif not been called, and if I saw this man, would this offend Dr Khalif?

Abdi looked at me. "We don't have any lights at night, Dr John. The generator doesn't work. What do you want to do?"

I am here now, I thought, and I have to think of the patient first. I can explain my actions in the morning. "Ask him to sit on the chair and open his nightshirt, so I can listen to his chest." Abdi obliged and through him I asked a few questions. Whilst I examined the man, Abdi hovered the lamp over the patient's head. The patient had a slightly raised temperature. He complained of general aches and pains, along with a cough, and a sore throat. I diagnosed a likely viral infection, and asked Abdi to translate this for me.

The old man and the group around him all nodded in a satisfied way and went silent. "This is one of the town elders," explained Abdi. "He heard you had arrived, and specifically asked for you. Although he didn't seem very ill, there was nothing I could do." Abdi searched his pockets, and he brought out a small packet of antibiotic tablets. "I have a small supply of these tucked away, what do you think?"

He wasn't that bad clinically, but he was old, it was after three in the morning, it was dark even with the oil lamps, and it was my first night. I didn't want to miss anything. I agreed he should have the medication, and I asked them to bring him back if he didn't improve. I had struck gold. There were very satisfied faces all around the room.

Abdi insisted he escort me back home. I was feeling tired en route, and attempted to walk on, but Abdi held my arm. "Not yet, Dr John." Once again on our precarious walk, Abdi swung his oil lamp in the dark, but there was no response. "I think he's asleep," murmured Abdi. He swung the lamp a second time, but higher this time to ensure it lit up his face. He said a few words in Somali. The soldier at the checkpoint gave a sleepy reply, and Abdi nudged me to walk on. I was not looking forward to taking this walk alone in the future.

As we entered the SCF compound, it then occurred to me, how did all those people get past the guards? I looked around, and I walked over to where the guards usually sat around their fire. They were nowhere to be seen. Then, I heard snoring coming from the small guardhouse in the corner of the compound. I was reassured to know that they had their ear to the ground, were ever vigilant, and on the case that night.

5.

THE ENGINEER ARRIVES

The line of waiting patients was much longer today. It went down the ward, through the door onto the veranda, and continued down the steps on to the dusty ground of the hospital compound.

Idris looked at me. "The news has got around town from last night," he announced. "They will all want to see the new doctor. Be warned."

Later, I returned to the house for lunch and a rest. I noticed that there was a second SCF Land Rover in the compound. Cathy and Gina had probably returned. There was also a truck loaded with building materials.

Jama walked towards me. "The engineer has arrived," he announced.

A bearded white guy appeared from around the back of the truck. "Hi, my name's Jerry. Where do you want the new latrines built?" he said, looking me straight in the eye.

This wasn't something I was expecting to be involved with when I accepted the job, and certainly not an area of my expertise.

Jerry probably noticed the blank expression on my face. "Only joking," he laughed, "but seriously you will need to help me make a few decisions." He then went to the back of the truck. He stood with hands on hips looking at the contents. Jerry was a muscular man, about five feet nine inches (or 1.75 metres), with brown, wavy hair, and a southern English accent.

"Are you taking all this to the hospital today?" I enquired.

"If we do, there's a chance it may not be there in the morning. Safer to keep it all here for tomorrow."

We strolled into the house, where Cathy and Gina were standing in the hallway.

"First, I have a little present for everyone," announced Jerry. He then flicked the light switches in the hallway, which had not been working before. The lights came on straightaway. He had already mended the old generator in the SCF compound. A huge smile erupted on Gina's face. Jerry reached into his bag and brought out a box. He then plugged something into the socket on the wall, and he placed it into a full bucket of water. "An immersion heater. Who wants the first hot shower tonight?" The look of joy on Cathy and Gina's faces was just fantastic.

He then fitted a new water filter to the water container. "Much better. You can now boil your drinking water and filter it." He was a man on a mission, and went around the compound sorting anything and everything. Later, he devoted the rest of the day to sourcing extra materials for the hospital. He wanted to make an early start the next morning. That evening Cathy and Gina were full of stories from Hargeisa, whilst Jerry eagerly had a second plate of spaghetti.

The following day, I was standing at the front of the hospital. Jerry had been beavering away all morning. The building materials had been delivered to the hospital, guards recruited to protect them overnight, and the ground all marked out for the new ward.

"Today, I really need you to decide where the new latrines are to be built," said Jerry. He was itching to get on with the job. He stood on the hospital veranda, feet tapping, waiting for an answer.

I'd been trying to postpone this decision, as I wasn't sure I had anything to offer. "Well let's take a look around the hospital compound. I'd really like to involve all the local hospital staff, what do you think? They will be using them as well don't forget," I said.

Abdi stood listening. "It's important you have workers who know what they're doing. The last time we had a major latrine dig one of them died."

"Died?" I said, a little shocked. "I hadn't realised it could be so dangerous. How did it happen?"

"The new latrine was dug too close to the old one, which was full. The rock between the two collapsed onto the man digging, and he drowned," added Abdi.

Good God, I thought, what a way to go.

"Heard that one before," responded Jerry authoritatively. He then laughed. "But I'm a man of experience, when it comes to digging myself out of a hole."

He sent his entire workforce to start digging out the hole for the foundations of the new ward, and then looked at Abdi. "While the doctor makes his mind up, can we take a look at the hospital generator?" This created a huge smile on Abdi's face, and they both disappeared into the bowels of the generator room. A few minutes later, Jerry reappeared covered in thick black grease, but with a grin. As an engineer, he had clearly been enjoying himself. "It's old, but I can probably get it going, although I will need to get my hands on a few spare parts." Wiping his fingers on an old rag, he returned to the depths of the generator room, where you could hear more clanging.

Later that day, I had a request from Abdi to meet him at the hospital entrance, and bring a torch with me.

"Everything is OK. Follow me, Dr John," requested Abdi.

"Where are we going Abdi?"

"You'll see, soon enough."

We walked to the old latrines, where Jerry was waiting outside. Abdi opened the door, and he ushered me inside. The smell was overpowering.

"Shine your torch down there," ordered Abdi.

I approached the two well-trodden footplates, leaned over, and pointed the beam of light into the darkness below. I could see cockroaches scurrying around to escape from the light.

"What do you see, Dr John?"

"I see cockroaches, Abdi."

"Yes, yes, but what else?"

I looked more closely. "I think I can see that the pit is nearly full. Are they all like this?"

"Yes, and some are worse. So, Dr John, when are we going to build the new latrines?"

"Exactly! So, when are we going to build the new latrines, Dr John?" mimicked Jerry.

Obviously, after their distraction this morning investigating the generator, they were back on track. I realised that I had prevaricated long enough on the topic. "Honestly, I don't know where it's best to put them, I keep saying that. In view of what happened last time, with the labourer who died, I want this to be a team decision, not mine alone. Jerry, why can't you suggest what you think is the best option, your guys are going to do all the work?"

"OK, but it's not so simple. Due to the accident last time, I'm finding it difficult to get the labourers to do the digging," said

Jerry. "In my opinion, I'd suggest that they go next to the old latrines, all around the hospital compound. They're already in the best place, and we can add a few extra onto each. But one thing," he paused, "we will leave at least double the usual thickness of wall between the new and old ones."

Leaving the cubicle, I noticed a bowl of stones in the corner, which puzzled me. "What are these for?" I asked innocently.

"Not everyone uses water to wash," murmured Abdi. "Sometimes, we don't have enough water. Water is precious."

"So, what are you trying to tell me, Abdi?"

"Do I really have to go into that level of detail?" remarked Abdi. "Some people use stones to wipe themselves."

"No wonder they've filled up so quickly," exclaimed Jerry. "They're probably half full of stones." He stood, pondering. "In view of the urgency, I'll try to make a start this week. The problem is that as you dig down it's almost solid rock, and we have to make these quite deep."

"Now who's making excuses?" I said.

"OK, OK. Abdi, I will need your help to find the right people for this job. There is one more thing. You need to think through who will be the latrine monitor. We have to get most people using water, otherwise we will be digging again very soon." With that Jerry shook hands with Abdi and the deal was done.

A short time passed, and I was walking through the hospital grounds, about to go home.

"Dr John, Dr John, everything is OK, but I think you need to come to the delivery room." It was Abdi, waving at me to follow him.

"What's the problem Abdi?"

"It's OK. It's OK but we need your help," replied Abdi.

A woman had just delivered a baby. The mother looked exhausted, and the baby was very small for a full-term baby. Cathy and Saynab stood looking anxiously at the mother.

"This is her fourth baby in three years," said Cathy. "She isn't bleeding, but I think she's just extremely anaemic." Indeed, she was, and later that day, despite our best efforts, the mother died.

That night was a solemn affair. I sat at the dining table, reflecting on the day. Choosing sites for latrines was not something I had anticipated when taking the job, and losing my first woman in pregnancy so soon was not easy. Cathy did not come to eat dinner, so I went to find her. She was sitting subdued on the side of her bed. She looked worn out, and she had clearly been crying. This was unusual for Cathy, who was normally the first to have a smile.

"You haven't eaten with us tonight, is there anything I can do?" I softly enquired.

"It's difficult, so difficult, when you look after someone for hours. Then, when you think they're OK, you lose them. You lose them to something so simple as anaemia."

She was right and I was not sure what I could say. "Cathy, you do need to eat—" But before I could finish, Cathy interrupted, "This is the fourth woman I've lost to anaemia in my short time here. What's the point when you can't stop them dying?" she wept.

This was news to me. I held her hand to comfort her. Gina had told me earlier that Cathy had not eaten all day. "Let's talk about it over dinner. If you don't eat, you won't be well enough to look after anyone."

Cathy finally stood up from her bed, and wearily walked to the dining room. I sat opposite. "We've saved you some chicken in white wine sauce, assorted vegetables, and croquet potatoes."

"Just as if," said Cathy, raising a slight smile and wiping the tears from her cheeks. She then tucked into her cold spaghetti bolognese, followed by papaya.

6.

EVERYTHING IS OK

Jerry was off prospecting for more building materials. Gina and Cathy had already left for work, and they had taken the Land Rover. I set off to the hospital on foot in the early morning sunlight. En-route I seemed to attract more and more excited children. I was surrounded by so many that it was like a scene from the 'Pied Piper of Hamlin'. They all wanted to hold my hand, and found my blond hairs fascinating, as they gently stroked my forearms. At the hospital entrance, they said their goodbyes in Somali and ran away into the distance, shouting excitedly.

Abdi Aposto was waiting on the veranda.

"Hi Abdi, how is everything today?"

"Everything is OK. They are OK," said Abdi. "But, Dr John, I think Gina and Asha want to see you immediately."

I could see a huge line of women and children waiting.

Gina already looked tired. "Thank God, you're here. I don't think we can cope with the numbers today."

Between us we worked our way through the line. Idris was the only interpreter, which made this difficult.

"How many interpreters do we normally have?" I asked.

"Usually one each, but some of them are more reliable than others," replied Gina.

"In what way?"

"It's difficult to explain," she muttered.

"Just spell it out," I insisted.

Gina looked across at Idris and Asha. "Well, it's mostly Ali Interpreter. He's not great at turning up on time, or sometimes even at all. Today being one example."

I decided not to pursue this sensitive conversation in front of Idris, but to explore it further back at the house.

It was quite a warm day. Despite the heat, there was a long line of sick people, sat outside in the open sun on the dusty floor, patiently waiting their turn. Occasionally, a better-dressed person would arrive, and walk straight to the front of the queue. Other patients didn't complain, and Idris gave the impression this was acceptable by inviting them in. This was a dilemma for me. It didn't feel right that I should allow this. I decided to leave Gina and walk down the line with Abdi. I briefly asked patients why they were here, and I generally looked them over to see how ill they appeared.

Halfway down the line was a woman with clothes that were very dusty, old, and faded. She wore a black headscarf and smelled of burnt wood or charcoal. On her back, she had a very large scarf wrapped around what I presumed was her child. I reached for the top of the scarf, and gently peeled it back to expose the child's head. At first, I thought the child was sleeping. I placed my hand on its forehead. It felt very cold and clammy. With my fingers, I gently raised one eyelid. The eye appeared completely glazed over. I could smell something quite unpleasant, almost like rotting flesh. The child was obviously very unwell. I asked Abdi

41

to explain to the mother that her child was very sick, and needed urgent attention. We whisked mother and child onto the ward.

The child was placed on a mattress on the floor. Once the scarf was removed, the full horror was exposed. It was a boy of about three years old. He was clearly unconscious, and in a state of shock. Under his left armpit was a hot swollen lump. It was an abscess the size of a very large orange. It was covered in what looked like a mixture of dried mud, and shredded plant leaves. It was oozing pus, which was the source of the smell.

"What's this?" I asked Abdi, while peeling off some of the mud.

"It's a form of traditional medicine," declared Abdi. "It's something people make to put on infections, and sometimes they might even add goat dung. It's very popular amongst nomads."

A well-dressed woman then walked past the whole line of patients and entered the ward, insisting on being seen by the doctor. She had glanced at the sick boy on the mattress, but she was not prepared to wait.

"Abdi, please explain to this lady that I am extremely busy with this very sick child. Ask her to join the line," I said.

"This woman is a relative of one of the town elders, and wants to be seen now," replied Abdi.

I had tried to remain calm, but under the circumstances she seemed totally unreasonable. I glared at the woman, and in a raised voice said, "Abdi, tell her this child is going to die if I do not treat him now, this second. If it was her child, what would she want me to do?" Without waiting for an answer, I turned back to the unconscious boy. Abdi spoke in a much calmer and gentler voice than me. The woman still seemed unhappy, but she walked away, and sat expectantly on a nearby stool.

42

We had none of the usual supplies that would be available in a western hospital. With Gina's help, we rapidly put up intravenous fluids and, from Gina's bag of limited supplies, injected some antibiotics. Asha looked on.

"What is the boy's name, Abdi?"

"Axmed," answered the mother, who was now in tears.

I now had to open the abscess. Nearby, an older woman had lit a small charcoal fire on the ward in a burner. She was about to cook food for her daughter. Abdi and Asha arranged for some instruments to be boiled in an old hospital saucepan over the fire. With freshly boiled instruments, I gently opened the large lump in the child's armpit. The stench was pretty grim, as copious amounts of pus poured out of it. Inside, the flesh was rotten. I carefully cleaned out the wound. At the bottom of what was now a large cavity, I could see all the large nerves and blood vessels deep inside the armpit. I prayed that none of the vessels ruptured.

My next instruction caused a few raised eyebrows. "Can we get some fresh ripe papaya from the market, as soon as possible?" Gina, Asha, and Abdi looked at me in surprise. "I'm going to show you 'Dr John's Traditional Medicine'. But it's much better than mud, herbs, and goat dung. I promise." They still looked at me. "Just do it, trust me."

Hearing the conversation, another patient on the ward pulled out a papaya from her bag, and willingly handed it over to Asha. I showed the team how to mash up the flesh of the papaya, pack it into the wound, and cover it with a dressing. They all stood observing me in amazement. "You just need to wash it out with salt water and repeat this every day until it heals." The team nodded in mystified agreement. "If it wasn't for the white doctor telling you to do this, you would have laughed, and ignored me.

43

But this is something I learned whilst working in a hospital in Jamaica. It does work. In fact, I have never seen it fail. It cleans out the wound, and helps it heal," I proclaimed with great confidence.

After a few minutes, the small boy lay in bed with one arm attached to a drip. The other had a large bandage dressing wrapped around his shoulder and armpit. The dressing looked a little big, but I didn't want any chance of the papaya oozing out.

That evening Gina and I went back to the hospital after dinner to check on Little Axmed and ensure he had been given all his injections. He was still unconscious, but his temperature was coming down. On returning to the house, I went to bed early. With Little Axmed improving, I could go to sleep peacefully. I secretly hoped that this was not going to be the first time the papaya dressing failed me.

The next day, we went straight to the women and children's ward, where Asha was already waiting. Little Axmed's mother was holding him on her lap. His sleepy eyes were open, and he turned his head very slightly in our direction, as we walked towards him. His mother's previously worried expression was now replaced by a faint smile. She said something in Somali.

"What did she say, Idris?" I asked.

"She says it's a miracle, thank you so much."

I turned to Gina and Asha. "Make sure you clean the wound out every day, any worries give me a shout."

At that moment, a feral cat appeared, ran across the ward floor, and jumped onto the mattress. It scowled, picked up some food from a bowl near Little Axmed's mother, and ran out. What a night for the family, and now the poor mum had lost her breakfast. A patient on the next mattress leaned over, and kindly offered to share the small amount of the food that she had. Having had to deal with the unreasonable patient who was queue-jumping the day before, this act of kindness helped to restore my faith in humanity.

Out of the corner of my eye, I noticed that a white female goat had walked onto the ward and proceeded to open its bowels all over the floor. I joined the other staff and as a group we shooed the goat back outside. Hospital ward rounds at home were never like this.

That night, I was awoken by a knock on my bedroom door. I opened one eye. There stood Abdi with his oil lamp. "Dr John, everything is OK, but tonight we need you."

"What is it, Abdi, what's the problem?"

"It's OK, it's OK, but the baby won't come out. We need you and Cathy."

I looked at the clock. It was 3am. I roused Cathy, and we set off to the hospital in the Land Rover with our bag full of equipment.

On arrival, we were led to the birthing room. It was dark, and we had one oil lamp. Lying on a mattress was a woman in labour, clearly in distress. An older woman was attending her.

"Who's this?" I asked Cathy.

"This is Khadiija, she's one of the local Traditional Birth Attendants, or what we call TBA for short."

We discovered that this was the patient's first baby. She had been in labour for many hours. Khadiija was not happy with the progress, and thought the mother needed help to deliver safely. Therefore, she had brought the woman to the hospital.

Cathy examined the mother's abdomen, and she listened to the baby's heartbeat. The baby was OK and not stressed. However, the mother clearly was. We agreed to use a ventouse suction pump (a suction cap you apply to the baby's head) to help ease the baby out. Cathy invited me to do the honours.

When I examined the patient myself, I was a little confused since I couldn't see how to get the pump attached. I thought it was just the light. There seemed to be only a very small opening to the vagina. "It's because of her female circumcision," said Cathy. I was shocked. This was something I had only heard about. I had no detailed knowledge of female circumcision, or female genital mutilation as some called it. I'd certainly been given no warning about this from a clinical point of view. I asked for the lamp to go closer, as I had never seen a woman who'd had a female circumcision before.

Whilst I was dithering and wondering what to do, I was pushed out of the way by Khadiija, who reached for the patient. She squeezed two fingers in the small opening, and she pushed them under what appeared to be an extra film of skin that was tightly stretched across the baby's head. Before I could say or ask anything further, and without warning to the patient, she made a big cut upwards in the skin, using a large pair of scissors. The woman let out an ear-piercing scream, and violently arched her back away from the mattress.

I looked on, still quite shocked. Khadiija gestured for me to get on with whatever I needed to do next. Now, I could clearly see the baby's head, and more easily attach the ventouse pump. Within a very short time, I had delivered a healthy, screaming baby boy.

"Better you than me," said Cathy, cleaning the equipment. My first Somali delivery had certainly been a baptism of fire, and an experience that I will never forget.

7.

GASTRONOMIC DELIGHTS

Today, I decided to explore the local market. Would I find anything different for the team, and perhaps encourage Deeqa to try a new menu? The scents of spices were in the distant air, so many different ones that I couldn't distinguish between them. I passed through the old, whitewashed archway, and into the main market square.

Dozens of people were passing backwards and forwards in every direction, talking and shouting. I noticed all the sacks and boxes, each coloured the same dull brown. These were mirrored by brown hessian sacks draped as canopies across upright sticks. Under each one sat a market trader in the shade.

I walked down the first aisle, peering into each container. Once opened, they revealed their individual scents and colours. There was cardamom, cloves, cinnamon, ginger, raw dark sugar, tea, coffee, and many more. In fact, there were so many scents that it was making me feel giddy in the heat of the sun.

I noticed that most market traders were women. They sat patiently in their brightly coloured dresses and headscarves, waiting for the next customer. In the corner of the square, I spotted a teashop under another hessian sack. Here it was all men. They were all wearing their traditional koofi hats. These were similar to that worn by Jama, almost like a fez but with no tassel, of varying colours, and heavily embroidered.

As I walked around, I passed into another section that included pots, pans, and thermos tea flasks. Nearby was a man with a very old black and gold Singer sewing machine. His foot was pedalling up and down under the table, as he stitched a garment. He sat beneath exotic and very beautiful materials that were draped all around him.

Surprisingly, there was a man selling what looked like French baguettes. I was so excited I didn't even ask the price. I handed over a clutch of Somali Shilling notes, and I asked for three baguettes. I was handed four baguettes in a white paper bag. I decided it was best not to try and explain that I only wanted three, and just accepted them.

The next section had meat; all freshly killed that morning. Some portions still had the animals tail attached. The meat had attracted a thick cloud of flies. One man was busily waving his fly swatter, which appeared to be made from a camel's tail.

My nose was then assaulted with a different aroma, something not easily defined among all the chaos. Ah yes, I was approaching the livestock area with donkeys, goats, camels, and their dung on the floor. I decided it was best to head back the other way.

I looked at my watch. Time had passed by quickly, and I should be returning home. I wiped the beads of sweat from my brow, and proudly clutching my French baguettes, I headed back towards the archway.

As I was leaving, I noticed a man with a donkey. On the back of his donkey were four old cooking oil drums, which had been cleaned and filled with water. He slowly made his way around the market. For a small fee, he refilled the flasks of the market traders, who must have been parched in the heat.

Idris was waiting for me at the archway.

"Where did you get the bread?"

"From the bread man in the corner. Why?" I enquired.

"Oh nothing, but just make sure you eat it soon. It goes stale very quickly, and it needs lots of jam."

"I will, I will. But it's a great surprise for everyone else, don't you think; who would have thought French baguettes?"

"Of course," said Idris with a quietly suspicious smile.

Back at the house, I warmed the baguettes in the gas oven, and placed them on the dining table for the team. With the rest of the team having been here for a few weeks, I couldn't believe that they hadn't already discovered the French baguette man. I carefully cut the bread into sections and sliced them open. The bread had an almost 'granary' like appearance. I eagerly smeared on some tinned ghee. This was followed by an ample spoonful of jam, which had recently been brought back from a French supermarket in Djibouti.

I noticed the rest of the team seemed less interested in my recent purchase, and had started reaching for other things to eat.

"Good?" enquired Cathy, nodding at my baguette.

"Not only good, it's pretty tasty with almost a nutty flavour," I replied.

As they were leaving the room, Gina looked at Cathy. "Shall I tell him, or will you?"

"Maybe not today," replied Cathy, "better he enjoys himself in his first week."

Not really listening, I merrily munched on through my

baguette, oblivious to their comments. I have no idea what those two are on, I thought to myself, complaining about the food all the time.

Many days and many French baguettes later, I was sitting at the dining table, munching through a particularly crunchy baguette. It seemed more crunchy than usual. I decided to take the partly eaten bread out of my mouth to inspect it more closely. I had to come to terms with the fact that the texture of the bread was not due to some granary style recipe, but weevils, extremely large weevils. The nutty taste, I later discovered, was caused by their excretions in the flour.

This was all part of my learning curve. From that day on I developed an acute taste and smell for weevils, and I could detect them in any loaf from ten metres.

That evening, Deeqa prepared spaghetti bolognese with papaya for dinner. My big secret was that I had borrowed a cook from Hargeisa, who would start work tomorrow. She had two days to transform Deeqa, and her weekly menu.

The following day, my intention was to introduce the new cook. However, after a busy night in the hospital, I awoke late but was still exhausted. I had a shower and walked down the corridor to the dining room. I could see Deeqa standing in the kitchen. Her hands were on her hips, and her face was like thunder as she glared at the new cook. They seemed to be arguing about today's shopping list. I was just about to intervene, when I heard Abdi at the door. I was urgently needed at the hospital.

That evening, I returned to the SCF house, and I eagerly went to the kitchen to see what we had for dinner. I found a small stack of smashed dinner plates in the corner. There was a note from the Hargeisa cook: 'Sorry, there was a slight disagreement this evening. There's a salad in the fridge'. Perhaps I needed to do something?

The following evening, a newly trained Deeqa prepared meat, which was perhaps a little chewy, with gravy and rice. This was followed by fruit salad for dinner. A world first. Whilst taking the dirty plates into the kitchen, I saw a note written by the cook from Hargeisa addressed to me. It read: 'I think it will take longer than two days!'

The Hargeisa cook eventually stayed well over a week. Although there were still occasional bouts of shouting, and banging of pans in the kitchen, she was beginning to have an impact. It was slower than expected, but there was definitely an impact. The menus were now more varied, but only time would tell.

The evening after the Hargeisa cook departed, a happier Deeqa greeted us. She was once again 'flying solo'. At my request, she had prepared a fruit crumble, as a surprise for the team. A little crunchy and burnt around the edges, but I didn't want to suppress her enthusiasm.

8.

AN EMERGENCY TRANSFER

I was leaving the women's ward, when I noticed that the SCF Land Rover was returning from the town with Gina and Asha.

"Been somewhere exciting?" I asked, as the vehicle came to a standstill.

"Just doing a home visit again," stated Gina sharply.

"A home visit again, I've been told we shouldn't do home visits?"

"Well, I think you learn a lot. You see the patient in their home environment, for example," insisted Gina confidently.

I didn't want to have this conversation right now. "Can we leave this for tonight, when we're back in the house?" I requested. As we turned the corner, it was noticeable that the line of patients had grown significantly in Gina and Asha's absence. It seemed I was going to be forced into what might be a difficult conversation regarding home visits.

That evening, I waited for everyone to sit down for dinner. "Before we start, can we discuss a few issues?" I asked, as politely as possible. "Home visits and also self-important people jumping the queue in the hospital. I think we need to agree a way forward."

Cathy sat timidly looking down at the surface of the table. Gina was straight in. "Well, I've already shared my view on home visits," she said briskly. "As for jumping the queues, I agree it's difficult. What do you suggest?"

I looked at Cathy, waiting for her to speak, but she remained silent. "Cathy, do you have a view before I talk?"

Cathy looked at us both. "Not sure, I can see both sides on this. I will go along with whatever is decided." I could sense this was perhaps already a sore point from before my arrival.

Jerry was reading a book at the end of the table. He looked up blankly. "Clinical decision, mate, leave me out of this one. But be my guest, just keep digging your hole."

I didn't want to create any upset in the team, but this had to be sorted. "My suggestion is that whatever we agree tonight we all need to adhere to it. Otherwise, we will all be played off against each other."

Everyone nodded.

"OK, let's start with the easy one. Jumping the queue. For me it's a big no, no. But the best option could be that we have someone reviewing the patients in the line and picking out anyone who is more urgent." I paused, seeking agreement from the team. "Think of Little Axmed recently, he could have died in the queue, whilst his mum meekly waited her turn. In comparison, the lady in the smart dress, who was not seriously ill with painful periods, would have been seen first." Both Gina and Cathy finally nodded in agreement.

"Excellent. Home visits next," I said cautiously. "More difficult, I sense." Cathy continued to look at the surface of the table. Gina stared into the air, looking bored already. "All my briefings have been very clear on this. They were also the departing words of advice from Donald. I don't understand all the issues. However, in my short time here it does seem that some members of the community will abuse home visits, as they do with the queue outside the ward."

Suddenly, Cathy looked up. "Can I just interject?" She paused and took a deep breath. "I can truly see both sides on this, but we could spend all day doing home visits in the Land Rover. We would see very few people in comparison to the hospital, where we are extremely busy. There, I've said it."

Gina still looked disinterested. "I can see I'm outgunned. I'll do my best," she replied. "But I still think there will be the odd occasion when we need to do them."

"That's settled then, kisses all round," said Jerry. "Can we finally eat? I'm starving."

The following day, I was just about to return to the ward to see Cathy and Gina, when all the interpreters arrived. Even Ali had turned up on time today. They invited me to the hospital teashop. It sat a few hundred metres away from the hospital compound and halfway to the area used for buying and selling livestock.

The teashop was a large aqal, which was only partially covered for a little shade. In one corner sat the owner next to a charcoal fire. On this was a large pan from which you could hear the tea constantly bubbling. On the other side of the aqal was a ring of stones, each one a seat for customers. We sat, and within seconds the owner had rinsed glasses in another pan of hot water. He poured out milky tea for everyone. The owner looked about fifty years of age. His face was weathered from the sun. He gave us a smile, which revealed slightly yellow teeth, as he passed us the glasses. The tea was very sweet and tasted of cardamom.

"Can we have a confidential word with you?" asked Ali Interpreter in a hushed voice. This was unusual for Ali. He normally talked quite demonstratively with arms waving, as if on stage playing to an audience.

"Well, I'm listening. What's this about?" I said.

Ali looked at the others, as if asking for permission to continue. He then glanced at me. "Are any of you travelling to Hargiesa soon?" he asked nervously.

"Not that I'm aware of," I replied. "Why?"

"We don't want to alarm you, but a military checkpoint was attacked last night."

I wasn't sure what to say in reply, and I stared enquiringly at Ali.

"If you do travel to Hargeisa, we must be with you," insisted Ali.

Ali's eyes looked around the aqal, as two other Somali men entered. They were well-dressed in western-style patterned shirts, and they were wearing sunglasses. Ali immediately stopped his conversation with me. He said something in Somali to the two strangers, which made them laugh. Ali then looked at me, and he nodded to the exit. We all stood crouched inside the aqal, shook the owner's hand, and went towards the exit with a stooped walk.

Outside, there were two more relatively well-dressed men wearing sunglasses. Again, they had western-style brightly patterned shirts and clean, uncreased trousers. As we walked away, I looked back.

Ali grabbed my hand, encouraging me to walk on. "Please don't stare," he insisted.

I obeyed and instantly looked away.

"NSS, secret police," he whispered. "Just monitoring us."

"Why us?" I asked.

"Well, more likely you. They're always suspicious of foreigners. Just a warning, Dr John, but they don't like outsiders understanding what is being said in Somali. They don't even like us visiting you at your house for any length of time."

I looked at Ali. "Can I ask about the military checkpoint?"

"Not now. There's nothing more to say, other than I think we will see a lot more of these guys in future."

Later that day, there was a surprise visit from Brad. His excuse was to see the progress with the building works, but he seemed quite serious, and asked all of us to finish early for a team meeting at the house. That evening he had news that was to completely alter our lives in Somalia.

"In the last few nights," announced Brad with a very serious tone to his voice, "there have been assassinations in Hargeisa." He paused, looked at us all, and poured himself a whisky. "I'm not sure how many were killed, but they were all government officials, including a senior person in the NSS. The response to this is that Hargeisa is crawling with military and secret police. There is also a curfew dusk until dawn."

"Will that affect here?" enquired Cathy.

"The NSS is the National Security Service or secret police. The KGB trained them, when Somalia was aligned with Russia. It's one of the few things in this place that's well funded and actually works. Will it affect here? Not sure. It's a different clan here, and they're considered neutral in all this. My prediction is that you will be safe. However, getting to Hargeisa will be far more difficult."

Gina looked more worried. "In what way?"

"Well, the number of military checkpoints will increase. I counted around fourteen on the way here. Also, you won't be able to transport patients to Hargeisa after 3pm, for example. Think about the journey time, any later than this, and you will be arriving too late. If you approach the city near dusk, your vehicles may get shot at. It's too risky."

There was a palpable silence in the room.

"Another thing," he added, "you can't set off in the morning before the military."

"Can you please explain why not?" I asked.

"Every morning at sunrise, the army will send a jeep out first to ensure the route to Hargeisa is safe. No one will be allowed to leave Borama before this."

The situation sounded serious, but we hoped things would settle down. That night, I sat on the steps of the house looking at the stars. Gina came outside. "Can I join you?" She sat and lit a cigarette. "I know you don't smoke, sorry, but this has started me off again." There was a faint tremble to her voice. "This was my third attempt to stop smoking since I've been here. This job is not exactly helping me to give up."

The next day, Brad returned to Hargeisa. Jerry was busy designing his new earthquake-proof buildings, repairing other buildings, and anything else in sight that needed fixing. Being as busy as possible was perhaps his way of dealing with the news. Gina, Cathy, and I dealt with the never-ceasing flow of patients.

Later in the day, a nomad arrived at the hospital with his pregnant wife carried on the back of a camel. She claimed to have been in labour for many hours and for even more than a day. It was her first pregnancy. After examination and observing her for a short time, Cathy and I concluded she was in obstructed labour, and it was unlikely the baby would be born by a normal delivery. She needed a caesarean section. With no way of performing this in Borama, we had to get her to Hargeisa Hospital. Fortunately, the baby did not seem too distressed at this point.

It was 2.30pm. The fastest drive we could make with a pregnant woman would take us at least two to two and half hours, and it would be very uncomfortable for her. Importantly, the gates of Hargeisa would close at 5pm. If we left immediately, it would still be cutting it very fine. However, our decision was made for us as the Land Rover and Gina were missing. We were then informed by one of the interpreters that Gina was on a home visit. Cathy and I decided we would have to look after the woman all night, and hope for the best. First thing in the morning, we would try to get her to Hargeisa.

At 4.00pm Gina returned, and alongside her was Ali Interpreter. Seeing me waiting with Cathy on the hospital veranda, she stepped out of the vehicle and lit a cigarette. Ali crept slowly out of the other door. I launched myself down the hospital steps. Enough was enough.

"What's the problem?" remarked Gina, whilst taking another puff on her cigarette. She looked at Ali, who, despite the seriousness of the situation, had his usual cheeky smile.

"I'm told you've been on a home visit," I said sternly. "The problem, if true, is you said that you wouldn't do them anymore."

Unfazed by my anger, Gina calmly carried on smoking. "Not quite true. I said I would try not to, and there may still be—"

Before she could finish her sentence, I interrupted. "Not only that, but we also desperately needed the vehicle to transport a pregnant woman in obstructed labour." By now, my raised voice was close to shouting.

Gina looked at the floor, and she stubbed out her cigarette. "I'm sorry, really sorry, what else can I say?"

"That this won't ever happen again would be good," I requested, in a calmer voice.

"OK, OK, this will definitely never happen again." This time she looked as though she meant it.

Cathy, Saynab, and I had all taken turns looking after the pregnant woman, through the night. At dawn, we had the Land Rover ready with our fastest driver, Mahdi. Although a risk he might not turn up on time, I had decided to take Ali Interpreter. The previous evening, I had given him a 'pep talk' about his timekeeping at work. He was early today and already sitting by my side. He looked somewhat 'glassy-eyed', his hair uncombed, and his shirt was only partly tucked into his trousers. He'd obviously had some difficulty getting out of bed at this time, but he had actually made it.

"Ready, Dr John," said Ali Interpreter. He then explained to the patient, who was lying in the back of the vehicle, that we were about to leave. The army jeep set off at great speed. We waited a few minutes and quickly followed. Time was finite, and we prayed there'd be no problems on the way.

After a while, we arrived at the first of many military checkpoints. There were no guards waiting. As we drove by, a yawning soldier appeared from his hut, brushing his teeth. He looked a little surprised, as we pelted past. Ali just waved out of the window. He was wearing his customary cheeky smile, and he pointed to the SCF logo on the doors, whilst shouting 'We have an emergency'.

59

The army jeep was beginning to pull away, and it was only just in sight. Ali Interpreter shouted in Somali to Mahdi Driver.

"What's the problem?" I shouted, over the roar of the engine.

"We need to keep up with the army jeep and take the same tracks. We don't want to risk any land mines," responded Ali Interpreter. Land mines. No one had mentioned land mines before we set off. But now nothing completely surprised me anymore. I slapped Madhi Driver on the back, and I urged him to drive faster. The poor patient grimaced, as her contractions set off again.

We were waved through all the other checkpoints, except the last one. Here, we were brought to a complete stop. Two soldiers circled the vehicle. They spoke in Somali to Mahdi Driver.

"What's happening?" I asked.

"They're expecting a bribe," declared Ali Interpreter.

"A bribe, can't they see we have a sick patient here?"

"That is exactly why they think you'll pay."

"No bribes, Ali. Absolutely not!" I was furious. "If we pay today, they'll stop us every time. This is simply not on."

"They don't get paid much, and sometimes not at all. This is how they raise money. Bribes, or you give them something off your truck."

"No, no, no." I insisted. "Tell them this woman and baby might die. Just say she is the relative of an important person in Borama. That should help."

Ali obliged, but only spoke a few words, which did not seem to have any influence.

"OK, ask them what they would do if this was their relative, or even their wife? Can you please explain that in full this time?" Ali interpreted for me again, and this time seemed to use a few more words. The two soldiers eventually shrugged their shoulders, and reluctantly waved us through.

The army jeep had now disappeared. Madhi Driver continued, whilst carefully looking for the freshest tyre tracks. Luckily, within fifteen minutes we were on the tarmac road, which led down to Hargeisa.

Our hectic journey had lasted just over two hours, when we arrived at the entrance of Hargeisa Hospital. The patient was handed over to a team of Chinese surgeons who rushed her to theatre. Within forty minutes, we were told that both mother and baby girl were fine.

"After all that, and now you're happy," announced Ali Interpreter loudly.

"I've done my job. No sorry, we've done our job, and earned our money today," I smiled.

"So, is this a good time to ask for a pay rise?" asked Ali, with his mischievous grin.

"That is not under my control, as you know. You'll have to ask the main office in Hargeisa. Please give a huge thank you to Mahdi Driver for me. Where is he by the way?"

"Oh, he has relatives here, and has gone to visit them, whilst you were in the hospital."

Ali Interpreter did not have a driving licence, so this meant I had to drive. "OK Ali, show me the way to the SCF office."

After our successful morning we were in high spirits, chatting and laughing as we drove along. A policeman suddenly stepped out into the road, and he waved me down. My first instinct was to look at my speedometer. I was driving very slowly. I wound down my window.

The policeman circled the vehicle, looking it up and down. He then said something in Somali.

"What's he asking?"

"He wants to see your driving licence," declared Ali.

"Oh no, I don't have it on me. It's in Borama."

Ali translated this, or at least I thought that's what he had translated, but the conversation was going on for some time.

"What do we do now, Ali? What's he saying?"

"He's waiting for a bribe. In fact, that's probably why he stopped you in the first place."

"A bribe, no bribes, Ali."

"I know what you think about bribes, but under the circumstance today, I think—"

I interrupted. "No bribes. Otherwise, we'll be paying bribes everywhere and anytime I come to Hargeisa in the future."

Ali obliged and translated. The policeman opened a door, got into the back seat, and said something forcefully in Somali.

"Ali, what's happening?"

"We have to drive to the police station immediately."

"Why?"

"Please, Dr John, no whys, no questions. This could get worse," appealed Ali.

9.

HARGEISA HOSPITALS

Following instructions, I drove slowly to the police compound. I parked outside the building, which looked in poor condition. We were waved inside, and then asked to stand in one corner. The interior appeared quite clean, and there was the smell of fresh paint in the air. The colour was very similar to the blue on the Somali flag. The station was not busy, and there was no one else from the public inside.

The policeman, who had arrested me, went over and had a short conversation with his colleague at the front desk. They both looked in my direction. Their conversation continued, and there seemed to be some disagreement. Eventually, the officer behind the desk waved for me to approach, and I was led through a gate. After passing through it, the gate was slammed shut, preventing Ali from following.

I turned to Ali. "So, what happens now?"

"Not sure, I'll be back," and with that Ali raced out of the station.

Without Ali, I was feeling quite alone, as I was taken down a short corridor. The police officer was looking nervous, as he stopped outside a police cell. He fumbled with his keys, and he tried a few in the lock. None seemed to fit. He looked at me, and then waved me to follow him. We walked through a door, and into what looked like an office. There was a desk and two chairs. The officer pointed for me to sit in one of the chairs. He then left, and I heard him lock the office door.

What now? I thought. My stubbornness regarding bribes was perhaps going to cost me dear. I looked around the room. There was the ever-present picture of the President, Siad Barre, and a picture of the Somali flag. Otherwise, the blue walls were bare. At this point, I didn't feel anxious. My view was that if I had broken the law, surely being new to the country, they would let me off. Perhaps the worst that could happen is that I would have to accept three points on my licence and pay a fine. But paying a bribe. No bribe.

Two hours passed by. No one had come to the office, and I had heard no activity in the corridor outside the door. Eventually, I heard the door being unlocked, and in a flurry, three Somali men entered. One was the officer who had been behind the desk, the second appeared to be a higher-ranking police officer, and the third was wearing a United Nations High Commission for Refugees (UNHCR) badge.

The man wearing the UNHCR badge spoke first in English. "Hello, I work as a pharmacist for UNHCR. You are Dr John, yes?"

"Yes, that's correct."

"This is the Chief of Police, and I will act as your interpreter."

"OK, that's very kind," I replied politely.

They all had a heated conversation in Somali. The Chief did not appear to be happy. The UNHCR pharmacist then continued in English. "The Chief says it is an offence, whilst driving, to have no driving licence on your person. This applies to everyone, whether Somali or foreign. The penalty is four days in prison." I suddenly realised the gravity of the situation. I was in Somalia, no three points, or a fine. Perhaps the bribe was a better option. I had to think of something in my defence and quick.

"Can I say something?" I pleaded. They stopped their conversation, and turned to look at me. "Today I had an emergency in Borama, I needed to save the life of a very sick pregnant woman and her child. The only way was to bring her to Hargeisa Hospital. In my hurry to get here, I forgot my licence. Can you translate please?"

The pharmacist turned to the Chief, but before he could say anything the Chief spoke in English. "No need. I understand."

"Then may I continue?" I asked. The Chief nodded.

"If this was your wife, or relative, would you want me to get her here as soon as possible, or waste valuable time looking for my licence?" I stopped to see his reaction. The Chief's face was unaltered. Unlike the military checkpoint, my plan did not seem to work this time.

Their conversation continued in Somali, before the Chief spoke again in English. "I think you should go, before I change my mind."

"Thank you, thank you," I said. "This will not happen again." I offered to shake his hand.

The Chief's face was still unmoved, and he did not offer his hand to shake. "I repeat, just go, I'm a busy man."

The pharmacist grabbed my hand, quickly dragging me out of the office and into the car park. Ali Interpreter and Mahdi Driver were both waiting in the Land Rover. We all clambered into the vehicle and hastily left the police compound.

"You owe me one, Dr John," laughed Ali Interpreter. His usual cheeky smile had returned. "By the way, the pharmacist here is my cousin. He has police contacts, sometimes useful."

I stayed in Hargeisa for two days. It was very productive and interesting. I visited the hospital again with Ali to see my patient and her baby. Both were looking very well, considering what they had been through. We were given a tour around the building, and we met a group of Germans, who were providing equipment for the hospital. I jokingly asked if they had any spare or old things that I could have. To my surprise, I was offered hospital beds and mattresses, enough for all our wards at Borama.

We then met the Chinese surgical team. They didn't speak any English, and neither did their Somali interpreter, who had been taught Mandarin in China. We had a protracted conversation, where Ali spoke to their interpreter and back again. With all the repeated translation, it became quite a confused conversation. However, the surgical team appeared very organised, and, by the end of our conversation, they seemed to have agreed that I could send any appropriate referrals directly to them in future.

"Just a moment," said Ali, looking perplexed. "Is it not a long way to send the patients to China?"

"I think they mean referrals here, to Hargeisa, not China," I clarified.

"Well, we will find out when we make the first referral," said Ali with a grin. "Can I test the system? If I'm lucky, I might get a trip to China!"

The hospital had basic operating theatres, beds on all wards, and a decent supply of medicines in the pharmacy. The lab however was very sparsely equipped, and it had few reagents. I asked where the mental health wards were. Ali explained they were in a different hospital, a short distance away, and he agreed to take me there.

The mental health hospital was not just in a different place, but also in a different universe. The buildings were in a terrible state, even worse than in Borama. Inside, it was like stepping back in time. Patients were aimlessly wandering around, bumping into each other, while talking to themselves in their own little worlds.

I entered another ward, which resembled a medieval prison and where every patient was chained to the wall. I looked at the first patient inside. He was in a shocking state, lying in his own urine and faeces. The smell of stale urine was overpowering. He had chronic sores on his limbs from the chains. His hair had not been washed, combed, or cut for a very long time. He stared blankly into the distance, rocking from side to side and occasionally banging his head on the wall.

The next patient was dressed in very torn clothes, and he was shouting loudly. His eyes glared at anyone passing by. He was continuously yanking his chains in a desperate attempt to free himself. His wrists were so sore they were bleeding.

As we slowly walked around, there were many similar cases. These were truly upsetting scenes. I didn't want to see much more. "Ali, I'm just a little shocked, I've never seen anything quite like this before."

"There are no medicines for these poor people. Their families, if they have any, cannot look after them. So, they are chained for their safety, and the safety of others."

"What about the nurses, Ali? There has hardly been any staff whilst we've been walking around."

"With the poor salaries, it's difficult to get nurses to work

67

anywhere in the government hospitals. The job here is so much more difficult, so they just don't want to work here. There is virtually no staff. However, there are a few untrained volunteers." We walked slowly back to the vehicle. I could still hear the patients' yells echoing around the courtyard. A truly sobering experience, but not one I could do anything about.

My time in Hargeisa had been somewhat mixed. But, on the positive side, we had saved the pregnant woman and her baby, and now had beds for Borama. Also, my time with Ali had allowed me to get to know him better. Although a bit of a lovable rogue at times, he had got me out of deep trouble when I needed it most. I just wondered what the expected payback would be?

10.

FIRE IN THE TOWN

I had been away two days. When I returned to Borama, we had two new members of the team. A giant tortoise had made itself resident in our SCF compound, and a feral cat had adopted our house. The cat had been found sleeping across our doorway each night.

I was informed that Abdi Aposto had encouraged absent nursing staff to return to work at the hospital, and Dr Khalif had been more prominent around the hospital. Jerry had also repaired the hospital generator, along with the main leak in the roof of the women's ward. In the absence of permanently employed qualified nurses, Gina and Cathy had developed a plan to improve the number of nursing staff. Their proposal was to take on local volunteers, and to train them up. The best candidates would be rewarded with a guaranteed place at Hargeisa Nursing School. The proposal seemed really good and quite feasible. The task left for me was to go along with Brad to meet the town elders, and to discuss the way forward for the hospital. With all this progress, I decided I should go away more often.

The bad news was that Jerry had injured his knee. This was a bitter blow. Jerry was shipped off back to Hargeisa, where he would travel to Nairobi, or even the UK, for treatment. However, during his absence, he had organised local workers to continue with the foundations and building of the new ward.

Following a very busy night in the hospital, I sat for a moment on the steps of the hospital veranda.

"Morning," said Abdi. "Everything is OK. Dr Khalif would like to see you."

Of course, I thought, where was he when needed last night? It always seemed to be the case that I was called out, but not Dr Khalif.

I walked wearily round to his office. Dr Khalif was all smiles. "I hear you did a great job last night."

"Hopefully, but only time will tell," I replied. Was this the time to ask where he was last night? In reality, I was too tired to be bothered.

"I'd like you to do a ward round with me this morning," requested Dr Khalif.

Either he couldn't read my body language or didn't particularly care. This was the last thing I wanted to do. Although I was tired, it was difficult to refuse, so I agreed.

Dr Khalif took one of my hands, and he held it whilst walking around the male wards. I had noticed how some men in Somalia did this with a friend. Although for me it initially felt a little strange, I took this as a positive gesture. On completing the ward round, Dr Khalif stopped and released my hand. "I have something I want to share with you."

"And what is that?"

"I received news yesterday that I am to be posted south, so I will be nearer my family."

"This is great news for you," I replied, but wondered when this would take place.

"Thank you, yes. I will be leaving in two days."

"Oh, so soon. Will you be replaced?"

"Yes, but I'm not sure when. Abdi will keep you informed. I have been very impressed since you have been here. I'm not sure you really need a Somali counterpart."

I was not entirely sure what to think, but this sounded ominous. Dr Khalif had been very easy to work with. For example, I had not been asked by him to be involved with the male wards. However, he was not very evident out of hours, and Abdi always seemed to approach us for any real emergency. I was not to see Dr Khalif again, as he left the very next day. We would have to wait for his replacement and start over again.

Finishing her lunch later that day, Gina stared across the table. "We're not too busy today. What about visiting our neighbours?" I had still not been to sleep. But I was expecting to walk across the road to a nearby house, and so I agreed. Instead, I was led to the Land Rover, and without much discussion we set off.

The countryside was quite scenic with acacia trees, cacti, and children herding goats. We passed giant termite nests, and we crossed a number of dry riverbeds.

"Where are we actually going?" I asked.

"We're going to see our nearest ex-pat neighbours, Nathan and Charlotte. They're French Canadians, and work in a nearby refugee camp called Dare Mann. It's about thirty minutes or so." I sat back, continued to admire the scenery, and briefly fell asleep.

Dare Mann was also a camp for refugees from Ethiopia, but it was a world apart from Tug Wajali. It was set in a series of valleys and was quite green in parts. There were large vegetable patches and fruit trees, and water appeared to be more plentiful. We pulled up outside two small traditional whitewashed circular mud houses. Nathan and Charlotte were sitting in the shade outside. They were clearly pleased to have guests. After introductions, we sat down for Somali tea, and were then taken on a tour of the camp.

Nearby, two men sat continually pulling the levers of an Oxfam water pump, which was in place to serve the gardens. Nathan explained that part of their role in the camp was to encourage farming and self-sufficiency for food. Looking at the greenery, I could see that they were clearly making an impact.

During the tour, I was introduced to the Somali camp doctor, who was extremely happy to guide us around the facilities. He appeared very proud of his work. He explained that the camp was now permanent, and like Tug Wajali, it was overseen by the Refugee Health Unit (RHU). The RHU was part of the Somali Ministry of Health and funded by UNHCR. RHU staff received relatively good pay, and he had a full complement of nursing staff. They used guidelines and treatment formularies for most common illnesses, and they had plenty of medical supplies. I now realised why so many Somali doctors and nurses were employed by the RHU. Although good for the RHU, this was draining staff away from working in government hospitals. The guidelines and formularies allowed mostly nursing staff to care for patients. This made me think. If they were good enough for the refugees, then why not use them in Borama Hospital.

Full of renewed enthusiasm from the camp, we returned to the house. I could hear Brad's voice. He had arrived whilst we were out and was waiting in the living room. I had forgotten that today we had a meeting with the town elders, and we had to prepare. This was my first official meeting with them. As he always seemed to translate more comprehensively, I decided to take Idris as our interpreter.

The meeting was held in a local government building in the town. We walked down a corridor. At the end we could see a door slightly ajar, and we could hear loud chattering coming from inside the room. We walked through the doorway. The room fell completely silent, as a group of men, mostly aged sixty plus, watched us take the seats being offered.

The elders then sat chattering again in a semicircle facing us. One elder stood up, and he started speaking in Somali. Idris looked a little nervous but began to translate.

"This is Hussein. He is one of the senior elders. He says thank you for coming to meet everyone, and that SCF are welcome here today."

"Tell him thank you, and we are glad to be here," responded Brad.

"They are interested to hear the plans of SCF for the hospital," continued Idris.

Brad then talked in detail about how previous projects had not completely worked out as expected. He suggested that whatever SCF did it had to be sustainable, and the work needed to be a partnership with the town. He mentioned the mantra from London regarding the training of local staff, and that the hospital should not be totally reliant on SCF, if it was to be sustainable. He also took the opportunity to remind the town that they would need to provide water, food, and fuel for the hospital as part of the partnership.

After a long translation by Idris, there was an initial

unnerving silence in the room. The elders looked at each other, and then started chattering excitedly again. There seemed to be some disagreement. Hussein started his reply. "So SCF are not going to pay higher wages or provide more ex-pat nurses? They are not going to provide fuel, water, and food?" Idris paused his translation and looked pensive. "He asks if there is to be any payment to the elders for allowing you to be here in our hospital?"

I could see where this was heading. Although Brad was leading the conversation, I couldn't stop myself speaking. "Idris, are they seriously expecting SCF to fund everything, and even offer bribes to the elders?"

"That would appear to be the case, Dr John."

Brad sat forward in his chair visibly irritated, and asked Idris to translate. "If the elders remember, when we last met, we talked about SCF repairing buildings, perhaps building some new sections to the hospital, paying for medicines, and training local staff. The aim is for the town to ultimately run the hospital itself in the future. The town does need to take over the hospital at some point. Meanwhile, a contribution by the town of providing water, food for patients, and fuel for the generator, once repaired, is vital." Idris delivered this message in a very calm and measured tone.

Hussein once again consulted his elders on either side. "Perhaps SCF are not doing all the things we want. For example, you didn't mention opening the operating theatre. Perhaps we should get another organisation, who will do all these things, to replace you."

I was not prepared for this, and I had not expected the meeting to take this direction. The warm reception from the hospital staff and local townspeople was obviously not reflected in the elders. Brad started to shuffle in his seat. "Tell Hussein and the elders that SCF are very keen to be here in Borama, I think he will find it difficult to attract another organisation to work here." He paused and then continued. "I am disappointed. These issues were all agreed with you, the last time we had a meeting."

The elders went into another huddle. Hussein spoke again. "We will allow you to run the hospital for now. But we will have to keep this under review." With that he ended the meeting, and he gave an expectant wave towards the door for us to leave.

Brad dejectedly ambled out. "We really need Jerry back. We have to give them something they can actually see as progress."

At home, we sat talking to Brad about the best way forward. Gina and Cathy went first, and they shared their volunteer nurse proposal. Brad sat listening intently.

"Brad, can I add that we've had too many deaths of women in pregnancy, or shortly after delivery. They are often so anaemic that only an urgent blood transfusion would save them," said Cathy. Brad looked at each of us, and he appeared surprised.

I decided to suggest a possible solution. "We need a very basic laboratory, with simple blood tests, TB smears, and malaria checks. To achieve what Cathy describes, we would also need to be able to cross-match blood and offer transfusions." This was almost certainly more high-tech than Brad was expecting. "However, I think re-opening the operating theatre is too expensive. Even if we did, in terms of being sustainable, they will never get a surgeon to work out here, anyway. They struggle to get any doctor to stay here." I peered at Brad, who now seemed more receptive. "It's better just to ship the patients down the road to Hargeisa. The Elders obviously won't like this, but it's for the best."

"The transfusion idea, I guess, is OK. The WHO has been

doing random HIV testing on blood samples in Mogadishu, and has found no cases as yet. Perhaps that is one of the few benefits of this government closing off their borders to neighbouring countries," declared Brad.

"So, what do you think?" I quizzed.

"All great ideas," said Brad, while pouring himself another whisky. "I suggest you put your list together, and I'll consider it all tomorrow."

After dinner, Brad sat nursing his bottle of whisky. For a short time, I sat on the steps of the house with Gina and Cathy. Our newly acquired cat nestled between us, purring. Gina lit a cigarette and passed one to Cathy. "All this stress isn't doing me any good, I've started smoking more."

"I'm allowing myself just one per week," added Cathy, looking pleased.

"You've managed to cut down, but your veggie diet didn't last long," commented Gina, gazing knowingly at Cathy.

"You're vegetarian?" I asked, a little puzzled.

"Well, it's too difficult here, so I've sort of given up," replied Cathy despondently.

I went to bed. I had been so busy recently it was the first time that I had thought of home for days. I wondered how my family and friends were all doing. As for me, I certainly didn't have much time to dwell on my woes anymore. Life here was very busy, but it was starting to be therapeutic. As I drifted off to sleep, I pondered whether Deeqa could stretch to a lentil bake for Cathy?

That night, as I was lying in bed, I could hear loud voices outside. I leapt from my bed, and I looked through my bedroom window. Coming through the gates was an excited group of four to five people, all carrying oil lamps. Abdi was at the helm. I went to meet them at the front door. "Dr John, everything is OK, but we have a problem. There has been a house fire and many casualties."

Not knowing quite what to expect, I woke Gina and Cathy, and we boarded the Land Rover. This time Jama was awake and already at the gate. He gave a military salute as we left.

Entering the hospital compound, we could see the night skyline glowing in the distance from the fire in the town. Abdi warned us that the fire had involved at least one family, including the parents, and an unknown number of children.

It was not long before the first casualties arrived. You could smell smoke, as two adults were brought in with their clothes still smouldering. As we were removing their clothing, another group arrived with the first child. The group was shouting and wailing, while a group of older women were loudly ululating. This was always a sign that things were serious.

I left Gina and Cathy to care for the parents, and I tried to force my way through the second crowd. Abdi shouted very loudly in Somali, and a gap opened for me to approach. The child lay unconscious. She looked about two years old, and she seemed to be burnt on every surface. I could see that any exposed skin was blistered, peeling, or slightly charred. In places, it revealed the deeper tissues underneath. As we tried to remove the last piece of clothing, she took one final deep breath and died before me. I didn't have time to take all this in, as another crowd arrived, carrying more children.

It seemed half of the town's people were now crammed inside the hospital ward, all desperately trying to assist. I was conscious that their attentions were not really contributing, and the many unwashed hands were likely to make things worse.

"What can I do to help, Dr John?" shouted Abdi, above the constant commotion.

"We need more space Abdi, more space. I know everyone has the best intention, but it would be better to get them outside quickly."

Within seconds Abdi was in action, and I could see we had two more injured children. Both were boys, one aged about three and the other around five. Their limbs had burns, but they were more superficial. Meanwhile, the parents seemed to be starting to recover from their smoke inhalation. They had severe burns to their arms from trying to save the children.

Of course, unlike a western hospital, we had no oxygen, no sterile dressings, and few instruments to help deal with all this. We had to improvise as quickly as possible with what we had. Wounds were cleaned with salt water, painted with purple gentian violet, and covered with gauze daubed with petroleum jelly. We had an active night with a rota for trying to prevent the distressed children from pulling off their dressings. Ultimately, all these patients went home, burns healed, and with minimal scarring. It was amazing what we achieved with the resources available.

Over the next few weeks, our project really progressed. Within two weeks, Jerry had returned, bounding around full of energy on his fully recovered 'bionic knee'. His injury had not been as serious as first thought. The building work was in full flow.

Our beds and mattresses had arrived from Hargeisa. We also obtained copies of the RHU/UNHCR guidelines and formularies. Gina and Cathy were doing a sterling job adopting these for the hospital. Our own medical supplies from the UK had been ordered, delivered, and temporarily stored in the SCF house for safekeeping. The operating theatre was cleaned, whitewashed, and the steriliser repaired. This would allow us to perform very minor procedures. We had even 'sweet-talked' the Finnish TB team into repairing the X-ray machine and providing a small supply of X-ray films.

An American trainer of lab technicians, based in Hargeisa, was involved in advising on requirements for a laboratory in Borama Hospital, should we get the funding. Also, the design of a lab was now on the 'Jerry to do list'. Because of the curfew in Hargeisa there was now a role reversal, where Hargeisa staff started to visit Borama for their days off. Gina and Cathy had also recruited the volunteer nurses, ranging in age from sixteen to early twenties. This was possibly one of the most exciting aspects of our work, as without nursing staff the hospital would not survive. The big question was would they respond to the training, and importantly, would they stay in Borama?

In a world before the Internet and smartphones, our only contact with the outside world was by handwritten letter and listening to the BBC World Service at night. I decided it was time to put pen to paper and construct my first letter home. We had to take any opportunity of a staff supply trip to Djibouti. All our mail came in and out of a PO box there, and a truck was to set off tomorrow.

11.

THE MAN WITH THE KEYS AND
THE MAN WITH NO LEGS

Following his departure, there was no sign of Dr Khalif's replacement. I now found myself also running the male wards. However, although small in number, the male nurses were a delight to work with, and they seemed clinically very able. Indeed, they appeared more knowledgeable than Dr Khalif. They embraced our new hospital guidelines, based on those from the RHU. Through these, they were managing the majority of the patients who presented to the male clinics. Our volunteer nurses were very keen. However, they needed many months of training before they could be let loose on the local population.

Jerry was well on track with his building and other repairs. He was having some frustration with overnight pilfering of certain materials, despite paying for night guards. Each morning, the new guards claimed to have seen nothing suspicious. This resulted in the guards ultimately being replaced. However, this did not rectify things. Eventually, Jerry had to revert to all the materials being returned to the SCF compound at night, and each day taking small amounts to the hospital as required.

I strolled with Abdi to the pharmacy, where we had placed some of the new pharmacy supplies. It was locked.

"The man with the keys has just gone," said Abdi.

"Where's he gone?" I asked, looking around at everyone.

The staff sitting outside shrugged their shoulders.

"Nobody knows," said Abdi.

"Which man is it?"

"I asked Abas to be responsible for the pharmacy," declared Abdi.

"Why Abas?"

"Well, I've tried to share out responsibilities for different parts of the hospital."

We then discovered that Abas had given the keys to another male nurse, but nobody knew who this was. We went to the male wards to enquire. On arrival, we were told the man with the keys had just gone, but this time he had gone with the keys. When asked where he had gone, nobody knew, but they thought he might be back in an hour. With a degree of frustration, I returned to the women's ward to do something more productive, and I vowed to be back in an hour.

One hour later, the man with the keys was back. We were finally able to open the pharmacy and went inside. Some of the stock looked suspiciously low.

"Abdi, can I see the stock book please?"

Abdi reached for a book on the shelf. A page had been produced for each drug to be recorded when used. However, very little had been written anywhere in the book.

I frowned at Abdi. "I have to trust the staff Abdi, and this is not good enough." Abdi looked at the floor, and then gently placed the book back on the shelf.

I was now on the rampage. "Whilst we're walking around, can we take a look at the food storeroom?"

"Yes, of course, Dr John."

The town had still not provided any food for the hospital. In the interim, SCF had purchased high calorie porridge powder, as used in the refugee camp nutrition centres. This was important, as we had quite a few patients who were very thin and malnourished.

A hospital worker was sitting outside the food store on a chair. He muttered something in Somali, and he pointed into the distance.

"What did he say, Abdi?"

"The man with the keys has just gone," he replied.

I tried to remain calm. "Gone where?" I asked, but quietly presuming the answer.

"Nobody knows," said the man.

I looked at Abdi. "Which man is it this time?"

"Axmed Theatre, I put him in charge of the food store."

Whilst we were talking, I heard voices inside the storeroom. I tried the door, it was not locked, and opened freely. Inside was Axmed Theatre, with a relatively well-dressed woman. He froze in the middle of filling her plastic container with porridge powder. It then occurred to me that during the morning I had seen the occasional woman walking out of the hospital gates, carrying similar containers.

"Is this a patient, or a relative of a patient?" I asked, looking at Abdi.

There was silence, and Abdi began to look even more sheepish. The woman casually closed her container, and walked past, as if nothing had happened.

"This woman is not a patient, or a relative of a patient, are they?" I asked forcefully.

"I think I have made a mistake. I will try to fix it," replied a disheartened Abdi.

My frustration was mounting, but, at this point, I was not sure what to do. I felt a tap on my shoulder. It was Idris. He had been following us around the hospital, and keeping very quiet. "Dr John, can I speak with you outside?" he said. We walked a short distance to talk in private. "I do not know all the women who have been involved here today, but I've noticed that some were relatives of either hospital staff or town elders. Even if the staff are usually honest, it's very difficult to refuse such people, if they ask for something."

I understood what he was implying and I also realised I couldn't run the hospital without Abdi. I promptly returned to the storeroom, and with a degree of exasperation, I took all the keys. I asked everyone to leave, and determinedly locked the door.

"What now, Dr John?" asked Abdi.

"Well, I am now the man with the keys," I stated firmly, "But I don't want to be, Abdi. This food is for the patients, and especially the poorer ones who have nothing, or no relatives in town. It also costs money, and what we spend on food, we cannot spend on something else. So, the hospital and the town lose out. Do you understand?"

"I understand," answered Abdi, somewhat forlorn.

Abdi was about to walk away, when I reached for his hand. I placed the keys in his palm, and I closed his fingers around them. He looked at me, surprised, with raised eyebrows.

"I'm now the man without the keys Abdi, and you are now the man with the keys." I started to walk away, and then deliberately stopped to look back. "I have to trust you. Please just fix all this the best you can, and that includes the pharmacy."

I returned to the children's clinic to find Gina and Asha struggling to cope with the numbers of patients waiting in the line. There had been a surge in activity since we opened the new ward. I strolled down the line, and I saw a seven or eight-year-old boy slumped on his dad's lap with his arm wrapped in a scarf. I gently peeled back the scarf to reveal an infected, rotting arm. There was virtually no skin on the outer side, from his wrist to his elbow.

"Idris, can you ask what has happened? How did he get like this?"

"The father says he was bitten by a snake a few days before, whilst sleeping at night on the floor of the aqal."

As she cleaned the wound, Asha looked concerned. "I'm worried he will lose his arm. We had one just like this before, and eventually he needed an amputation in Hargeisa."

Our guidelines didn't cover snakebites. "It's very infected, so we should obviously give him some antibiotics," I instructed. "But we should try Dr John's papaya dressing." I could see the doubting faces. "Trust me, I've never seen it fail," I said confidently with my fingers crossed behind my back. The following day we had a similar case following a spider bite. Asha applied papaya dressing without me even suggesting it. Over the next three weeks their arms remained clean and healed with very little scarring. Both boys went home with a supply of dressings. It was yet another success for the papaya dressing.

In the middle of the morning clinic, Abdi appeared on the ward. "It's OK, everything is OK, but can you come to the theatre now?" Abdi didn't seem too stressed, so I was in no hurry walking back with him. I then noticed a military jeep in the hospital forecourt, and a group of soldiers standing anxiously on the front veranda.

As I approached the theatre, I could hear screaming and shouting. I was not at all prepared for what I was about to see inside.

Lying on the newly cleaned operating table was a soldier in absolute agony. There was blood all over the table and floor. A number of male nurses and soldiers were trying to hold him down on the table. His left leg was missing from the mid-shin down. His right leg was partly missing from just above his knee. What remained of his leg was so badly injured it looked like strips of ribbons. The skin and other remaining tissues were splattered with stones and grit. It was like 'pebbledash' plastering on the side of a house. "He trod on a mine," shouted Abdi, over all the commotion.

The male nurses were attempting to set up intravenous fluids, whilst also forcefully scrubbing the stones and grit out of his flesh. This must have been adding to the poor man's distress. I asked them to stop the scrubbing immediately, but no one was listening. "Stop, for pity's sake, stop!" I shouted loudly. The staff stopped and looked at me. "Abdi, tell them that's not important at this time. We need to stop the bleeding. Tie something around the stumps of his legs."

They took the injured soldier's belt from his trousers, and they placed it tightly around one thigh. Another soldier, standing mystified in the corner of the room, was asked to remove his belt, and the nurses applied it to the other thigh. Meanwhile, the patient became more distraught. He started to try and hit everyone before suddenly slumping, semi-conscious, onto the bed. I managed to get IV lines into each of his arms. There was no strong pain relief medication in the hospital, so other than injecting some antibiotics that was all we could do.

It was almost midday, and we needed to get the injured

soldier to Hargeisa as soon as possible. We transferred him to the army jeep. I was about to get inside, to help escort him, when another more senior soldier placed a hand on my shoulder. He pulled me back.

"You can't go," ordered Abdi.

"But he's seriously ill; if I go, he may stand a better chance."

"It's too dangerous," pleaded Abdi, "and personally I cannot see him making this. I think you're wasting your time." The jeep then set off, before the back door was properly closed, and, in a swirl of dust, it headed out of town.

I later discovered that although the soldier had survived the journey, he died in the corridors of Hargeisa Hospital on the way for surgery. I was also told that he hadn't unknowingly trodden on a mine by accident, but that he was part of a team planting them along the border. One had exploded.

The whole affair was quite shocking. Although it was my first experience of a land mine injury, unfortunately it was not to be my last. For several days, I could not get rid of the image of this man. Wherever I was, and whatever I was doing, he was always there. Always. Always there, lying in front of me screaming, with the staff scrubbing the stumps of his legs.

12.

A RARE DAY OFF

Gina and Cathy befriended a number of the volunteer nurses, including a very capable nurse called Safiya. They all regularly visited the SCF house to spend time together. The nurses offered Somali cooking lessons, and eventually even convinced both Gina and Cathy to have intricate henna drawings on their hands and feet. In return, Gina and Cathy taught them English, and shared their books and magazines. It was really great for everyone to interact and get on so well.

One morning, it was my day off, and so I got up late. Before having a wash, I decided to go for breakfast. Wearing my sarong, I wandered into the living room. There sat five of the volunteer nurses with Gina. They all started to giggle.

"Gosh, guests for breakfast!"

"Sorry," replied Gina, "I think our little joke has backfired."

"What joke is that?"

"Well, Cathy and I were talking about Valentine's Day in the UK. I think something got lost in translation, and they all thought it was today."

"So, tell me more, how does that explain this morning?"

"Cathy jokingly said something about coming around to the house, at some point, to see Dr John in his shorts or sarong. And here you are," exclaimed Gina, her face beaming with satisfaction.

"And where is Cathy?"

"Ahem, well, err, realising her mistake, she's already gone to work. Her excuse was that she would be able to head off any others coming this way."

"Any others?"

"It was one of our large teaching sessions, so they all heard the joke. Or should I say they heard the translation of our joke by Ali."

"You let Ali, of all people, translate the joke?" I exclaimed.

"But the good news, Dr John, is that they've all brought sorghum pancakes and ghee for breakfast. Your favourite I believe?" Gina smiled, knowing that it was not.

As they sat around the table, they all presented their stacks of pancakes. With no interpreter present to help us, this was a slightly embarrassing situation. So, I offered a big thank you, and did my best to get through one pancake from each nurse. Everyone seemed very happy, and then they all suddenly left for the hospital.

Later, with a very heavy stomach, I made my own way to the hospital, where Ali denied all knowledge of translating any jokes. "I didn't realise that was a joke," implored Ali. "Gina and Cathy talked about a custom in your country, where unmarried younger people send cards and gifts to someone they like. I just did my job and translated as asked." He paused for a second and then continued. "It could have been a lot worse Dr John, trust me," he said with a wink. I did not realise that one day this episode would come back to haunt me.

The conversation quickly moved on, and as it was my day off, Ali Interpreter and Idris had organised a day out. A picnic in the gardens of Amuud, and a challenging walk to the top of a local mountain. We clambered into the Land Rover and set off.

Amuud was like another world, situated close to the banks of a dry riverbed and bristling with fruit and vegetable gardens. We sat on our blankets in the shade, under giant eucalyptus trees, their leaves swaying and rustling in the gentle breeze. Lying before us was a veritable feast, with samosas, fruit, salad, dates, and fresh bread. This seemed a million miles from the woes of the hospital.

The team were relaxed and chatting away. Interestingly, they took me into their trust, and started to share information about themselves. I discovered that Ali Interpreter was married, and had previously been an English teacher, but earned more as a translator. Idris was originally from Ethiopia. He had left during their famine and other political problems. This explained to me why he could talk in different languages to some of the patients. They also started talking about Abdi Aposto. He was widowed, and had few relatives left in Borama. The hospital was his entire life. Aposto was his nickname because Aposto (*tutto a posto*) meant 'everything is OK' in Italian. This was his favourite phrase, which made sense.

After our picnic, we drove a short distance to climb the mountain. It took us about forty-five minutes to get to the top, where we had a fantastic view across the mountain range. However, we had an unwelcome surprise as we reached the summit. Dug into the ground was a trench. It was partly covered with a tarpaulin, from which a large tripod-mounted machine gun poked out over the top. There were old dusty water bottles, and jerry cans strewn around an old tent, which was leaning

89

on one side. This small military lookout post seemed recently unused. On closer inspection the gun was dust-free.

We decided to leave hastily, before we were noticed. Suddenly one of the tent flaps opened, and a soldier emerged into the daylight, shading his eyes with his right hand. We anticipated that we would now be in serious trouble. Instead, the soldier was very happy to have some company, and started to talk in a friendly manner to the team. After a relatively short conversation, we said our goodbyes, and walked down to the vehicle.

"Appears he was taken from his village a few months back, and conscripted into the army," explained Ali. "After a few weeks' training, he's been posted here with one other soldier."

"Is it normal to just be taken and conscripted like that?" I asked.

"Very," huffed Ali.

"Where's the other soldier?"

"He's down the other side of the mountain, in the defaecation zone. Let's head on."

Near the Land Rover was a small herd of goats, being tended by a nomadic woman and her small son. As we approached, the woman looked up, and appeared surprised. Suddenly she screamed loudly, waved her arms in the air, grabbed her son, and started to run in the opposite direction.

I looked at Ali. "What's that all about?"

"She's probably never seen a white man before. She's shouting the devil has come." Ali set off after her, and eventually convinced her to come back.

"Say something," Idris ordered.

"Say what exactly?"

"Anything. Just let her see you can speak. Say 'hello' in Somali."

I obliged. Although a little happier, the woman did not want to come any closer. She started to speak to Ali.

"What is she saying, Ali?"

"That your eyes are the colour of the sky. She thinks they're really piercing, and can see right through her, almost evil."

Ali tried to comfort her, but whatever he said made no difference. Meanwhile, her son, who seemed about five or six, had slowly drifted towards us, looking at my arms and muttering in Somali.

"What's he saying, Ali?"

"He wants to know if it's OK to touch your arms."

I bent down on one knee, and I stretched out my right arm. He stepped a little closer, and he reached out to gently stroke the blonde hairs on my forearm. He seemed entranced, but then promptly heeded his mother's request to return to her side.

I offered them the little food and water I still had in my rucksack, which they gratefully accepted from Ali. I thought it best to leave them in peace. We all climbed in the vehicle, drove past slowly, and waved out of the window. The woman still looked hesitant, but eventually raised one hand. Meanwhile, her son waved enthusiastically with both hands in the air. We set off to return to Borama before sundown.

The day's experience made me realise just how remote it was in the countryside. I hadn't realised that men could just be taken from their village and conscripted like that. As for nomads coming into Borama Hospital, it was probably quite intimidating to see the white SCF staff.

In Borama, I wasn't taken to the house, but I had another surprise. I found myself sitting in an open-air cinema, watching a

Bollywood film with English subtitles. The audience was mostly men, but about a third were women. Although not my usual taste in films, it was still a welcome change. Ali explained that the exotic Indian dancers were considered quite revealing by Somali standards.

When the film finished, I was escorted home. I walked into the living room, which was thick with cigarette smoke. Gina sat with a ferocious expression on her face, and she blew out some smoke. "Where have you been all day? We've been worried sick about you."

Sitting in the room was Brad. He had a cigarette in one hand, and a glass of whisky in the other. He said nothing, but just peered over his glasses at me. Cathy put down her cigarette and smiled. "Thank God, at least you're home and safe."

I was surprised by this emotional reception. Gina looked across at Brad, who seemed a little agitated.

"What's going on, why is everyone so upset?" I asked.

Brad explained that the French MSF team based at Tug Wajali had recently been kidnapped at gunpoint. They were released the next day unharmed in Ethiopia, but their vehicle was taken. There had been student anti-government demonstrations in Hargeisa, and a number of Somali villages along the Ethiopian border had been attacked. But it was not certain by whom. Importantly, one of the Somali SCF admin team in Hargeisa had been arrested for two days, and then released with no reason given. My absence all day had therefore caused great concern.

Brad continued with his news. "There's also a temporary ban on airmail posted from Mogadishu and Hargeisa. An ex-pat in Mogadishu was recently arrested for the contents of his letters, too much detail for the government apparently. He was given a fifteen-year prison sentence, until he received a presidential pardon, and was ordered to leave the country."

"Is there any good news?" I asked.

"Yes. In contrast, Borama seems very safe, and your mail goes through the post box in Djibouti. But all unnecessary trips are now cancelled, and, if things get worse, you may need to get out at short notice. All the hotspots are south of Borama. Therefore, your exit will be north, overland to Djibouti." Brad opened his bag, and he pulled out a map of northern Somalia. He proceeded to pencil in the route we would need to take.

"None of us have ever made that journey alone," said Gina.

"True, but the Somali staff should be with you," responded Brad, trying to be reassuring. "One more thing," he continued, "we need to install a radio here so that the Hargeisa office can communicate, even when we can't drive up to see you."

I sat back trying to take all this in. I looked down the table. Jerry seemed oblivious to the whole conversation.

"Nice lamb stew," reported Jerry, unfazed, and quietly sitting at the dining table. "Deeqa's best effort yet."

13.

THE NEW SOMALI DOCTOR

With all the problems along the Ethiopian border, and south to Hargeisa, there were no Djibouti supply trips this month. This also meant no mail in or out, which was an important blow to team morale. We had so little contact with the outside world that our letters were something we all really looked forward to.

"Your first patient is waiting," declared Ali, pointing me towards the women's ward as I arrived at the hospital. "I think her name is Amiina laba xabxab (pronounced hob-hob), or at least I think that's what she said," he continued with his usual smile.

On entering the clinic there was a line of patients, and I was directed to a woman sitting on a chair in the corner. After a short conversation I examined her chest. She was a large lady with very large breasts, which made the examination a little awkward. However, she clearly had a serious chest infection and I decided to admit her to the ward for a short stay.

I instructed the nurses to give Amiina laba hob-hob her antibiotics immediately. The nurses looked at me strangely.

"What's the problem? Let's get on with it. There are many more patients to see, besides Amiina laba hob-hob."

"A little harsh," said Aasha reprimanding me.

"Is there a problem?" I asked politely.

"Well, I know we all have, or are given, nicknames, but you could have been a little more discreet," she declared wagging her finger at me.

I still did not understand what I had said to cause this reaction. So I followed Aasha to the medicines locker and asked for an explanation. To my horror, I discovered laba hob-hob was not the patient's name. I had been on the end of one of Ali's many jokes, and had been calling the patient Amiina two watermelons in front of everyone in the clinic.

After completing my morning's work, I sat in the shade of the veranda outside of the women's ward. "When do you think we will have a new Somali doctor?" I asked Abdi.

"I guess now is as good a time as any to let you know we already have one," declared Abdi. "He arrived one week ago."

"Where is he then?"

"We were waiting for him to report to the hospital, but that hasn't happened yet."

"Abdi, is that not a little strange?" I enquired.

Abdi just shrugged his shoulders. "Everything is OK. He's from the south, Dr Omar. He's from the President's clan. I'm told he's setting up his private clinic first in the town, including home visits."

This all seemed rather bizarre. More to the point, I was doing all his work, and the town were fine with this situation.

"Well, Abdi, I expect to be one of the first to meet him when he does appear."

A week later, Abdi had arranged for me to meet Dr Omar, my new Somali counterpart. I stood outside his office door and knocked. It seemed very formal, compared to Dr Khalif. There was no reply.

"Is he in, Abdi?"

"Definitely, knock again."

I knocked a second time, and I heard someone shout in Somali from inside.

"We can go in," announced Abdi. "Everything is OK. Remember he doesn't speak any English, but he does speak Italian," he continued helpfully. This was of little help to me, as I did not speak a word, other than my newly acquired '*tutto a posto*'.

We entered to find Dr Omar sitting behind a different desk. There was now a picture of President Siad Barre, and a picture of the Somali flag on the wall. The office had been repainted in the light blue of the Somali flag.

"Hello, Dr Omar, my name is John," and I held out my right hand.

Dr Omar looked at my hand, remained seated, and after a few moments gave me a very limp handshake. He said something in Somali, and then continued to look at the papers on his desk.

"What did he say, Abdi?"

"He asks what is it that you want?"

"Oh, I simply wanted to say hello, and perhaps talk about how we are going to work together."

Dr Omar didn't seem remotely interested, as he continued to gaze at the paperwork on his desk.

"He says he's busy right now," continued Abdi.

"OK, can you ask if he wants to suggest another time? Perhaps later today?"

"He said not at the moment, but he will let you know. We can leave now."

Dr Omar's gaze never left his desk, and Abdi ushered me out.

"Friendly chap," I quipped.

"Not exactly," said Abdi, my sarcasm wasted.

"The office has changed."

"Yes, its furniture from the storeroom. Dr Omar removed the newer furniture, and he has taken it to his private clinic in the town," Abdi informed me, through gritted teeth.

A few days later, I had a visit from the nurses on the male wards. They looked annoyed. A long conversation took place between Idris and the nurses. There were raised voices, and much waving of arms.

"It seems they're having problems with Dr Omar. He spends very little time in the hospital, and is making some very strange clinical decisions, when he does," said Idris.

"So, what do they expect me to do about it?"

"They would like to be allowed to at least use the hospital guidelines again."

"I wasn't aware we had stopped using them."

"It would appear Dr Omar has said that he doesn't need guidelines, and he has removed them from the wards."

The following day, Dr Omar was in the hospital. I decided to confront him, but diplomatically, if possible. He was doing a ward round, and I was made to wait. "Idris, can you ask if we can talk now? I need to carry on with my own work too." Another fifteen minutes passed, before he finally agreed to speak.

"Idris, can you ask him about the guidelines, and does he find them useful?"

Dr Omar gave a very long answer, with a stern face. The

two nurses on the ward flicked their eyes, with raised eyebrows, from Dr Omar to me, and back again. At one point, the nurses attempted to interrupt, but Dr Omar raised his right hand, and they stopped immediately.

Once Dr Omar stopped speaking, Idris turned to me. "I'm not really sure how to interpret this politely."

"Well, just try me."

"Dr Omar said this is his hospital, not yours. You are only invited here to help out with the women and children. He suggests you stay on your side of the hospital, and he will stay on his. If you want to use guidelines, because you can't remember what to do, that's your choice. He doesn't need them."

I had worked with some very rude consultants in the UK, but I had never been spoken to quite like this before.

"Idris, can you explain these are not just my guidelines. They are mostly from the RHU, so actually from his own Ministry of Health. We have just adopted them for the hospital. Is he fully aware of this?"

"Dr John, I really don't think this will make any difference. The nurses have previously explained all this."

"Idris, please try again for me."

"I've translated as nicely as I can. If I translate what he has just said to you word for word, then I doubt you would ever speak to this man again. Trust me."

I was stumped. "Can we just try? This is important?"

"Dr John, this man is from the President's clan. I really do not want to upset him further. I strongly suggest we stay polite, say goodbye, and leave." Without waiting for me to reply, Idris said goodbye in Somali, and ushered me away.

"Dr Omar has a lot of contacts," continued Idris, as we

walked away. "He could make life very difficult for all of us if we push him too far."

"OK, I sort of understand."

"Whilst we were waiting," continued Idris, "I heard him telling some patients that they couldn't get the right treatment here at the hospital, but, if they came to see him privately, he could cure their problems." I could see we were going to have a challenging time with Dr Omar.

As we walked away, I remembered that we needed some medication for the ward, so we walked over to the pharmacy. When we arrived, it was closed. We were told, 'The man with the keys has just gone'. When I asked where, the answer was 'Nobody knows.' Nothing seemed to change.

A few days later, it was particularly warm, and rain clouds were beginning to form on the horizon. We had German friends, who worked in Hargeisa, staying in our house. The husband, Karl, had left the day before on a business trip to Djibouti. His wife, Brigitte, was to stay with us for a few days, until he returned. I had just finished my morning's work, when the SCF Land Rover arrived with Mahdi Driver. He had an urgent conversation with Idris.

"We need to go to your house as quickly as possible. Brigitte is ill."

We discovered that Brigitte was eighteen weeks pregnant, which was the reason for her not travelling with her husband. She was having occasional abdominal contractions, and she was obviously worried. I gave her my room, as it was more comfortable for her to rest in. The contractions seemed to ease, and she eventually went to sleep. I left her with Cathy, and I returned to the hospital.

In the labour room, Saynab was in a heated argument with Abas.

"Idris, what's going on?"

"Saynab thinks Abas has stolen some medication from the ward."

I could see a bulge in one of his trouser pockets. "Idris, ask him to empty his pockets onto the bed, just here." Abas refused, but Idris spoke again in a far more forceful tone. Abas pulled out packets of antibiotics, and an injection of Oxytocin, something used to stop bleeding after delivery of a baby. We had only recently acquired these supplies.

The medication was returned to Saynab, and we marched Abas to see Abdi Aposto. We found him sitting, twiddling with his keys, outside the pharmacy. As I was explaining what had occurred, I remembered when Abas had the keys to the pharmacy, and some of the stock seemed low. Now Abdi had the keys, I presumed he had to obtain things by other means. "It's up to you to sort this, Abdi. As you know, Dr Omar has told me that this is not my hospital. Therefore, I presume I have no power to discipline any staff. So, you'll have to involve Dr Omar," I suggested ironically.

Clearly, I couldn't completely trust all the hospital staff. With some sadness, I went back to the SCF house. I could hear crying coming from my bedroom. Cathy was sitting on my bed trying to console Brigitte, who was having more contractions. Sadly, within forty minutes she had a miscarriage.

I wondered how Karl would take this. As he was away, we couldn't get any message to him. At home in the UK, the doctor's job would be almost done at this point, as the hospital team would deal with the aftermath. I had to talk to Brigitte and discuss what she wanted to do. Under the circumstances, she was naturally very upset, and still coming to terms with the realisation that she had miscarried her baby. I decided to leave it for now, whilst she slept.

After an hour or so, I walked to the bedroom window, and looked out at the dry garden. Only three metres away were the orange trees. On his knees, beneath one of the trees, was Jama. With a small shovel, he had started to dig a hole at the foot of the tree. Meanwhile, Deeqa was wandering around collecting wildflowers.

On completing the hole, Jama stood, and straightened his sarong and hat. He then went about the garden, collecting large stones, which he placed one by one into a mound next to the hole. He reached into a plastic bag, and pulled out a small roughly cut wooden cross, which was tied together with string. He must have made this himself. He stuck it in the ground at the head of the hole. Deeqa then laid her small bunch of flowers by the side of the stones.

Brigitte was beginning to wake up. I asked if she could stand, and I took her to the window to show her what they had prepared. "What a lovely gesture," she wept. "Just perfect."

Later that day, we carried out the burial. Jama insisted on placing most of the stones on top of the grave, and then he gave us all one stone each. Once completed, he stood straight, gave a military salute, and walked calmly back to the guardhouse. Cathy escorted Brigitte back to the house to rest. This experience made me realise the risks that people take when they decide to leave home and work for an NGO in a faraway place. I remained in the garden and sat quietly, contemplating life.

14.

FEMALE GENITAL MUTILATION

It was time for a break, and we headed to the teashop. On the way, I noticed the men from the secret police in their sunglasses and smart patterned shirts. They were often hanging around the hospital, watching everyone passing in and out of the compound. Why, I was not sure, and this was something nobody seemed willing to talk about.

Later that day, Abdi interrupted me. "It's OK, everything is OK, but I think Cathy needs you." By now, I was used to the usual 'OK expression' of Abdi, but I was never really sure what to expect. I walked briskly to the labour room. On the bed was a young woman lying in a pool of blood.

"She's about twelve weeks pregnant, very anaemic, in mild shock and seems to have had a miscarriage. But the bleeding is quite bad and won't stop," said Cathy.

I noticed the woman was semi-conscious, and Cathy had already put up an IV fluid line.

"I can't lose another woman like this; we have to do something," Cathy said.

Despite our best efforts, the woman continued to bleed profusely.

This was a dilemma. We had agreed no major surgical procedures in Borama. However, she was not going to make a trip to Hargeisa, and it was already 3pm. It was too close to the curfew time. "Abdi, get the theatre ready," I ordered, "I'm going to clean out the uterus." We whisked her to the theatre room. Axmed Theatre was all smiles. He had wanted to hear this ever since I arrived, to open his theatre for a real surgical procedure.

We had no general anaesthetic, but we had recently acquired some injectable intravenous Valium to sedate the patient. We also had a painkiller, which could be given intramuscularly. Within a short time, the procedure was finished, and the bleeding had stopped. We decided to keep the patient on the ward for a few days to ensure she fully recovered. I didn't realise at the time, but in the following weeks and months, I would perform this same procedure several times. Not what we originally planned, but it was saving lives.

After two days on the ward, the patient was recovering. She was still quite weak and very anaemic. She could hardly stand, or get out of bed, and really needed a blood transfusion. However, all we could offer was a high iron diet, and many weeks of iron tablets to assist recovery. The local diet was not rich in iron, especially for women, who in many families would generally eat after their husbands. When you added malaria and frequent pregnancies to the mix, iron deficiency anaemia was extremely common.

We were considering the best course of action, when the husband appeared on the ward. He wanted to take his wife home. We had a long, protracted conversation with him about how sick his wife was, and how she was not well enough to go home.

"But I have children; who is going to look after them, and the home?" the husband asked aggressively.

Despite what I thought were all convincing arguments for her to stay, the conversation was going nowhere.

"Idris, tell him that if he takes her home, she could die."

I was to be completely shocked by the reply.

Idris looked at me. "He says he can always get another wife."

Cathy was so outraged she had to walk away.

I turned to Saynab. "What do you suggest?"

"This sometimes happens, Dr John. Tell him if she dies, he may get another wife, but who will look after the children in the meantime?"

This had the desired effect. However, this was to be short-lived. Two days later, when I went to the ward, her bed was empty. The husband had appeared that night, and, without our knowledge, he had taken his wife. We never knew what happened to her.

Shortly after, we had a similar story with a malnourished child, who had a severe chest infection. The mother had been looking after the child in the hospital. The father appeared, and he wanted the mother and child to go home. He was told the child was too ill and could die. His answer was that there were other children at home for the mother to look after. He could always have another child. Against our advice he took them both away, but he did accept antibiotics to be given at home.

That night, whilst lying in bed, I reflected on my last month in the hospital. Here, suffering severe pain was regarded as quite normal, and life was seen to be so cheap in the eyes of many people.

The following day, a young seven-year-old girl was carried into the hospital. Her legs were bound together, and she had a large cloth between her legs soaked with blood. She looked very pale, anaemic, and in mild shock.

"Idris, what's happened?" I asked, expecting her to have been in some sort of accident.

"She's been cut," he replied, following a brief conversation with the group of women. "They can't stop the bleeding."

"Sorry, what do you mean cut?"

"She's had her female circumcision; this sometimes happens afterwards."

Saynab unbound the girl's legs, and Cathy stood ready with large gauze swabs to act as a pressure dressing. I gently eased the bloodstained cloth from between her legs. Blood immediately pumped out from an artery, and Cathy pressed the wound with her dressing.

"Idris, how long has she been bleeding?"

"A few hours now," said Saynab, her English improving all the time. "She's very pale, I don't think she can afford to lose any more blood."

The situation was not improving with the pressure dressing. I needed to insert a stitch around the clitoral artery. With no local anaesthetic left in the pharmacy, I had to do this procedure without pain relief. The staff held the poor girl down. Five minutes later, the stitch was in place, and the bleeding had stopped. The family wanted to take her home, but we decided to keep her overnight just to be sure.

This experience prompted me to talk to Saynab and Asha about female circumcision, and how this was performed locally. I realised that this was going to be a sensitive, and potentially difficult, conversation. I asked if they were happy for Idris to translate, and we went to a quiet area of the hospital.

They seemed very willing to talk at great length, and described, what was to them, a perfectly normal part of life in quite horrifying detail. All girls, when reaching seven years, have their circumcision. In Somalia, it is what some describe as being the most extensive type of circumcision. This is performed largely by the same older women who act as TBAs in the community, in return for a fee.

Relatives have to hold the limbs of the screaming child, whilst the procedure, which uses a clean razor blade and no local anaesthetic, is performed. What remains of the vulva is then held together, and the legs are bound to stop the bleeding. The child stays like this for some time, which could be for many days. This is to allow a sheet of scar tissue and skin to grow across the vulva area. Once healed, this leaves a small pencil-hole-sized gap, allowing urine to pass, and blood once their periods start. Only having this small gap explained to me why so many young women presented to the hospital clinics with urinary tract infections, and painful periods.

Once Asha and Saynab had finished, I looked at Cathy and we sat for a moment to absorb this tale. I turned to Idris. "I'm not sure their English is up to this, so can you please ask if they are OK with you continuing to translate?" Idris obliged and they agreed.

"Can I ask you both, what do you think and feel about this?" I enquired delicately.

They looked at each other, both willing the other to speak. Eventually, Asha went first. "It's complex, Dr John. It is something that is expected. Personally, I would like to see a time when we don't do this. In fact, the government has made it illegal, but it's so deep in our culture that it hasn't stopped, and the government do nothing in practice to prevent it."

I thanked them for their honesty, and I thought the conversation had ended there. Then, Saynab finally spoke up. "One more thing," she said quietly, "women here always say there are two days that are the most painful two days in your life. Your circumcision day, and the night of your wedding, when you are opened."

I reacted by leaning right back in my seat. "Opened?" I questioned.

"Yes. Part of the wedding ritual is for the skin to be opened slightly with a knife. We are both single, so we still have this to come in our lives."

Slightly stunned by this conversation, I went back to the ward with Idris to ensure the girl was well, and that the bleeding had not returned. She lay on the bed, and she was now sleeping after the ordeals of the day. At the time of inserting the stitch, I had felt quite guilty about performing this with no pain relief. But having heard what the child had already been through, I realised that this was obviously minor in comparison.

A number of weeks later, around mid-morning, a small group of very well-dressed women from the town appeared on the ward.

"They want a confidential meeting with you alone," said Abdi.

"Do you know what this is about, and surely I will need someone to translate?"

"Everything is OK. That's why I'm here, it's a sensitive matter, and they don't want you to use the interpreters."

I was a little confused, but I agreed to the meeting. Abdi then guided us all into the empty office of Dr Omar.

"This lady is Muuna," declared Abdi.

Muuna began to speak, and Abdi translated. "I have come

to discuss a delicate matter," said Muuna. "It's about female circumcision."

"Oh," I said, surprised, as this was an issue so rarely openly discussed.

"You know that this is part of our culture, but of course it has its problems, and it is painful."

"Yes, I understand that."

"As a group of female elders, we have come to ask you a question. Could you do it in the hospital safely, and with pain relief?"

This was certainly not what I was expecting. I could understand why they might ask this of me, but my initial reaction was to refuse outright. Then I thought momentarily that if we cannot actually stop the practice, perhaps their proposal would at least reduce the trauma it caused. I stood in a slight daze, whilst my brain tried to get around this issue.

Abdi, ever helpful, looked at me. "May I speak?" he asked. "What are you thinking, Dr John?"

"That I cannot really do this for all sorts of reasons. However, it has probably taken some courage to come here and talk about this so—"

Before I could finish my sentence, Abdi interrupted. "I understand, but you are right. This is not for you. You are already too busy."

"Abdi, I don't think being too busy is the main issue here."

"Perhaps not, but diplomatic. Professionally this is something a doctor should not perform in a country that has legally banned it. I think it is best you do not get involved in this issue. It could make more enemies than friends." He was of course correct. "Shall I reply for you?" he enquired.

"Err, yes please do, but ensure you explain this with a degree of tact." Abdi turned to Muuna, and carefully explained my reasons for declining. The women looked at each other with disappointment, said thank you for listening, and left the hospital.

"A little story for you," said Abdi. "Muuna herself does not believe in female circumcision, and she has tried to persuade others to cease this practice. I suppose she is looking at alternatives. In fact, she stopped her own daughter being cut." He paused and sighed deeply. "However, she had to visit a sick relative in another part of the country. Whilst she was away, the mother of her husband took the granddaughter to be cut. When Muuna returned she was outraged, and even more so when she discovered her daughter nearly died from the bleeding. That's why she is worried about safety. It's important you realise that not everyone agrees with this practice. But it is just so deep in our culture. For example, many believe you will not be able to marry if you are not cut." He hesitated and looked a little mournful. "Do not forget that some of the TBAs who work in the hospital also do circumcisions. There is a lot of money to be made by some older women in the community."

It was an important point. I hadn't thought about this before. There was a definite conflict of interest for the TBAs, who we relied on. We were training them in the hospital. Yet, they were perhaps doing something quite different once in the community. I thanked Abdi for helping to respond to such a sensitive situation, and I was truly glad he was there.

I thought about our recent experiences of female circumcision (or Female Genital Mutilation). We had to deal with the consequences almost daily, but we had no way of influencing the practice. Although it was a constant issue, and deeply troubling for the team to come to terms with, it was something we simply had to accept as part of local life.

15.

THE RAINS

"OK, so plug in, switch on, ready to rock and roll. This is Red Falcon. Do you copy? Roger, roger that, over. This is Borama calling, is anyone out there?"

"Just what are you doing?" asked Gina.

"Err, just practising for our first transmission," I said, blushing. I was holding the microphone of our new radio. "I can be Red Falcon. I was thinking Cathy could be Phantom Deliverer, and you, well err, Smoking Gun. Or are you trying to give up again?"

"Boys with their toys. What about Jerry?"

"Now the latrines are all built, I was thinking something appropriate. What about Black Hole?"

"I want to be Jupiter Rising," exclaimed Jerry excitedly, appearing from his bedroom.

It was 9am and time for our scheduled call.

"This is Red Falcon in Borama. Borama calling Hargeisa base camp, over," I said. There was no reply.

Jerry eagerly reached for the microphone. "This is Jupiter Rising. Hargeisa, do you copy? Over."

"This is Hargeisa office, we copy. Please be aware that others might be listening, like the police, for example. Do you copy that? Over." We looked at each other like naughty children being reprimanded.

Cathy peered at Jerry and Gina. "Can I still be Phantom Deliverer?"

"I think your microphone is still on," replied Hargeisa. "I suggest we stick with 'Borama Office' for now, over."

"So, so boring," said Jerry.

"I suppose Smoking Gun isn't very appropriate," said Gina.

"As I mentioned before, your microphone is on," said an exasperated voice from Hargeisa.

Our conversation with Hargeisa then continued in a more serious tone. The recent problems had stopped, so travel would be allowed again. This was great news. Jerry had almost completed his construction and repairs. He was eager to return to Hargeisa for other projects. Djibouti supply trips were also now possible.

I went outside the house, and I pulled up a bucket of water from the water tank, for my shower. The morning sky was unusually dark, and it shared its first few drops of rain for months. Within minutes, it was absolutely pelting down, and it didn't stop all day. Water started gushing through the main compound gates. It split into two fast-flowing streams, which went around each side of the house. It then passed out through a gate on the other side of the compound into the street. We were effectively trapped inside.

Jama, Malik and One-eyed Hussein sat in their guardhouse, and occasionally opened the door to peer outside. Our feral cat friend sheltered on top of one of the front tyres of the Land Rover, under the wheel arch. It was cosy for now. The tortoise had clawed its way to higher ground, and it lay in the corner of the compound near the shed that housed the generator.

The torrential rain was deafening, as it hit the tin roof of the house. Quite late in the day, we heard a loud knock on the door. I rushed to open it, and there stood the three guards. They had a plastic sheet over their heads, and they were carrying their belongings and blankets. Their sarongs were folded up to the middle of their thighs, as they had waded through the water to the steps of the house. I pulled them safely inside.

I looked out of the door and into the compound. The water was now lapping against the top step of the guardhouse, and it was halfway up the Land Rover's tyres. The cat was still nestled under the wheel arch. Perhaps a rescue mission might be needed later.

The next morning, there was a lull in the rain. Gina and I decided to see if we could get to the hospital in the Land Rover. The water level had dropped slightly. I gently trod through the muddy floodwater, which was quite precarious in flip-flops, and managed to get to the vehicle. Gina then quickly followed. Mission accomplished, we set off slowly to the hospital.

The short journey was not easy. Fast-flowing streams of rainwater had formed everywhere. The front of the hospital had turned into a deep paddling pool. Aaden TB and his team, trousers rolled up to mid-thigh, were wading their way to the TB hospital. In the Land Rover, we ploughed through the water onto higher ground, and pulled up next to Abdi. He was sitting in the shelter of the veranda. With his hat propped on one side of his head, and his shirt slightly ruffled, he looked as though he had been at the hospital all night. Never without his hat, I wondered if he even slept in it.

Jerry had clearly done a great repair job, as all the roofs were watertight. Most staff had not made it to work. Faithful Asha, despite potentially jeopardising her dignity, had hitched up her dress, and waded through the water. She had already been around the ward to ensure everyone was OK. Interestingly, a number of the volunteer nurses had also turned up for duty.

It proved to be a very quiet day. As the rains continued over the following days, we had fewer patients to see. Then everything changed. In Borama, large numbers of townsfolk developed chest infections, and severe diarrhoea. They were especially from the poorer parts of town. I could understand the dampness and poor housing causing the chest infections, but I was not sure about the diarrhoea.

On a drier day, I decided to take a walk through the town with Idris. I had previously seen water tankers in the town delivering water. This was pumped from an underground water source and chlorinated. But today, in the poorer part of town, I saw the donkey man from the market, delivering water in his old vegetable oil containers. The water was placed into old oil drums outside each dwelling.

I asked Idris where the Donkey Man obtained his water. I was taken to the edge of the town. There was a myriad of small flowing streams in what was normally a dry riverbed. We watched the donkey man scoop the water straight from the riverbed and pour it into the old oil containers on the back of the donkeys. Nearby were herds of animals standing in the water, women washing clothes, and men washing their trucks and cars.

The reason for the outbreak of diarrhoea was now quite obvious. What to do about it was less clear. The water from the tankers was more expensive, so poorer people could only afford the cheaper donkey man option. In addition, the streets were often too small to accommodate the tankers in the poorer areas. I asked the team what we could do. Abdi headed into town to talk to the elders about this situation. I later discovered they had met with the donkey man. They banned him from doing this in future, insisting he took chlorinated water from the tankers, and sell this to the people in the town instead.

The rain transformed the countryside. The dusty, rocky terrain became green, and flowers erupted everywhere. But for me the most magical thing was the colourful yellow weaverbirds. Their activity was a delight to watch, as they built upside-down nests in trees and bushes all over our garden. There was one just outside my bedroom window. It was so close I could no longer open the window, as it would disturb the nest. But I had such a great daily show to watch.

A week or so after the rains had started, there was loud shouting and knocking on the door of the house, during the afternoon. Jama, along with the other guards, burst in. "Dr John, quick, we must close all the doors and windows." He pointed to the horizon, where there was a dark cloud rapidly developing. Initially, I thought this was a large rain cloud, but then I realised it was moving too fast. The weather was also too wet for a dust storm. The sky was becoming darker and darker, as the cloud moved with extreme speed.

"Termites, Dr John. Flying termites. They sometimes come after the rains."

We rushed around the house, closing whatever was open, including any inside doors. Unfortunately, the old metal window frames were not airtight. I also noticed a little sunlight coming under the front door. We had no more time, and Jama ushered us all into my bedroom. He had obviously lived through this before.

Minutes later the house went dark, as it was hit by a giant swarm of termites, battering against the windows and the roof. It seemed to pass just as quickly as it arrived. We gingerly opened the bedroom door. Despite our attempts to lock them out, there were still thousands of large brown termites, crawling in every direction. Not long after landing, they began to shed their wings all over the floor. The house was in a terrible state. Many hours later, we had managed to sweep them out of the house, but we kept finding their wings for days afterwards.

With the rains there was a noticeable increase in flies, which was especially annoying for the hospital patients. One morning, Ali Interpreter was playing to the audience. He was waving away the flies, whilst giving his theatrical translations in the clinic. He was joking, making both staff and patients laugh. Despite some of his annoying attributes, I had to admit he was very entertaining.

I noticed our NSS friends in the sunglasses, and smart patterned shirts, lurking around the hospital again. I didn't understand why they thought the hospital was so interesting. They were leaning against a small, white, Suzuki jeep. This was the same jeep that had often followed us around the town in recent weeks.

"You're on good form this morning Ali, are you up for some fun?" I asked.

"Fun is my middle name," replied Ali, with his usual grin.

"Have these guys nothing better to do?" I nodded towards the men in sunglasses. "What about going for a fast drive on a visit?" I continued.

I herded the team into the Land Rover, and I moved Mahdi Driver into the passenger seat. "Dare Mann, anyone?"

"Do you have your driving licence?" asked Ali Interpreter, with a grin. I nodded in reply to confirm that I did. Once all were strapped in, I put my foot down, and we hurtled out of the hospital gates.

The men in sunglasses were taken by surprise, as we raced past, spraying a little water from the back wheels. They jumped into action, clambering into their Suzuki. The chase was on.

I decided not to take the direct way, but the roughest route possible. The capable Land Rover took all this in its stride. I looked out of my rear-view mirror. I could see the already troubled Suzuki bobbing around on the rocky surfaces.

We reached one of the normally dry riverbeds. It was now a torrent of water, which was cascading down from the mountains. I stopped on the edge of the river, and I turned to Mahdi Driver. "Will we make it?" He nodded. Slowly, I descended the vehicle down the steep riverbank, and gradually we waded across the river.

In my rear-view mirror, I could see the Suzuki arrive. Initially, it started to try and descend, but obviously the driver changed his mind and reversed backwards to safety. I looked for a gentler exit point, put my foot down, and the vehicle lurched up the bank. The back wheels struggled slightly in the mud, but we made it out onto the opposite riverbank.

The Suzuki was still on the other side. The driver was now out of the vehicle scratching his head, looking at the water gushing by. Gently, we eased through some mud, passed by some bushes, and we were finally out of sight. Everyone cheered with satisfaction, and we carried on to see Nathan and Charlotte in Dare Mann.

We found them both well, and busy with their work in the camp. However, recent experiences had made them think about life. They informed us that they were missing home, and that they were likely to leave in the near future. They were our nearest ex-pat neighbours, good friends, and regular picnic buddies for 'timeout' in the gardens of Amuud. We understood, but we would miss them.

Returning to Borama, we reached the same river crossing. To our surprise, the Suzuki was now sitting completely stuck in the middle of the river, having made a failed attempt to cross. The water was almost up to the windows of the vehicle. Two men were sitting on the roof in patterned shirts, with wet trousers. They were wearing their sunglasses on the top of their heads, and they were looking very sorry for themselves.

I was tempted to drive by, but sense prevailed. In the middle of the river, we pulled up alongside the Suzuki, and we allowed the secret police to scramble onto the roof of the Land Rover. We churned through the water, whilst they held onto the roof rails. Secretly hoping that they might fall into the mud, we surged up the steep riverbank on the far side. We then stopped, allowed them into the back of the vehicle, and offered a lift back to Borama. The journey was very quiet, with little conversation. Even Ali Interpreter refrained from making any jokes. As we pulled up outside the police station, I did wonder how they were going to explain losing their vehicle.

Eventually, we arrived at the SCF house. It was time for our scheduled radio link to Hargeisa.

"Borama Office, this is Hargeisa, do you copy? Over."

"We copy, over," said Gina.

"Is that Phantom Deliverer? Sorry couldn't resist it. Over." It was Jerry. "You have a surprise today, Borama."

"Ooh, we like surprises. Is Jupiter Rising coming tonight? Over." said Gina.

"No, but you have a new ambulance."

"New ambulance?"

"Yeah, that's right. It's already en route, as we speak. Brad decided that you shouldn't be without a vehicle. So, you no longer need to use the SCF Land Rover to transport patients."

Later that day, a covered Land Rover pick-up truck arrived. It had SCF and Red Crescent logos, and it was parked outside the front of the hospital. Within a very short time, Dr Omar entered the hospital for the first time in days. He wanted to take the ambulance for a drive. Unfortunately for Dr Omar, 'the man with the keys' had just gone. Where he went, nobody knew.

16.

TRIP TO DJIBOUTI

In early April, the rains were beginning to disperse. From both a security and a weather perspective, it was safe to make a supply trip to Djibouti. We drew straws, and yes, it was Red Falcon and Jupiter Rising's turn to make the trip. The blue SCF Isuzu truck arrived from Hargeisa, along with a Land Rover. The scouting party consisted of Hargeisa staff, Mahdi Driver, Jerry, and myself.

This was an incredibly, bone-shaking journey, but the scenery was majestic. Initially, we followed the Ethiopian border. The mountains were now green, following the rains. We stayed overnight in a deserted house used by travellers, where we all slept on the floor with blankets.

The next day, we descended into the lower plains, where there was no sign of rain. The earth was scorched and deeply cracked. The heat over the lowland plains was oppressive, and the Land Rover had no air conditioning. Normally, whilst driving in the mountains, you could open your window for a little fresh air. However, here, the breeze was more like having a hot hair dryer blowing on your face. The windows stayed firmly up to keep out the heat, and the swirling dust.

There was very little vegetation. The occasional animal carcass lay on the road, partly eaten and mummified in the heat. The ground was so parched and lifeless. At one point, there was an amazing sight: goats standing on branches in a tree. They had somehow climbed the only tree to find something to eat. Further along the route, a male ostrich appeared from nowhere, and seemed to race the vehicles just for fun. We also occasionally passed large herds of animals that were being driven by nomads to Djibouti, where they would be sold for markets in the Middle East.

Our journey took around fourteen hours. At the border, the formalities were straightforward, and we crossed into Djibouti. We decided to stop at a café and eat. We sat in the shade, sipping ice cold drinks, but with the coastal humidity my shirt was completely wet through. The waiter appeared from the kitchen, holding a plate of rice, with what looked like raisins mixed into it. As he plopped the plate on the table, the raisins flew into the air, and buzzed around our heads. I decided I wasn't that hungry.

I was about to take another sip of my drink, when I noticed two large flies had landed in my glass. I picked them out and carried on drinking. I was given the thumbs up from our truck driver. "Good to see you're settling in."

"What do you mean exactly?" I asked.

"An old joke." He laughed. "When you first come to Somalia, if a fly lands in your drink, you throw the drink away. Later, you pick it out and carry on drinking. Eventually, you drink with the fly in, and leave the fly in the bottom of the glass. You're nearly there!"

After a short drive, we entered the main city area of Djibouti. There was obvious wealth in this place but also dire poverty.

121

There were many people sleeping rough in the street, something I had not seen in Borama or Hargeisa. Going to live in Djibouti was seen by many Somali people as something to try and achieve. It was clear from these scenes that this was not always a successful experience.

We stayed in a simple but clean hotel, which was close to all the shops and warehouses. Although the room had no windows, crucially it did have air conditioning. With the heat and humidity, I felt like stripping off, and just lying on the bed. But we only had forty-eight hours to obtain all the supplies, including the collection and delivery of our mail.

Everything was generally more expensive than in Borama, but there was so much choice, and the goods were of a better quality. At a French supermarket, we could get extra treats, and we had a special licence to buy alcohol for personal consumption. Whilst the Hargeisa staff went about sourcing bags of concrete and other building materials with Jerry, I had my own shopping list. This included a tray of beer for many of the SCF staff, whisky for Brad, rolled tobacco for Cathy, and packets of nicotine chewing gum for Gina. This time she was serious about stopping smoking.

Djibouti sits at the outlet of the Red Sea. The port was full of seafood restaurants, and Yemeni fisherman from across the water. It was also a large military base for France, and many ships and navies from around the world stopped off there, after passing through the Suez Canal. We walked through the streets, and I noticed sailors and soldiers everywhere. There was the normal-sized variety, usually a French conscript doing his national service. Then, there was the larger, more frightening variety from the French Foreign Legion, which was also based in the town. With all this activity came prostitutes. I don't think I have ever seen so many. Sit down in any seemingly quiet bar or café, and you were immediately approached by a clutch of women from a variety of ethnic backgrounds. The bar in our own hotel was the only place that we could sit peacefully and safely.

Having perused the shelves in the French supermarket, followed by lunch in a French restaurant, the day was already offering guilty pleasures. I'd even strolled along a nearby beach. This made me feel a little guilty, as it was in stark contrast to life in Borama. Back in the hotel, I was introduced to a French military doctor, who invited Jerry and me to the local hospital. It was simply another world, with facilities such as those you would find in Europe.

Later, he asked if we were interested in going to the 'naughty bar'. I was not entirely sure what he meant, but Jerry seemed keen, and before I could say anything he had already agreed to the visit. Shortly after we arrived in the marina for lunch, at the very smart 'Bar Nautique'. Jerry looked at me. It was probably not what he was expecting. "Not exactly something lost in translation, but perhaps in the French accent," he said disappointedly.

Over a drink, the French doctor indicated that if we wished, we could send patients from Borama over the border for free treatment at the military hospital. All they needed was a letter from myself and even without a passport this would be possible.

We were then dropped off at our hotel, and later that evening I was sitting with Jerry in the hotel bar. A small group of men were drinking on the other side of the room. When they heard us speaking English, they asked if they could join us. We presumed they were also staying at the hotel. They were all from Britain, and seemed to be really interested to learn what it was like on the Somali side of the border.

They wanted to take us on, what was promised to be, a short bar crawl. Although we tried to decline, they were not taking no for an answer. As we went around the bars, 'with wine speaketh the truth'. We discovered that they were all in the French Foreign Legion. Each in turn shared the details of their life story, and why they had needed to join the Legion. Generally, they came from Liverpool, Glasgow, and the East End of London. Their stories varied, but they included being involved in organised crime. Some were trying to escape vengeance from their own gang or others. The Legion offered them a second chance in life. The exception in the group was a more innocent character. He had just wanted to seem tougher than his dad, who had been in the Marines. Joining the Legion would hopefully impress his family. All very interesting, but as time passed, we were beginning to wonder exactly where we were in the town.

Six bars later, or perhaps more, I can't remember, and the bar doors were flung open. In walked four giant, rather tough-looking, hombres. They had no visible necks. Their arms were the size of most men's thighs, and their thighs the size of most men's waists. As in a gangster movie, they looked around, and existing customers quickly moved to either side as they approached the bar.

"Grab this," instructed one of our Legionnaires. He was holding out a giant glass ashtray. "These guys are Tahitian Legionnaires and really rough. They can't handle their drink, and they are always looking for a fight. If there's any trouble, smack them over the head with it. It's the only thing that will stop them."

He thrust the ashtray into Jerry's hands. Jerry promptly took it, and, as if it was a hot coal, he gave it straight to me. I looked at the ashtray in horror. Before I could really take in this situation, a second Legionnaire ordered, "Get behind me, we need to head for the nearest exit."

Slowly, we edged around the outer wall of the bar towards the toilet, where we pushed open a fire exit door, and ran out into the alley. I dropped the ashtray. Behind us, we could hear a huge fight breaking out inside.

"Sorry pal," said the second Legionnaire. "We didn't intend, or plan for this."

"I think we need to do the right thing here, Jimmy," said the first Legionnaire. "Let's get these lads home safely." We were escorted through the streets, and we were delivered unscathed back to our hotel.

"Next time, eh lads?" said Jimmy, waving goodbye.

"Sure," said Jerry, "next time." Jerry turned to me. "Great guys, don't you think?"

Back in our room, I began to count how many lives I had used up since I'd arrived in Somalia. I lay on my side of the double bed, staring at the ceiling. The air conditioning unit was belting out cold air, but I was still sweating after the evening's antics.

"Good night, darling," said Jerry sleepily. "Just kick me if I begin to snore. Great story though for when we get back."

"Oh yeah, great story, but I'm not sure Gina and Cathy will be so impressed."

I vowed never to go out of the hotel again after dark. Who would have thought that a night in Djibouti would be more dangerous than living in Somalia?

The following morning, we were to have our first haircuts since arriving in Somalia. Jerry and I walked to the nearest recommended barbershop. Any requests could be made, but the Arab barber chopped away, and everyone came out looking the same. American Marine style! Whilst on our travels, I had decided to start growing a beard, and had this tidied up. I was transformed. The team would have a shock when we returned home.

Strolling back from the barbers, we noticed a burnt-out building. The charred sign said 'Café Historil'. Later, we discovered that there had been a bomb in this café on the 18th of March that year, which was probably meant for local French soldiers. Instead, it had blown up a group of German academics, who were visiting from Kiel University, and a number of other civilians. The bomb killed twelve in total. In the past, SCF staff had often taken a coffee there. "Heavens," said Jerry, "that could have been us." I thought long and hard about 'Lady Luck' and being in the wrong place at the wrong time.

17.

THE MAJOR'S WIFE

"While you were there what did you do?" Ali enquired on my return from Djibouti.

"Oh, this and that, and I made contact with my mother," I replied while examining the next patient.

"You had contact with your mother?" Ali asked looking very surprised.

"Yes, and my sister too."

"Your sister too?" Idris questioned standing nearby.

"Well, it's been a long time out here in Somalia. My mother would have been disappointed if I didn't."

"A long time, disappointed he says," stated Ali looking at Idris with raised eyebrows. I then noticed that a number of staff had eagerly gathered to listen to our conversation.

"And your sister, would she have been disappointed too?" Idris asked.

"Of course, in fact she would have been jealous if it was just my mother," I replied.

"These Europeans, I struggle to understand them sometimes," Ali continued.

"Was it not a long journey for your mother?" Idris enquired seeking more information.

"Not really," I replied cautiously and becoming a little puzzled with the flow of the conversation.

"May I interrupt?" requested Abdi, who had been intently listening to everything we said. "Perhaps we are all jumping to conclusions here," he exclaimed, holding his arms out and appealing to the small crowd surrounding us.

To my embarrassment, I then discovered that the term 'having contact' had a very different connotation in Somalia. It was used as a term for having sex with someone. I had unwittingly dug myself into a very large hole from which I needed to get out. I rapidly explained that I had merely had a phone call with my family, and from that day I removed 'having contact' from my vocabulary.

Late at night I heard noises in the kitchen. I got out of bed, and sleepily padded down the corridor with my torch. The kitchen floor seemed to be moving. There was a crunch under my left foot. I peered down to see what I had trodden on. The whole floor was alive with cockroaches, which were scuttling away in all directions from the light of my torch. I turned to shine the torch on the kitchen work surface, which had a number of drying saucepans. There were cockroaches there too, but also about ten mice.

The next morning, we obtained anti-cockroach powder and mousetraps to place around the kitchen. The following day, the floor was covered with dead cockroaches. However, the mousetraps sat empty, although the bait had been eaten. I was stood in the kitchen with Cathy, wondering what we should do next, when Jerry appeared. "These are no good," he said, pointing to the mousetraps. "I have a much better idea." He promised to sort everything that night.

The following morning, I could hear squeaking noises coming from the kitchen. There were more dead cockroaches, and the floor was scattered with sheets of cardboard. On the boards were mice, which were alive, but they seemed to be stuck to the boards. I was still trying to fully focus. I looked more closely, and the boards were smeared with some sort of gel. Jerry appeared from his room. "Ah, good job done."

"What's all this?"

"Mice glue, very effective. One of the guards recommended it."

"Yes, I can see that. The mice are stuck, but still alive. So, what do we do now?"

Jerry put his hand in a small bag, and pulled out a hammer, which he handed to me. "You hit them with this," said Jerry, with a faint grin.

"I hit them with this?"

"Well, you can't get the mice off the glue. It's that, or you'll have mice all over the house. Your choice."

Cathy and Gina arrived. "What's all the noise about?" enquired Gina. After a brief explanation, they both went to the dining room for breakfast. "Well one of you will have to do it," instructed Gina.

I looked at Jerry, and Jerry looked at the hammer in my hand. "You've got the hammer," said Jerry.

"Yes, but who put the mice glue down in the first place?"

Jama appeared on the front step with a bucket of water. "Much better," he said, handing me the bucket. He must have seen my vacant expression. "You put the board, with the mice, in the water," he muttered with some irritation, as if it was obvious. I went outside into the garden, but I couldn't do the dirty deed. Jama impatiently snatched the bucket and the mice. With a huff, he disappeared to the back of the guardhouse. This was yet another area of expertise I was not expecting to develop, when leaving the UK.

As I returned inside the house, Cathy came screaming out of the toilet. "Get them out, get them out," she shouted, as she kicked off a pair of her knickers from around her feet across the floor. A number of cockroaches appeared from inside the toilet, and they scuttled across the tiles. Jerry and I immediately stamped on as many as possible, making the familiar crunching noise underfoot.

We both ventured into the toilet. Our Princess Anne prized possession was alive with cockroaches, streaming out of the pit latrine. Returning to the corridor, we were met by Jama. This time he was holding a large tub of insecticide and a bag of lime powder. "Much better," said Jama, "this is what we use in the guard house." He was right, and we never had such a problem again.

At the hospital, the arrival of the new ambulance had taken the pressure away from using our own Land Rover for patient transfers. However, it had increasingly become the personal taxi for Dr Omar. He was not a great driver. This was evidenced by two dents, which had already appeared on the left side of the vehicle. Not easy to achieve, as Borama was not exactly endowed with much traffic. The ambulance had formally been given to the hospital, and as we were frequently reminded, it was Dr Omar's hospital. The fact that Dr Omar was rarely at the hospital, and mostly at his private clinic in the town, was incidental. We were also suspicious that Dr Omar mostly used the ambulance to transport his private patients.

However, in terms of pest control, the positive aspect of all this was that the male nurses went about their jobs with minimal interference from Dr Omar. This included secretly using the RHU/hospital guidelines. Once or twice a week, Dr Omar would appear for a ward round. He would make a mixture of clinical decisions, good and bad. Then the nurses would alter his decisions, using the guidelines, as soon as he left the premises.

A key event this month was the arrival of officers from SCF London, escorted by Brad. They were visiting to review progress with the project. They were really keen to understand exactly how it was on the ground. The visit went well. Even Dr Omar turned up at the hospital, and a ceremonial tree was planted to mark the occasion. The town elders seemed suitably impressed that the visitors had come all the way from London. We were offered new contracts for a further six months and one day later they returned to Mogadishu.

We were all excited about the new contracts. Then, I wondered how my parents, family, and friends would feel about this. In just over five months, we had achieved a great deal, but I thought there was so much more to be done. As part of my post-graduate training, I had undertaken an assessment of my personality. The results indicated that I had a strong tendency towards wanting to complete and finish pieces of work. So, with regards to the offer of a new contract, the 'completer-finisher' in me took the helm and I accepted. That night, I lay in bed, trying to get to sleep. I was pleased to be staying another six months, and overall I was quite enjoying life. My feelings of depression and self-doubt, from when I left the UK, were an almost distant memory.

The day after our London visitors departed, I was walking down the line, reviewing those waiting for the clinic. There was a boy aged about nine years old, with his worried mother. He was extremely thin, and completely wasting away. This in itself was not unusual, as we had malnourished children presenting virtually every day. However, his parents had shaved his head, and he was covered in white marks all over his body, some of which had blisters. "Traditional burning remedy," declared Idris. "It's very common, especially amongst nomadic people. They take a cigarette, and stub the burning end, wherever they think you have the illness."

I had seen this before applied to small areas, such as a painful knee, TB glands in the neck, and even a sore throat, but never so extensively. After careful questioning and examination, I diagnosed probable TB. This was supported by the chest X-ray. We also needed to consider whether anyone else might have TB in the family contacts.

TB was rife in Somalia. It was so common in some nomadic people that, as with anaemia in many women, you could almost predict TB by tossing a coin as they walked into the clinic. I had seen TB not just in the chest but also in lymph glands, bones, and even TB meningitis. The TB hospital was packed. Aaden TB and his team did a fantastic job keeping the hospital running, encouraging patients to stay and complete their lengthy treatment. Although not formally part of my job, they did need clinical help. I had agreed to organise ward rounds in the TB hospital every two weeks. Something not provided by Dr Omar.

Aaden TB would also undertake outreach to family members in the town, and he frequently brought back patients who absconded. However, nomads were a different issue. Family tracing, and getting them to stay to complete their treatment, was never easy. I knew, when I handed the boy over to Aaden TB, that as soon as he started to improve, he might abscond. Three weeks into treatment, and on my morning ward round in the TB hospital, his bed was empty. His father had arrived and taken him during the night. We would never know what happened to the boy, but his TB was certain to return.

"Dr John, everything is OK, but I think Cathy needs you." It was Abdi. Following my TB ward round, I was taking a break in the hospital teashop, and I was marched back to the hospital compound. There was an immaculately uniformed soldier, waiting with his wife in the labour room. The couch already had a small pool of blood. "This is Major Yussuf," declared Abdi. "He speaks English, but perhaps either Idris or I should stay, just in case."

The woman did not look well. She was pale, quite listless, and had probably lost quite a lot of blood.

"She has blood for some days, with lumps," said Major Yussuf, "and it will not stop."

"How many days has she had blood?" I asked.

"At least three or four. Please, you must do something. She is getting very serious."

Abdi pulled Cathy and me to one side. "Major Yussuf is an extremely important man in the army. He has many contacts, you understand. You must look after his wife, and with care."

I asked a few more questions and examined her carefully. She was pregnant and having a miscarriage. I did not think she could afford to lose any more blood. Cathy was anxious we might have another anaemic patient dying in pregnancy.

133

"What do you think Cathy, another operation to clean out the uterus?" Cathy nodded.

After a full explanation to the Major and his wife, Abdi was dispatched to prepare the operating theatre. The patient was sedated, and I began the procedure. "No pressure then," said Cathy. "Just the wife of a very important senior army officer."

To my surprise, I did not remove large blood clots, but rather very large lumps of jelly, covered with blood. The patient had something quite rare called a 'Hydatidiform Mole', which is a rare complication of pregnancy. There is either no foetus, or it is impossible for the foetus to survive. In these cases, the pregnancy does not grow properly, and the placenta develops into a large bunch of gelatinous grape-like tissue. This causes bleeding, and although rare, can sometimes lead to cancer. I knew this was not going to be a quick operation, and with the old instruments available, it took much longer to complete than expected. Eventually, I finished. I was thankful that it went without complication, and the patient returned to the ward.

Later that day, an army fuel tanker arrived at the hospital to fill up the tank for the generator. This was quickly followed by an army water tanker, which filled up the hospital water tank. Finally, a truck arrived with sacks of porridge for the hospital kitchen. This was all courtesy of the Major. Although the town elders agreed the town would provide these types of supplies, they rarely arrived, and SCF often had to purchase them. This meant our budget could not be spent on medicines and equipment. Thank God the operation had gone well.

After forty-eight hours observation, the patient was much improved but very anaemic. Once started on iron tablets, and a high iron diet, we agreed to let her go home. This was on the understanding that she should come back after two weeks to be reviewed, or earlier if there were any problems. I explained to the Major that his wife's problem, although rare, could lead to cancer. I suggested that it would be good to have her checked at the military hospital in Djibouti. I agreed to write a referral letter to get her across the border.

"Thank you, Dr John. I am forever in your debt," said the Major, who, in the short time I had spoken with him, seemed a decent man. "If ever you need anything, just let me know." At the time, I didn't fully appreciate these fleeting words of thanks, and how important they would be in my life.

18.

A PICNIC IN AMUUD

"Hurry up, finish your breakfast, today's a big day," exclaimed Jerry.

Indeed, it was. The laboratory building had been completed. This was exciting for all of us. We had appointed the technician around one month before, so they could start training in Hargeisa. Axmed Lab was starting work today. We were truly lucky to have him. He had previously trained as a nurse, and he was definitely the most enthusiastic person I had met in Somalia.

This morning, we had a new temporary SCF team member. Jed was the lab technician trainer in Hargeisa, and he was to stay for a short time in Borama. Jed was all-American. Short, wavy blonde hair, tanned complexion, and a build like an American footballer. With his Levi T-shirt, Wrangler jeans, Aviator sunglasses, and baseball sneakers, he was a walking advertisement for American brands. This was a fashion combination not often seen in Somalia, other than on the secret police.

Jed appeared in the dining room for breakfast. "Sorry I'm late," he drawled. Cathy and Gina sat with their eyes wide open, staring at him across the table. Gina offered him a plate of bread.

"Any eggs?" he asked.

"Err, I'll try to find some," replied Cathy, just beating Gina into the kitchen.

Jed continued to sit at the table, enjoying the attention. "Nice morning fellas, you have a great place up here in the mountains."

"Yes, we do, and much safer than down in Hargeisa. Anyhow, what's the plan today?" I enquired.

"I'll be here a few days until Axmed Lab is up and running. Then, I'll drop by occasionally to see how things are."

Jerry sat enviously watching as Gina returned with a plate of eggs. "Hey, John Boy," he whispered, "why don't we get this treatment?"

After breakfast, we decided to walk to the hospital, so that Jed could find his way on foot in future. It was already starting to feel hot. Jed sent his driver ahead with a pick-up truck full of boxes.

In the shade of the hospital veranda, there were three smiling faces. Abdi, Aaden TB, and Axmed Lab were observing the boxes being unloaded. They helped carry them to the lab, and then they watched excitedly as they were opened. I left them to set it all up. I walked to the women and children's wards, where no doubt I would find the lab's first customers. By the end of the morning, I had two suspected cases of TB, and four anaemic women. They were all asked to report to the lab the next morning.

At the end of the day, I called back to the lab. All the equipment had survived the journey without damage. It sat gleaming on the shelves and lab worktop. Axmed Lab sat on his new wooden stool, next to his microscope. "Dr John, I cannot thank you enough for this opportunity to work here. It is truly my dream. You cannot imagine how long I have waited for this."

He carried on thanking us, hardly taking a breath for another five to ten minutes.

"Axmed, can I just say something?" I asked. Axmed stopped and sat back on his stool. "It's great to see you so happy. Now we're set up the real work starts tomorrow. I hope you're just as happy by the end of the first week here."

"Oh, I will be, I will. This is a fantastic opportunity…" and so he carried on.

I could still hear his overflowing enthusiasm as I walked back to the clinic.

The following morning, I went to find Abdi. "Is Dr Omar around? We arranged to show him the new lab this morning."

"I don't think so," said Abdi. "Perhaps you had better check with Axmed Lab."

I walked to the lab with Idris. Inside, Axmed Lab was setting up the equipment for the day ahead and polishing his already clean worktop.

"Good morning, Dr John. I am ready, really ready for my first patient this morning." It was so early in the day, and his enthusiasm was already beginning to wear me out. Perhaps I need a holiday, I thought. He had no news about Dr Omar, so I wished Axmed good luck, and set off for the clinic.

"You do realise that Axmed Lab has applied for a job before?" enquired Idris.

"Yes, I do Idris, I do. He met me on my very first day here. He was waiting at the hospital and asked for an interpreter job, but we didn't have any at that time. He then asked for a nurse's job, but SCF are not funding the nurse's posts here. Hence, I couldn't offer that either. He's a great guy, so when this post came up, I asked Abdi to seek him out for the job."

"Oh, I didn't realise, I thought you might not recognise him now he has a beard."

"I recognise him fine. Do people not recognise me, with my beard?"

"Not sure, you do look different. The main thing is that it has a red tinge. People respect that."

I stopped. "Really, why's that?"

"Have you not noticed that some of the men have henna in their beards? They henna their beards when they have been on the Haj to Mecca." He laughed. "So, some people think you've been to Mecca."

"I just thought it was some sort of fashion."

Idris looked at me. "Well, you do a lot of 'just thoughting'. Perhaps you don't ask enough questions." He stopped, fearing I was annoyed, but I felt this was quite brave of him.

"Idris, go on. Tell me more? Perhaps I need some feedback."

"You're a great doctor, and we all respect you for that. But you are so into your job, and looking after patients, that you don't look after yourself sometimes. Perhaps you don't see what is going on around you." He stopped with a guilty look. "I think I have said too much."

He'd made a good point. I was so low mentally when I came out to Somalia that I threw myself into my job. I completely immersed myself with all my energy, and I was totally pre-occupied with work. I had been working with little time off.

"Perhaps I need a break, Idris."

"You need to know a little more about what is going on in this country. Who are your friends, and who are not," he paused and looked at me. "Principles will only get you somewhere if you are dealing with principled people. Not everyone is like you."

I thanked him for his honesty, and I decided to reflect on his comments later that day.

A few days later, Brad was waiting in the house. He asked us all to sit down for a team meeting. The conversation quickly turned to holidays, and how Gina and Cathy had been away, but I had not. I was starting to feel slightly under attack. Brad suggested that I should take a break myself.

Forgetting my conversation with Idris, I looked at Brad with a pained expression. "But there is so much to be done, and the lab has just opened, which is really exciting."

Brad's face tightened and he gave me a hard stare. "I'm not really asking. I'm telling you to take a break."

I was somewhat annoyed. I looked at Cathy and Gina hoping for support.

"You do need a break; you're tired and a little more short-tempered than usual. Trust us," said Cathy.

"Too right," said Gina, in total support.

I guess this was one of those moments in life when you just have to sit back, and recognise you're outvoted.

"So where to go, any ideas?" I asked, looking at Brad.

"Think of somewhere you've mentioned that you'd love to see."

"Not sure, there are so many."

"What about leaving for Djibouti, where you connect to Addis for 10 days in Ethiopia and then fly on to Nairobi. You can pay for the flights, but SCF staff can meet you, and let you stay with them. What you do in each place is up to you. Anyway, I thought you wanted to see what it's like over the border?"

He was right. This suddenly sounded great, and I would probably never get such a chance again. We agreed that I would go in early September.

The following day was my birthday. The team had organised a picnic in Amuud, and around twenty staff came along. Nathan and Charlotte also joined us. This was to be the last time we would see them, as they were returning to Canada the next day. We were going to miss them. The day was lovely, relaxing under the eucalyptus trees and being surrounded by flowers, fruit, and vegetable gardens. As a tranquil spot, it couldn't be beaten.

On the way back home to Borama, Mahdi Driver decided to take a small but bumpy detour, mainly as a bit of fun. We were all being thrown around the vehicle, as the Land Rover lurched around potholes, and over bumps in the road. Sitting next to me was Safiya. She was one of the volunteer nurses who had become a close friend of Gina and Cathy, and regularly visited our house. At one very bumpy section of the road, her hand went to grasp the handrail on the back of the seat in front of her. Her hand missed, and it landed on top of my right hand. Instead of being removed, it stayed there holding mine. I couldn't decide if this was only due to the incredibly bumpy ride, or it meant something else.

I wasn't sure what to do. I looked at her face. She gently smiled, and very slowly took her hand away. I looked behind me. This small gesture had not gone unnoticed, as Ali Interpreter sat with his usual grin looking directly at me. I wondered if anyone else riding in the back had noticed. I moved both of my hands away to the left-hand side of my handrail to prevent this happening again. Regardless of what I might think about Safiya, or anyone else, I was here to do a job. I couldn't afford to allow any romantic intentions to get in the way. Culturally, I wasn't sure what people would think, and I especially did not want any problems for Safiya.

141

The next day Safiya did not turn up for work, and she remained absent for a further three days.

"Is Safiya unwell?" Cathy asked Idris. "It's most unusual for her to have any time off work."

"I'm not sure," said Idris quietly, whilst looking sideways at Ali Interpreter. Ali stayed very quiet and started looking at his feet. This was always a giveaway sign with Ali.

"Ali, do you know anything?" asked Cathy.

Ali began to shuffle and muttered something in Somali to Idris.

"Ali, please tell me what's going on," demanded Cathy.

"She's not able to come to work at the moment," murmured Ali very softly.

"And why is that?" enquired Cathy further. "Can we go and visit her?"

"Not a great idea," added Ali.

"Sorry, I'm really puzzled by all this. If you won't take me, I will go by myself," insisted Cathy.

"Ali, has this got anything to do with the drive back from Amuud?" I asked.

"Yes and no. Well not really," said Ali.

Cathy then looked quite irritated. "So, is anyone going to tell me what happened during the ride?"

"Well, she accidentally held my hand during a bumpy part of the journey, perfectly innocent, nothing more," I added.

Idris began to look quite sorrowful. "I think you should know that there is a rumour amongst the nurses that you are sleeping with Safiya."

"What!" I was completely astonished. This was clearly much worse than I envisaged.

"I think there is one nurse who feels that she spends a lot of time at your house," he continued.

"But that is completely crazy; she comes around to see Gina and Cathy. They cook together. I'm not always even in the house when she's with them," I insisted.

"Perhaps the other nurse is jealous," suggested Ali. "Remember the Valentine's Day joke that I didn't realise was a joke? She didn't get invited that day, for example." I had forgotten about that day. At this point, Cathy took a deep breath, and looked up at the ceiling. She had of course been the source of the joke at that time.

"Well, it was just a rumour, but her father then became aware. So, she's been disciplined," continued Idris.

"What does that actually mean?" asked Cathy.

"It means he's hit her," commented Ali. "In fact, he's hit her quite badly for bringing disgrace on the family."

Gina had entered the room halfway through the conversation, and had been staying very quiet. "Men!" she declared angrily, whilst she was pointing at me. "And you should keep your hands to yourself," she continued. "Look what's happened to the poor girl."

"It was an accident, a bumpy car journey, nothing more." I tried to defend myself, but no one was listening.

Gina and Cathy walked outside together. I sat on the examination couch in the clinic. This was all very exhausting. I stood and angrily looked at Ali.

"Truthfully, have you said anything to anybody about the Amuud trip?"

"No, nothing."

I was not sure whether to fully believe him.

"But I don't know if anyone else noticed, and with the rumour perhaps someone might have exaggerated the story," suggested Ali. "Anyway, the rumour existed before the trip."

Abdi entered the room. "Apologies, Dr John, but I couldn't help but overhear the conversation. Everything is OK. It's not the first time such rumours go around, and it won't be the last. Please don't think this is your entire fault. I think I know who might have started all this, and they need to apologise to Safiya's father."

"Thank you, Abdi," I said appreciatively.

"At some point, a visit to the father would help. I can ask if he will agree to meet you and Cathy, so you can explain."

Two days later, we sat with the father. Idris gently translated our side of the story, which the father accepted. Safiya quietly remained in the shadows, sitting in a corner of the house, listening to the conversation. You could see her face was still quite swollen and bruised. Of course, that was what we could see, and I wondered how badly injured she was elsewhere. Seeing her like this was quite soul-destroying. In the UK, this would be considered outrageous, but Abdi had informed me that it was quite common practice here in Somalia. A clash of cultures, and one small incident led to this.

The meeting finally concluded, and we departed their house on the understanding that Safiya was innocent. The father agreed that Safiya could continue to visit Cathy and Gina, as long as she returned home before dark.

As we walked away, Idris wanted to tell me something. "Apparently the father has also been visited by your guard, Jama."

"What has Jama got to do with all this?" I inquired, rather puzzled.

"Jama might be old with a cataract, but if you think he doesn't know everything that goes on in your house, you're much mistaken. He was your character witness," hinted Idris. "By the way, the rumour might have been started by another nurse, but the father says he was actually informed by Dr Omar."

Very helpful! The ever-thoughtful Dr Omar strikes again.

19.

ERIGABO EXPEDITION

"Borama, this is Hargeisa calling, do you copy?"

"We copy, Hargeisa. How are things? Over," replied Gina.

"We have a mission for you from Brad. SCF are considering renovating a community clinic in an area of Erigabo, at the request of the Ministry of Health. They need someone to visit and make an assessment. Brad thinks it would be good to see how Borama Hospital survives without you all for a few days. Over."

"When do we go? Over."

"Brad asks you get ready to go in three to four days."

The following week we set off, heading towards the district of Erigabo, which was further along the north east coast, towards the Horn of Africa. Although it was good to have a break from Borama, the team were a little jaded from the pressure of work. It was also a very long, arduous, and dusty journey, with no tarmac roads and little sign of any civilisation between each small village.

I travelled with Jerry in his Land Rover pick-up truck. In the back, we had tents, camp beds, spare tyres, a drum of water, and another two of diesel. The main Land Rover had the rest of the team, more spare tyres, and the food supply in cool boxes. The dust clouds spraying from the back of each vehicle were enormous. So, travelling in convoy made it difficult to see where you were going. Therefore, where possible, we travelled in parallel.

After a short break for drinks and food, Jerry and I set off first, followed by the other vehicle. It was hot and after eating lunch I must have had a nap for a few minutes. I opened my eyes and sleepily gazed across at Jerry, who already appeared tired. His eyes were continuously trained on the bumpy dust track ahead. He had been doing the bulk of the driving.

When I fully woke up, I looked in my door mirror and couldn't see the other vehicle. I sat up and checked out the back window. I couldn't see anything through the dust cloud.

"Jerry, where's the other vehicle?"

"Not sure, it's so dusty. But they'll be there somewhere," said Jerry confidently. I convinced him to stop. The dust gradually settled but the other vehicle was nowhere to be seen.

We were near to a giant termite mound, so we parked as close as possible to the foot of the mound. We climbed onto the roof of the vehicle, and we scrambled onto the top of the termite mound for a better view. Even with binoculars, we couldn't see any other vehicle.

"There, over there, I can see a dust cloud," I pointed in the distance.

Jerry scanned the horizon. "No, just a dust devil, no vehicle."

We waited a further five to ten minutes. We were just about to climb down, when from behind some acacia bushes a nomad appeared. He looked hot and tired, with his single camel in tow. He stopped nearby and pointed to Jerry's water bottle.

"I think he wants a drink," I hinted.

Jerry handed over the bottle. The nomad downed the whole

flask in seconds and handed it back. He raised his right arm in thanks, bid farewell, and, without actually speaking, walked off into the distance.

Jerry looked at his empty water bottle, amazed. "How did he do that so quick? Stop him. We need his number and sign him up for the Christmas drinking competition!"

As we turned back to the horizon, there was still nothing to be seen. "We need to head back; maybe they had a puncture, or have broken down?" I suggested.

As we climbed back into the pick-up truck, I noticed a wet patch in the back. A tent pole had come loose and had punctured the old water drum. On closer inspection, we had lost a lot of our water and it was still leaking.

"I don't have anything to repair it with," said Jerry, "and if we try to turn it upside down, I don't want the risk of the cap coming off. We could lose everything."

I was rather concerned. "So, what now Jerry?"

"We have to accept we'll lose the water down to the puncture site. We will still have half a drum, so we should be fine," replied Jerry. "I hope," he added.

We clambered into the truck and retraced our path as fast as possible. After driving for about thirty minutes, there was still no sign of anyone.

"Let's just do a recap here." I peered across at Jerry. "We've lost the rest of our team. We've lost at least half our water. A nomad has drunk your water flask. We have no food, and we're in the middle of nowhere, miles from any village."

"But we do have a map, extra drums of diesel and as yet…"

"As yet what?" I asked.

Jerry slowed the vehicle down and worriedly looked in my

direction. "I was just about to say, as yet we haven't had any tyre punctures, but she's not steering too well."

Jerry brought the truck to a standstill. We had a puncture in the front left tyre. In the heat of the afternoon, we had to change the tyre. It took us around twenty minutes. Other than nearly losing a wheel bolt in the sand, we were fairly slick. Now, we only had two further spare tyres to get us there and back.

"Jerry, we've been driving for thirty minutes or so and it's taken us twenty minutes to change the tyre. I can't see that they would be that far behind us."

Jerry agreed. "They must have taken a different track. On the map, I'm certain we took the shortest route while you were dozing."

We turned and drove more slowly looking for fresh tyre tracks heading off in a different direction. After fifteen minutes, we came across an acacia bush. Where we had previously taken a right there, other tracks went off to the left. "Must be them," stated Jerry. So, we turned left, and Jerry put his foot down. It was almost the middle of the afternoon. We needed to find the rest of the team, and then get to our destination before dark.

One hour later, we arrived at a very small village with around ten dwellings. An old man was sitting in the shade of an acacia tree near his aqal. "Not sure I can do this, but I will try talking to him in Somali," I said hopefully, as I left the truck.

The old man was surprised to see a white man walking towards him across the hot dusty road. He looked a little apprehensive and sat up straight in his seat. I bent down to his eye level and asked if he had seen a white car, pointing to the SCF logo on our vehicle. White people, had he seen any white people? He nodded and instantly pointed down the village to where the road exited on the other side. I could see the road then split into two tracks. So, I asked left or right, and waved my arms for each option. The old man pointed right. I thanked him profusely and got back in the truck. As we left the village, reassuringly, there were fresh tyre tracks to the right.

Forty minutes later, we could see another village down the track, which was a little larger than the last. I looked on our map. It seemed that we had travelled two sides of a triangle, and were then back on the road that we had taken originally, before losing the other vehicle.

Entering the village, we could see what looked like a teashop. Parked outside was a white Land Rover with an SCF logo. We slowed down and drifted slowly towards the other vehicle, before coming to a standstill. Jerry and I were so glad we had made it that we gave each other a big hug.

A small group of people, including two white women, emerged from the teashop. With faces like thunder, they walked out into the heat of the day. Like a scene from a Western movie, they formed a defensive line of gunslingers across the road in front of their Land Rover.

Jerry looked at me and swallowed. "I think we're in trouble mate." We gingerly stepped out of our truck and closed the doors. We had only taken two steps when we were met with shouts of 'And where the hell have you two been all this time?' "Nice knowing you," murmured Jerry, striding forwards. In no mood to stand down, he went into battle. "Well, we could ask the very same question," he shouted back.

This was not a good idea. I will not bore you with the rest of the conversation. It was of course our entire fault for not being attentive, and it would never happen again. The only way out was to apologise and retreat gracefully. To regain some self-esteem, Jerry quietly pointed out the tracks on the map to the guilty-looking Somali driver, indicating where they had detoured. We eventually left the village, which confused and disappointed the local population, who had thought we were there to build them a new clinic.

We trailed closely behind the other vehicle and made our destination just before nightfall. On arrival, we had to register with the local police station. The two police officers looked puzzled, as they read through our travel papers. We were told to go to our accommodation, and they would call round later to return them.

On the way to the hotel we stopped at the existing small health clinic. We were told the man with the keys had just gone, and of course nobody knew where he was.

The old hotel was very small. It looked as though it had been deserted for some time. It was dusty, with very little furniture in any of the rooms. In the back of the pick-up truck, we had some camp beds, but not enough for all. However, we did have plenty of blankets. Nearby was another building, a restaurant, which served rice and meat. We all ambled down to eat.

As we returned to the hotel, one of the police officers appeared. According to a local NSS officer, our papers were not in order. For some reason, the town was not expecting us, and we were all placed under house arrest for the night. "Great welcoming party," exclaimed Jerry.

It had been a long and difficult day. Gina and Cathy were happy in their comfortable camp beds. The Hargeisa staff huddled up, deep in conversation, around the charcoal burner. Idris was already fast asleep, and Jerry was doing his best to wake the town with his snoring.

The next morning, although under house arrest, Mahdi Driver had already sneaked out. He brought back sorghum pancakes with ghee and flasks of tea for breakfast. Another senior member of the Hargeisa team, Abdirahman, had gone to the police station to hopefully resolve our situation.

We waited an hour and a half.

"It's been some time now," said Cathy. "What if he's been arrested?"

"True. One of you men should go and check?" said Gina.

We were still thinking about the best course of action, when the door opened and Abdirahman entered in a flurry. "OK everyone, get your things together we're leaving," he said.

"Leaving," exclaimed Jerry, "we've only just got here. What about the community clinic?"

"That's their problem. Our papers were put together in Hargeisa. They plainly state the Ministry of Health have asked us to come here, and the reason why. There should be nothing wrong with them. We're clearly not wanted. There was someone in the station from the secret police, looking over our papers. To make life more difficult, they've now kept them, so we don't have any to travel back with."

"So, what now?" I asked.

"If they've decided they don't want us, then we need to go. We're still effectively under house arrest. We have two hours to pack and leave town. If we're still here, we could all get arrested and put in the local prison. Not a good idea. There's no communication with the outside world. No one would know where we were or what's happened. They could do anything, and nobody would ever find out."

"Ridiculous, what a complete waste of time," exclaimed Jerry.

"It's taken two days to get here, and it will take two days to get back. Ordered to leave by the local NSS, but we're only here because the government requested it." He was clearly disappointed, and especially looking forward to another new building project.

"I suggest we stop moaning and get out in less than an hour. We don't want to give them any excuses," said Abdirahman. "With no papers I just hope that the SCF logo, and travelling with white people, will help if we get stopped at any remote military checkpoints."

The long journey back was just as difficult, but this time we religiously swapped drivers every two hours and kept close together. Amazingly, no checkpoint asked for any ID or papers. Mahdi Driver just pointed to the white man with the red beard and the SCF logo on the vehicle door. Each checkpoint just waved us through.

20.

A WELCOME BREAK

It was August and this month the SCF team based at Tug Wajale packed their bags for the last time, and they handed the camp over to the RHU. It was still a dusty wind bowl of a site to live. But no one seemed to want to move the refugees anywhere else.

Jed was now visiting intermittently to ensure Axmed Lab was coping. Axmed was still full of enthusiasm and doing more than OK. I had only a few days left before I would be on holiday. Although initially reluctant, I was now really looking forward to having a break and getting out of Somalia.

I was in sorting mode, trying to finalise as many things as possible before leaving. I was completely unaware that in the town there were important visitors arriving that day. I was in the middle of seeing a patient with Idris, when Abdi appeared. "Dr John, everything is OK, but you need to come. We have surprise visitors. They want to see the hospital, it's an honour."

"Who is it exactly?"

"I am not sure, but it is a senior government minister with military escort."

I walked with Idris promptly to the front of the hospital. A small convoy of five vehicles, with very dark windows, pulled up outside the compound. Out of the middle vehicle stepped a well-dressed Somali man in a western-style business suit and an open-neck shirt. He was followed by a far more imposing figure, dressed in a very smart army uniform and wearing dark sunglasses. A welcoming party lined the path to the hospital. I recognised many to be town elders, and I noticed that even Dr Omar was present. There were enthusiastic handshakes as they walked down the line, and Dr Omar eagerly whisked them off to see the male wards.

Abdi suggested I waited patiently, as I might be needed. About twenty minutes later, they reappeared from the direction of the lab and the operating theatre. They marched towards me but carried on straight past. Dr Omar did not introduce me or even look in my direction. The two visitors suddenly stopped and came back to speak with Abdi, who was now standing by my side.

"This is the Minister for Interior Affairs and General Bashir," said Abdi calmly, as they both started to shake my hand. "They are very impressed with the progress SCF are making in the hospital."

"Thank you, Abdi, most kind. Would they like to see the women and children's wards?" I enquired.

Abdi asked but they shook their heads. "Not enough time," said Abdi.

They walked briskly back and disappeared inside their waiting vehicle and drove away.

"Abdi, can you explain who they were again?"

"The Minister oversees internal matters, including the police and the secret police," replied Abdi.

"And the soldier?"

"That was General Bashir," replied Abdi in a puzzled tone, suggesting I should already know him.

"Who is General Bashir exactly?"

"He oversees all the army in the North, and he's based in Hargeisa. Very important person you understand."

"And not to be crossed," commented Idris.

I assumed I would never see or hear about this man again, and I went about my business.

In September, I flew out of Hargeisa on a Somali Airline twin prop Fokker, which gently skipped over the mountains and touched down in Djibouti. Here, I had my connecting flight to Addis Ababa with Ethiopian Airways. The journey from Djibouti to Addis was uphill all the way from the coast, to an altitude of approximately 2,400 metres.

En route, we touched down in the town of Dire Dawa. As we came to a halt at the airport, I noticed the tarmac was lined with Russian-made fighter jets. At this time, the Russian military had a significant presence in Ethiopia. We were asked to pull down the window shutters for security reasons and not to take photos. Most of the passengers boarding the plane seemed to be air force personnel, including two white men speaking Russian.

The plane taxied back down the runway and took off. We had only been in the air for a short while, when an air steward started to speak on the intercom. "Please will all passengers stay calm and remain seated. The plane will shortly be turning round, as we need to land. Thank you." I had no idea what was happening, but it didn't sound particularly positive.

The plane took a swift turn and sharply banked to the left as it circled back to the airport. When the plane had first taxied down the runway, my hands were relaxed on my lap, but now they crept towards the armrests and gripped tightly.

The plane quickly landed back on the tarmac, and it taxied for a second time to the airport terminal. However, it did not come to a complete standstill. Instead, the plane swerved around, and, with no explanation from the staff, it swiftly took off again.

This was all very unnerving, but the plane continued to gain height and head towards Addis. The air stewards then started strolling along the aisle to check on all the passengers.

"Excuse me, may I ask what the problem was before?" I inquired.

"No problem, sir. Someone left the back door of the plane open, and we needed to close it," was the reassuring answer.

In Addis, I was met by SCF staff and taken to the main office. I had a great time, visiting really interesting places such as Dese, Gonder, the source of the Blue Nile, and Harar. I stayed in some fantastic buildings that had previously been palaces belonging to Haile Salassie, the former Emperor of Ethiopia. They had been converted into wonderful hotels. At each hotel, lines of welcoming staff greeted me. But I would be only one of possibly three or four guests. There were more staff than customers. In one hotel, at breakfast, it was just my guide and me, along with three Ethiopian secret policemen watching us.

One sunny morning, I was sitting on a patio in Northern Ethiopia, overlooking beautiful, mountainous scenery, including a huge gorge down below the hotel. The waiter arrived with my cooked breakfast. I took my knife and fork, and was just about to start eating, when there was a rustling noise in some nearby bushes. I turned to see what was causing the noise. A large baboon appeared, and casually walked the short distance over the patio to my table. It sat comfortably in the chair opposite, joining me, as

157

if it was a fellow guest. The baboon was big, and it began to look at the breakfast on my plate. It yawned, baring huge teeth. Then one hand darted out to snatch a sausage. I wasn't going to argue. Within a minute or two, my plate was empty.

The baboon got up, and, just as casually, walked back towards the bushes. At this moment, the waiter returned to see the departing baboon, and my empty plate.

"I was just going to ask if you were enjoying your breakfast, but I see you've met Abel."

"Yes, indeed. Able to take my breakfast," I replied.

"Exactly right, sir, best not to argue. I shall bring you another."

On the arrival of my second breakfast, Abel joined me for seconds. I gently pushed the plate into the middle of the table to make it easier. The baboon cleared the plate and returned to the bushes. I decided it was then safe to get up and I went to eat inside. I just hoped I wasn't being charged for all this food.

I asked the local SCF team if I could visit Jijga. This was the nearest town to the Somali border. Both Borama and Hargeisa were not far on the other side. I just wanted to see what it was like. I hitched a ride in an NGO vehicle that was heading that way with supplies. I couldn't afford to be noticed, so I wore sunglasses and a chequered Arab headscarf, and I had to remain in the vehicle throughout the trip. Although I can say that I achieved my ambition to see over the border, the place was basically very similar to the Somali side, except not quite as run-down.

More interestingly, in Jijiga, I saw large quantities of qat being sold in small bundles in the market square. Qat looks like stems of privet hedge leaves, tastes very bitter, and contains an amphetamine-like stimulant. I had seen men in Somalia chewing it, their cheeks puffed out like a hamster's and teeth all green with qat juice. Their bloodshot eyes would be wide open, with the eyelids retracted right back, due to muscle spasm caused by the stimulant. This gave them a wild and scary appearance. Men could spend a lot of their money on qat and not leave enough to feed their family. Recently, I'd noticed that there had been more for sale in Borama. It was delivered fresh each day, being somehow smuggled over the border from Ethiopia. This market was a likely source.

On my return to Addis, I was taken to a very upmarket Italian restaurant. Many international organisations were based in Addis. The international and Ethiopian Government staff had money to spend, and this place obviously catered for them. Not what I was expecting for a country whose population was recently seen to be starving on the world stage.

A well-dressed Ethiopian man leaned over. He asked me where I was from, and where I was going next. I explained that I was British, and was heading to Nairobi.

"Oh, you're going to Africa next," he said. "You should really enjoy it. I'm told it's nice there. Have a great time." He then went back to the conversation with the colleagues on his table.

I paused momentarily, as I thought his response rather strange. Were we not already in Africa? I wondered, as I proceeded to eat my desert, which was labelled as traditional Ethiopian tiramisu on the menu.

From Ethiopia, I went to Kenya, where this time I could relax. Being a tourist on safari in Kenya, with so much wonderful food, was both a luxurious and yet weird experience, compared to my life in Somalia. But my happy jaunt came to an end, and it was time to head back to Somalia. Just like the first time, I would go through the capital and be briefed by Brad, before returning to Borama.

21.

TENSIONS RISE

It was October, and, after a long journey, I stepped down from the Land Rover. I looked around the SCF compound in Borama. Everything was quiet. The guards were having an afternoon siesta in the guardhouse. The giant tortoise was munching some plants near the gate, but, as usual, it did not care to venture outside. A small white goat was tethered to a bush.

I grabbed my bag, waved goodbye to Mahdi Driver, and walked up the steps of the house. The washing had been done that day, and the large aluminium pan, used by Deeqa, was leaning against the steps to dry. Clothes were draped over the bushes in the compound, as well as over the small clothesline. I stepped carefully over the adopted cat, which was lying in the sun across the doorway, and walked down the corridor. I could see Cathy sleeping, as I passed her bedroom. Otherwise, the house was empty, and all seemed tranquil.

I walked into the dining room. My only welcome home was from the resident praying mantis, which was standing poised to attack on the dining room table as usual. His head turned to give me what was now a familiar stare down, as I approached.

His head then turned back to focus on a fly that had just landed. I went to the fridge and poured myself a glass of cold water. I decided to sit and read my new book.

I had reached page five when the door to the house opened. I could hear Gina stomping down the corridor, and loudly muttering. "Unbelievable, truly unbelievable." She entered her bedroom and slammed the door.

This must have woken Cathy, who came into the dining room, a little bleary-eyed. She opened the fridge and started to scan the mostly empty shelves. She slowly poured herself some water, and then sat at the table yawning.

"Oh, hi. I didn't see you there. I didn't realise you were back today."

"Yes, are you OK? You look a little tired." It was not usual for Cathy to nap in the afternoon.

"Oh, I was up all night with some difficult deliveries, and only got to bed just before lunch. I need to go back and check they're OK. Anyhow, did you have a good time?"

I started to tell her about my holiday, but I could see Cathy was shattered and not really listening.

"Did you see the goat?" enquired Cathy. "It's my new pet. A present from a patient."

Before I could answer, the dining room door swung open and in walked Gina, who seemed very bothered by something. "Thank God, you're back. We've had a hell of a time," she exclaimed.

"I need to go," said Cathy. "I'll leave Gina to tell you all that's happened whilst you've been away."

Gina launched into her tale, as she paced the floor. "Men, men are unbelievable."

"What about men?"

"I can't take all this. Whilst you've been away, some of the male staff in the hospital won't take any notice of us. Why? Because we're just mere women, that's why. As for Dr Omar, I could strangle him." Her hands were wringing his neck, as she spoke.

Gina came out with a long list of issues. Dr Omar would not speak to them on any clinical matter. He had also started to bring all his private patients to the hospital lab for tests, demanding that they should have their tests first. Patients from the male ward came second and the male clinics third. Women and children were after that, if there was any time. "Thank God we're not testing animals, as even they would be more important. Quick open the intensive care unit, my camel is sick," exclaimed Gina.

Ali Interpreter had also returned to his old ways, coming to work late or not at all. The hospital had been very busy, and this had made life very difficult. Idris, who was supposedly on holiday while I was away, had been asked to cover for Ali on a number of days.

"Is Cathy OK? She looked tired," I asked.

"That's another thing," said Gina, launching into another set of problems. "Now the lab is up and running, we've been able to check levels of anaemia, and they're really quite shocking. I'm not sure how some of the women are still alive, let alone walking around and having babies. So, we have given some blood transfusions."

"Important stuff, but can we just go back to Cathy for a second?" I asked, determined to get an answer.

"That's exactly it. You know how passionate she is about her work and how she has been really upset in the past if any mother has died. Well, we've had some very sick and anaemic mums who have needed transfusions. But we couldn't get donors for them all, so Cathy has donated blood where her blood has cross-matched. I think she's done it twice in the last three weeks." Gina finally took a breath, and went quiet, before speaking in a more hushed tone. "If I'm truthful, she might have even given blood to a third woman, but I'm not sure. She knew I'd be cross with her, so she won't be honest with me." Gina looked me in the eye. "But I didn't tell you all this, OK?"

"Anything else?" I said, already feeling exhausted.

"The pharmacy stocks are low. The latest delivery shipment hasn't arrived, and some of the stocks have disappeared in the hospital. I'm thinking Dr Omar?"

I was trying to digest all this and decide a way forward. Then it came to me, book another holiday.

The following morning, I decided I must first talk to Cathy. I was just about to ask her for a confidential chat, when Ali Interpreter arrived slightly late on the ward. He had obviously not combed his hair that morning, and his shirt was not buttoned up properly. His eyes were bloodshot, eyelids slightly retracted, teeth still green, and he was talking even more than usual. He had all the signs of having been chewing qat late into the night. Although I had suspected him of chewing qat in the past, he had never been as bad as this at work.

"Ali, good to see you this morning. How are you?" I asked.

"Good and you? You're back from holiday already."

"Yes, I am, Ali. Is that a surprise?"

"Err, well, I didn't realise you'd be back at work today," stuttered Ali.

"Did you have a good time last night?" I enquired.

"OK. It was OK."

"How was your wife last night and this morning?"

"My wife?"

"Yes, your wife, Ali. Have you been home? Did you see your wife this morning?"

Ali began to stare at the ground. He had no cheeky grin this morning.

"Have you had any sleep, Ali?"

He continued to stare aimlessly at the floor.

"Ali, I suggest you go home, I don't think you are in any fit state to work today. Just go home, and we will talk about this tomorrow." I knew discussing it now was a complete waste of time. Under the influence of qat, he would promise me the earth, and then completely forget our conversation. He walked out of the clinic slowly, shoulders shrunk, and head slightly bowed.

"Can I tell you something confidentially?" asked Idris, who had been quietly standing in the corner.

"Of course, Idris. Please do."

"It's not good, Dr John. The qat is getting everywhere. For example, Ali is chewing more and more, but he's not the only one. It's not only bad for his health, but also, he can't afford it. His wife sometimes doesn't have enough money for food. I think he's getting addicted. Please, don't let him know I've told you, but she's pregnant, and the baby is due in February."

This was worse than I feared.

I turned to Cathy for a second time, and she was just about to speak when Axmed Lab appeared in the doorway. "May I have a word, Dr John, in private, please, back at the lab?" He appeared unusually perturbed, so I agreed, and followed him through the hospital compound. He stopped at the lab door and unlocked it. He invited me to sit on a stool.

He repeated Gina's story about Dr Omar and his private patients. "Also, I think some of my reagents have disappeared from the lab, whilst I've been taking urgent results back to other parts of the hospital. I can't walk anywhere, even in an emergency, without having to lock the doors."

"Do you know who might take them?" I enquired.

"I don't understand, why would anyone want them without the equipment? No one can use them, unless they're being sold to private pharmacies in the town. But I don't know of any that have lab equipment, even Dr Omar sends his patients here."

"Thanks for letting me know. For now, we'll keep the doors locked, even when you are rushing around."

I returned to the ward, and eventually I managed to speak with Cathy. Without any prompting, she explained fully what she had been doing, in terms of donating blood. She already realised she had gone too far. "I know it's not sensible, but what do you do when someone is so ill, and they and their baby might die? I do have mothers and babies walking around because of my blood. They are still very anaemic but at least they are alive."

"I totally understand—" I said sympathetically.

"I can feel a 'but' coming on," said Cathy.

"—but we, and that's all of us in the team, we can't save Somalia by ourselves. If we're not well, we can't help anyone else. Do you hear me? We have to try and get blood another way. Perhaps there will be times when we have to give blood, but that should be a team decision not an individual one." Cathy nodded.

That evening, I visited Ali Interpreter at home with Idris. He was in a much better state. I talked to him about his use of qat, and the impact of it on his family. He informed me his wife was pregnant. Although I could try to be supportive, I left Ali with

165

the message that ultimately I had to think of the team. Qat could cost him his job. I had deliberately said it rather sternly, hoping it would have the desired effect.

I passed by the hospital on the way home. Abdi was sitting on the veranda. I hadn't seen him all day. He waved me over. After he asked me about my holiday, I asked how he was feeling. He seemed a little flat, and 'everything did not seem OK' for him, today.

"I tell you this as a friend, Dr John, so you can understand. The hospital has no money, not even to pay the nurses. They earn very little as it is."

"Gosh. How long has this been a problem, Abdi?"

"For a while now, many weeks in fact. I'm not sure the nurses will come to work for much longer. We will only have the SCF volunteer nurses."

"Why is there no money, Abdi?"

"The money comes through Dr Omar. He says nothing has arrived, but I'm not sure. I suspect he's keeping it for himself."

"Should I say something?"

"Dr Omar is not an easy person to talk to. Don't forget he has friends in high places. He is from the President's clan. For now, it is better for you to keep quiet. He can cause a lot of problems for you, if you get too involved."

A number of days later, we had a visit from Jed. At last, our team meeting had an injection of enthusiasm. He bounded into the house, eager as always to see Gina and Cathy. Jerry had come with him to see how his buildings were holding up.

Abdi and Axmed Lab were waiting for us on the hospital veranda. Both had very stern faces.

"I need to show you something," declared Abdi. He and Axmed Lab led us all to the hospital lab.

Jerry, presuming the worst, raced off ahead and circled the building. "No cracks, roof and walls intact," he said happily.

"The building is not the problem," confirmed Abdi.

"There's nothing inside," said Axmed Lab. "It's been emptied overnight."

We all stood and looked at each other. Jerry examined the doors and windows. "No evidence of a break in, or vandalism."

"Does anyone else have a key?" I asked Abdi.

"Only Dr Omar," replied Axmed.

"Abdi, is that right?" I asked.

Abdi nodded. "Yes. He is the only other man with a key. Whilst you were away, he insisted he needed one."

We went inside. All the equipment and reagents were gone. There was nothing left.

"This morning I had a note delivered for Axmed Lab," Abdi informed us, handing the sealed note over.

"Axmed, please open it," I insisted.

With some trepidation, Axmed opened the note. "It's asking me to meet with Dr Omar at his private clinic, to start working there this evening," replied Axmed.

I could see Jed was fuming. He started to stomp off to Dr Omar's office.

"Wait a minute. We need to tread carefully," I pleaded.

Axmed Theatre had been standing quietly listening to the whole conversation and said something in Somali.

"What did he say, Abdi?" asked Jed.

"That Dr Omar came early this morning to clear out his office, and he's still there."

Before Abdi had finished his sentence, Jed was off.

I placed a hand on his shoulder. "Jed, just stop a second, let's both go in with an interpreter. We need to stay calm whatever happens."

I took a deep breath, as we approached the office door. We could hear furniture being moved around inside. Despite knocking on the door, no one answered. Jed burst through the door. Dr Omar looked surprised, and he went to sit behind his desk.

"Where has all the lab equipment gone?" Jed demanded, in a raised voice.

"I presume you are wanting me to translate?" asked Idris nervously. I nodded. Dr Omar replied in Somali.

"What did he say, Idris?" insisted Jed.

"He doesn't know what you're talking about."

"Tell him that everything has gone from the lab, and ask him where it's gone."

Dr Omar appeared disinterested, shrugging his shoulders as he muttered a reply. "He has no idea," translated Idris.

Jed was getting very agitated. I decided to intervene. "Idris, please tell him everything has gone. There's no sign of a break in, we know he is the only other person with a key."

Idris obliged. "He still doesn't understand why you are asking him about this."

"God damn it," shouted Jed. "How can he sit there brazenly lying to us?"

Idris stood silent not wanting to translate this.

Dr Omar stood up, fixed a steely-eyed gaze on us, and spoke.

"Idris, what did he say please?" I asked calmly.

"This is very serious, Dr John. He says this is his hospital, and if he wants to relocate the equipment to his private clinic, he is able to do so."

"I can't believe what I'm hearing, this is outrageous," shouted Jed. "Tell him this is actually my equipment, purchased with my budget, and I brought it here for the hospital. If it's not here, I will take it all back."

I was having difficulty staying calm. I'd put up with this man for months, and now my gasket was about to blow. I took a few deep breaths, and then I started to count to ten.

Idris continued. "Dr Omar says you have no control over what happens in this hospital, and you must now get out of his office."

I looked Dr Omar in the eye and thumped the desk. "I can't take this anymore. I'm leaving," I declared and stormed out of the office.

Outside, the staff had gathered, and were leaning in towards the door listening. They reeled back and parted to let me walk through. I briefly stood outside, and I could still hear Jed and Dr Omar shouting at each other. I strode along the veranda for some fresh air. The diminutive figure of Abdi was walking alongside struggling to keep up. "Dr John, you're not actually leaving are you, surely you can't leave? What will we do without you and the team? You have done so much, please don't leave."

I had to compose myself, and not say anything more I would regret. Eventually, I started to calm down. Abdi's words were ringing in my ears. I could see Gina and Cathy racing over from the other side of the hospital.

"Abdi, what I meant was I'd had enough of this conversation, and I'm leaving the office. The conversation was going nowhere."

"Oh, thank goodness," said Abdi, more relaxed.

"What we do next has to be a team decision," I said.

"Good," said Jerry. "We can't leave. I've not long finished the buildings, and the new latrines have hardly been used."

Abdi went back, and he encouraged Jed to step outside and calm down. Dr Omar came outside his office, and he demanded to know what everyone was staring at. He slammed the door shut, stepped into the ambulance, and drove into the town, scattering the few pedestrians who were in his way.

Jed was still agitated, and he was trying to wind down. "This was supposed to be a quick visit and I have other things to do today. I'll leave you to try and sort this out. We can radio in two to three days for an update." He charged off to the waiting vehicle.

"What a thoroughly exciting morning," smiled Jerry delightedly. "Jupiter Rising will orbit this way again soon." He climbed into his pick-up truck, alongside Jed, and they set off for Hargeisa.

I decided to leave the team discussion until later in the evening. We hadn't seen any patients and we all needed time to think. Walking across to the wards, I noticed some of the patients looking very alarmed by what they had witnessed. Some were related to the town elders.

22.

A SURPRISE VISIT TO HARGEISA

I had an early lunch at home, and I then visited the teashop to collect Idris on the way back to the hospital. I noticed a white Suzuki jeep following me. Inside were three men with their expensive patterned shirts and sunglasses. The vehicle overtook me, and then it stopped between the teashop and myself. Two men got out. One leant against the side of the jeep. The other walked a few steps away from the vehicle. The third remained on the back seat with the door open. I had to walk between two of the men to get to the teashop. Suddenly, one of them grabbed my right arm. "In. Get in," he said, pointing to the open car door.

"Why?" I asked, whilst trying to pull my arm away.

"In now," the man said, more sternly. The other man, who was leaning against the jeep, took my left arm, and bent it behind my back. I was bundled into the jeep onto the back seat. The door closed and the vehicle rapidly set off.

Idris and Ali were standing outside the teashop. They had watched the whole affair in horror, but had wisely not tried to intervene. I was not sure what this was about. I could not think of anything that I had done to alarm the secret police.

It was a bumpy ride in the small jeep. There was no conversation. None of them seemed to speak much English, or at least, if they did, they weren't going to answer any of my questions. The only thing I really understood was that we were heading towards Hargeisa.

We arrived in Hargeisa before nightfall, and we drove into the compound of a police station. The jeep door was opened. "Out, out," shouted one of the men. I stepped out onto the dusty ground, and I was waved towards the front door of the station. Inside was the familiar blue painted finish with a Somali flag and a picture of President Siad Barre hanging on the wall.

I was taken straight past the police officer on the front desk, and down a dark corridor to a grey solid-iron door, which had a small window. The door was opened, and I was led inside. They asked for my watch. I noticed it was almost half past five in the afternoon as I handed it over. Then they all left and closed the door. I heard the key turning as it was locked.

I looked around the cell. There was a concrete slab in the corner, built against the wall. It was well worn, and it had obviously seen many previous occupants. It was the only place, other than the concrete floor, to sit or lay down. There was a very small window higher up the wall. It was too high to see out of, but just large enough to allow in some light. It was not large enough to get out should you wish to try, and it had three rusty iron bars just to make sure. There was nothing to drink, and nowhere to go to the toilet. I wasn't sure how long I sat there. All I knew is that it had become dark outside, so now I could see very little inside the cell.

I was almost dozing off, when I heard a key in the lock. The door creaked open. There was a faint light in the corridor outside, and a uniformed police officer stood silhouetted in the doorway. He said something in Somali, and he waved for me to walk outside. He led me past three other cell doors, and into an office. In here, there was a brighter light on the ceiling, a desk, and three chairs. I was invited to sit in the solitary chair on one side of the table.

As the police officer left the room, two men with expensive patterned shirts, and one with sunglasses even at this time of night, then entered the room. They sat in the two chairs on the other side of the table.

"You are Dr John?" said one of the men gruffly, his gold upper tooth glinting in the light.

"Yes, I am," I replied. "Can I ask why I am here?"

"You are not here to ask questions, only to answer them," he replied assertively, as he leaned over the table. I presumed he was looking at me, but I couldn't tell through the mirrored sunglasses.

"Why are you here?" he asked.

"I don't know. I've just asked you that question, as you have brought me here."

"No, I mean why are you here in Somalia?" he replied, somewhat irritated.

"I am a doctor in Borama, and I work for Save the Children Fund."

"No, why are you really here? What information are you trying to find?"

"I'm not sure what you are talking about," I replied, getting more puzzled.

"We believe you are spying."

"Spying, spying on what exactly?" I was trying to stay calm, but this was getting more serious.

"Why don't you tell me? It will be easier for both of us."

"This must be some sort of mistake. I have no idea what you are talking about." I was now quite bewildered by the questioning.

"You are a spy, yes?"

"No, I am not. I've just told you."

"Why are you living so close to the Ethiopian border?"

"Because I was posted to work in Borama, and Borama is close to the border."

"You could go anywhere in Somalia, why Borama?"

"That is where I was sent by Save the Children Fund."

He paused and changed the line of questioning. "Do you have a camera?"

"Yes, I do have a camera, but—"

"Just answer the questions. Do you have a radio in your house?"

"Yes, but—"

"No buts, just answer the questions," he said, raising his voice. He stood up and started to pace around the room. "We've been told you have taken pictures. Is that true?"

"Only of patients, with their permission," I clarified.

"Why patients?"

"For teaching purposes; we use them to train the Somali nurses."

"You use your radio?"

"Sometimes, we all do—"

He interrupted again. "Where is your licence for this radio?"

I had no idea if we had a licence, but I presumed that this had been sorted by head office. "In Mogadishu," I said confidently. I was learning not to say any sentence with the words 'and' or 'but' in it.

I continued. "Do I have any rights, to—"

174

"I said no questions, you do not make questions." He sat back down, took out a cigarette from a packet, and he lit it for himself.

"I want to speak to the SCF office in Hargeisa or Mogadishu," I insisted. He just smiled, the glint of his gold tooth becoming even brighter.

"Or the British Embassy," I said.

"British Embassy," he laughed cynically. "So, you are a spy. British Embassy, they are all spies," he said, waving his cigarette at me.

"I am not a spy. I am a doctor."

He puffed cigarette smoke over the table and directly into my face, making me cough. "You are not making this easy. Why don't you just admit it, and tell me why you are really here?"

I coughed again and then replied. "I'm only a doctor, I use the radio with all my team to speak—"

"So, you are all spies, all the team. Now we are getting somewhere," he said, sitting back contentedly and folding his arms.

"No, we are not all spies. We have a radio to talk to colleagues in Hargeisa."

"Now we are getting near the truth. With people in Hargeisa to share information, to spy."

I could see that whatever I said would be twisted back to being a spy. The man was obsessed.

"So, you work near the Ethiopian border, you have a camera, admit taking photos, you have a radio in your house, and you share information with Hargeisa," he continued.

I decided to say nothing.

"You see, you have nothing to say now because it is the truth. Is it not?"

The other secret policeman just listened. He wasn't taking any notes, and there was no recording of this conversation. I had noticed he was carrying a small plastic bag when he came into the room, which he had placed on the floor. I could no longer see the bag as it lay behind the table.

The first man continued with the questioning, "If you have nothing more to say, we may have to take this a step further." I didn't know exactly what this would entail. At this moment, the second man reached down for the plastic bag. I wondered if the bag contained something to help them 'take this a step further'. He placed the bag on the table, and he pulled out a few branches of qat. I was relieved, as he picked a few leaves off the stems. He put them in his mouth and started to chew. He offered some to the first man, who hesitated and then declined.

"I can see you're going to be stubborn," the first man continued.

"I'm not stubborn. I am answering the questions as honestly as possible."

"Honestly, you say honestly, and yet you don't admit to being a spy."

"It doesn't matter how many times you accuse me of being a spy, my answer is the same. I am not a spy."

"We shall see. We have reliable information from Borama that you are a spy."

"From Borama. Who, who says I am a spy?" I said, getting a little annoyed. My emotions were starting to get the better of me.

"This I am not able to tell you. I remind you that you are here to answer questions, not to ask them."

"I need to go to the toilet," I requested, changing the subject. The two men spoke to each other, and the second officer pointed to the plastic bag.

"OK, you can go to the toilet. I'm finished here, at least for now. We'll continue this in the morning." They stood and left the room.

The police officer from the front desk returned and took me outside. I could see the two secret policemen were now sharing the bag of qat, as they sauntered down the corridor. I was taken to a pit latrine, and continually observed, whilst I was using it. I hadn't been to the toilet for ages. What a relief. I was then marched back to my cell. I could see my police guard had red eyes, retracted eyelids and teeth green with qat juice. Once I was inside, he locked the door.

Locked up here all night in a police station full of supposedly 'on duty' officers, who were soon to be high on qat. Although I had possibly been saved from further questioning because of it, I was worried. All sorts of thoughts whirred through my mind. The humming of the generator outside stopped, as it was turned off. It was very quiet. I lay on the cold concrete slab looking up at a ceiling that I couldn't see in the dark. How was I going to talk about this in my next letter home? Would there be a next letter home?

I had an uncomfortable night and was woken by the early morning light. A small, but bright, ray of sunshine came through the cell window, and it lit up a panel on the wall opposite. Just to remind me, the silhouettes of the iron bars confirmed where I was. My forearm was sore, and I rubbed it automatically. I could feel three lumps. As the light improved, I noticed I had large mosquito bites. The still of the night was replaced by the sound of engines, as vehicles were being readied for the day ahead. I could hear Somali voices outside, and there was a smell of cigarette smoke, as it drifted through the window into my cell. What would

I give for a drink? And, of course, I needed to urinate. As I walked around, I accidentally kicked a tin can that had been lying in a dark corner of the cell. I had found a makeshift toilet.

I'm not sure how much time had passed but it was now quite light. It was probably mid-morning. I had heard voices outside the cell, but no one came to unlock the door. I was so tired that I drifted back to sleep.

Suddenly, I was awoken by a number of voices outside the door. There was one voice that I thought I recognised for a brief moment, but I wasn't sure who it was. A key turned in the lock and the door swung open.

There was a tall man standing in the doorway. I could see he had a neat army uniform, but his face was still in the shadows. I wondered what was in store for me this morning. He stepped forward into the cell. To my surprise, it was Major Yussuf. He stood there with a very serious face. Was he also going to be involved in all this, I wondered.

"Dr John, put on your shoes," he commanded. "You need to come with me."

"To go where?" I asked. I had just asked a question, and then remembered I was not here to ask questions.

"I am taking you out of here."

"To go where exactly?"

"We're going home to Borama."

I had never tied my shoelaces so fast in my life. "Thank you, thank you," I said, clasping my hands together with absolute joy.

He held out his hand to shake mine. "Will you accept my apology for what has happened to you? I cannot believe you have been treated like this."

We calmly walked out of the cell and down the corridor. The

Major pinned any nearby officers to the wall with his steely gaze, as we walked past. At the front desk, he took out a document from his jacket, showed the piece of paper to the duty officer, and then signed another on top of the desk. I was handed my watch.

"There, you are free to go, free to go. Someone will pay for this," he declared, scanning the office. He then led me out of the building and to his army vehicle.

We climbed inside, and he drove out of the police station compound.

"I have one thing to ask of you," said the Major.

"What is that?" I enquired, wondering what the payback would be.

"What has happened to you is very embarrassing for us. I ask that you never speak of this to others, especially your senior team at SCF. We cannot have them being scared away and leaving, you or your team leaving. Will you do this, and I promise this will never happen again to any of you?"

"I will try my best and thank you. You cannot imagine how relieved I am. Who is it that organised my release?"

"I cannot say, but I have been to a very high level to arrange it. Do you understand? No one would dare challenge his authority. What is happening in this country at the moment is for the Somali people to sort out. You should not be involved or put in any danger."

I nodded wondering whom this might be, and if I would ever be able to thank them personally.

After a few minutes, we arrived at an extremely large official-looking compound.

"Where are we going exactly?" I inquired.

"I have to share the news you are released, and I have

something to collect. I will only be a short time," replied the Major, as he tooted the horn on the jeep.

The large gates creaked open, and we entered. The armed soldiers on duty peered inside the vehicle and looked apprehensively at me. The Major said something in Somali, and the guards waved us further inside.

"What is this place?" I asked.

"It is the residence of General Bashir," declared the Major, as he climbed out of the jeep. "You are allowed to step outside, but please stay with the vehicle," he instructed.

Initially, I sat inside the jeep, looking around. It was a strange mixture between gardens and a small army base. The Major had been gone for about twenty minutes. I decided to stretch my legs. I carefully climbed out and stood in the bright sunlight. I could hear a cat-like purring noise so casually turned around to look behind me. I was startled to see a cheetah standing about twenty metres away. I completely froze. It started to walk slowly towards me, and then veered away to investigate the front of the jeep.

I tried to stay calm and backed up towards the closed door of the jeep. I was attempting to get back inside the vehicle, when the Major suddenly reappeared, holding a file of papers.

"I see you've met one of the General's pet cheetahs?"

"Pet cheetahs?" I exclaimed.

"Yes, there are two of them, quite gentle really." He grinned. "Just don't try to run away."

We both climbed in the jeep. The Major slowly edged the vehicle forwards, encouraging the cheetah to move to one side, and we left the compound.

I was eventually taken back to Borama, and another soldier dropped me at the hospital. I walked back to the SCF house. If this had to be a secret, what was my story line going to be? I told the team that I had been on a confidential trip at short notice in Hargeisa. This was to discuss the situation with the hospital lab. I apologised for any worry I had caused anyone. Jerry spotted that I looked as though I'd had a rough night. He thought I'd been at a party, or even had a secret girlfriend. He gave me wink. It was Idris and Ali who gave wiser, and more knowing, looks in my direction.

The following day an army vehicle arrived, and it delivered all the lab equipment back to the hospital. The driver gave Abdi a note. When translated, it read as follows: "This is to inform you that Dr Omar has been removed from Borama. He has been transferred to another hospital in the south of Somalia at short notice. This is to be nearer his family, with effect from today."

No one in Borama claimed to actually see Dr Omar before he left. However, as he so rarely attended the hospital this in itself was not unusual. Perhaps he had been escorted from the town. The actual truth we would never know.

Following this episode, I was invited to meet the elders of the town. They seemed very positive about the SCF team, and made encouraging noises about us staying. I was given a formal letter to say that the team had 'Freedom of the town' status, and we had permission to take photos in the town as we pleased. I was also offered a Somali passport and the opportunity to become a Somali citizen. This was a great honour, and I thought perhaps it would be cool to have a Somali as well as a British passport. I could imagine the confusion it would cause at airports. It was Abdi who took the shine off this proposal, when he reminded me, in a fatherly manner, that I would be eligible to be called up for national service and conscription to the Somali army. I hastily found a diplomatic way to decline this offer.

Later in the month, the whole team was invited to the annual Revolution Day Parade in the main square of the town. We were told we could take photos, including of any military hardware taking part in the procession. On the day, we were invited to sit in the main stand, alongside other local dignitaries. This was a great day for the town. The procession had many floats, using a variety of vehicles. Even the hospital took part, using the SCF truck. This was all a complete turnaround for the team.

That evening, Deeqa had cooked a special goat curry with rice for dinner.

We had almost finished our delicious meal, when Gina excused herself. When she returned, she sat next to me. She leaned across and whispered in my ear.

"Did you notice there was no goat in the compound, when we came home?"

I had not and shrugged my shoulders.

"I've just asked the guards, and they said they'd killed it to celebrate today," continued Gina. "Not sure Cathy has realised yet. But I think we should leave it until we've completely finished dinner."

Poor Cathy, she was going to be heartbroken. Not only was she a failed vegetarian, but a failed vegetarian who was eating her own pet.

23.

SOMALI POST-MORTEM

Everything was running more smoothly, especially the volunteer nurse project. The students sat their end of year exams, and the best ones were awarded a formal place at Hargeisa Nursing School. This was good for each successful volunteer nurse but less so for the hospital, as we then had fewer committed staff. The hope was that, after graduation, they would come back to work in Borama. The scheme had been so successful that we decided to take on a second wave of students to fill the vacancies.

SCF agreed to replace the hospital generator as it had broken down on many occasions. This was on the understanding that the town supply the fuel. Although this might have been our understanding, fuel from the town was not always forthcoming. When we were short of fuel, a message to the local army camp usually resulted in an army tanker passing by to top up the fuel reserves. The same applied to the hospital water tank. The hospital guidelines were officially typed up and printed, with copies given out to all the staff. We even distributed copies to local pharmacies to try and encourage them to adopt more sensible prescribing. The Finnish team also upgraded the X-ray machine.

Unfortunately for me, it was not all entirely good news. I broke a tooth on a small stone in a salad. Jerry reminded me that this would never have happened if I had let Deeqa focus on cooking just spaghetti bolognese. I needed to have dental treatment, which was non-existent in this part of Somalia, so I was flown out by SCF to see the military dentist in Djibouti. This made me feel very well cared for by SCF. In stark contrast, some other organisations seemed to be less concerned about their staff on the front line. There had been a number of episodes over recent months where, were it not for our SCF team, staff from some other organisations would have been left to fend for themselves.

On return to Hargeisa from the dentist in Djibouti, I was informed that someone had discovered an old squash court, which had been built during the time when the British were based there. Cathy was on a day off in Hargeisa. She had not played squash before, so I agreed to give her a lesson. The court hadn't been used for sporting purposes for some time. The first task was to sweep away the litter and all the dried animal droppings, as it had been used to corral goats at night.

We were loaned squash racquets and ball by staff in another NGO. I smacked the squash ball against the back wall a few times to test it. I then demonstrated to Cathy how you had to thump the ball, rather than stroking it, as in tennis. With her first vigorous swipe of the racquet, she shot the ball straight into my right eye. My eye became instantly bloodshot, and I had blurred vision. Having only just returned from the dentist, I was whisked off to the Help the Aged (HTA) eye surgery team in the local town of Sheikh.

The journey was a good two and a half hours drive, but mostly on tarmac roads. I was more concerned about my eye than I had been for my safety when sitting in the prison cell. As a casualty doctor, I had seen patients seriously damage an eye in a squash accident. The squash ball is just the right size to fit into the eye socket, should it strike your face in just the right place.

I was given eye drops, a large eye pad, and the spare room at the HTA house. Four to five days later, my vision had returned to normal, and I was discharged back to Borama, sporting a red eye as my war wound. Although I wasn't bearing any grudge, Cathy decided to give me a wide berth for the first day back. In the absence of protective goggles, I decided it was to be my first and last game for the Somali National Squash Team.

On my first day back in Borama, there was a rabies alert. Someone had seen a wild dog they thought was acting strangely and frothing at the mouth. I was asked to go out searching with the police to find it. They wanted me to confirm if the dog was rabid. I was not sure why I would be any better than the local police, but it was better not to argue. When we found the dog, before I could say anything about my opinion, they just shot it. They didn't want any risks, which made me wonder why they had made such a fuss about me going in the first place.

I returned to the hospital. Abdi was very excited standing on the veranda. Whilst I had been away, a new Somali doctor had arrived.

"Good morning, Dr John. Everything is OK. A new doctor, Dr Muktar, has arrived. For once, we have a more local doctor. He is from Hargeisa, and not from the South. I think you will like him, and maybe he is more likely to stay." I was whisked off to what would now be Dr Muktar's office. Abdi knocked on the door, and, without waiting, he just opened the door and walked straight in. This in itself was a refreshing change.

"Welcome, welcome, Dr John. I am Dr Muktar. I am told life

has not been easy since you arrived. I want us to work together." He placed his right hand on his heart. "I promise that I am keen to improve this hospital."

Hospital life was perhaps on the up. Could it last? A few weeks later, we had a day that would test us all.

Abdi and Dr Muktar were waiting for me outside the hospital. There were no smiles this morning, and I was hurriedly taken to the office.

"Everything is OK," said Abdi, "but we have a problem this morning."

"I really need your help," pleaded Dr Muktar.

"Just ask," I said, wondering what this was all about.

They escorted me to the operating theatre. Outside the door were two soldiers on guard. After a few words, the guards stood to one side. Abdi reached into his trouser pocket for his keys and unlocked the door. Dr Muktar rushed me inside. He then asked Abdi to lock the door. He pointed to the theatre table, which was draped with a slightly bloodstained white sheet. It was covering a dead body.

"This is a recently deceased soldier. He is a local man and I have to do a post-mortem. He died yesterday," said Dr Muktar apprehensively.

"Why a post-mortem?" I enquired. I had not seen or heard of anyone having a post-mortem since I had been in Somalia.

"He's died mysteriously. I'm told he died after coughing up a lot of blood, so he probably had a chest infection. The family have not seen the body, but do not believe this." He pulled back the sheets. My first impression was that this was someone who had been badly beaten up.

"Before anyone touches the body, can we just talk for a minute," I said.

Dr Muktar stood back. "I'm no post-mortem expert," I continued, "so can I just be clear what you're expecting of me?"

Dr Muktar looked uneasily at Abdi and then replied, "We need to do this to find the cause of death."

"Yes of course, I understand that. But you haven't answered my question. Can you do a post-mortem? For example, I've seen a small number of them performed, and even helped with a few during my training when I was a student, but that's all."

"I can do a simple PM, but like you, I am no expert," replied Dr Muktar.

"So, who is this PM for exactly?" I asked.

"Well, it might be used in the local court, if it gets that far, so it's for everyone," replied Abdi.

"In which case, should the body be sent somewhere else where they do have an expert?" I suggested.

"This is not possible. This is a local confidential matter," replied Dr Muktar, almost whispering.

"So, is this really for the family, or the army?" I quizzed further.

"It's for both, for both. If people agree with the results, it will go no further."

"So going back to my original question, my role in this PM is what?"

"To watch me do the PM, and help me agree the findings," said Dr Muktar.

Having just experienced the cells in Hargeisa, I was not sure I really wanted to do this. I needed time to think it through. "When are you planning to do the PM?" I asked.

"As soon as possible. But first, I have some really sick men on the ward, and my morning clinic. Some patients are already waiting. So probably it will be early afternoon."

I agreed to think about the request and meet up before lunch. I walked over to the women's ward with Idris who had been waiting outside.

"What is this about?" he asked.

"Not sure Idris, but it doesn't look good."

On reaching the ward there were around ten to twelve excited people, waiting to see me. Idris spoke to the crowd to see what they wanted.

"They say you have just seen their dead relative. The mother and father are sitting over there." I noticed an older couple sitting on chairs in the corner. They were both in tears.

"Idris, can you ask them to explain what they believe has happened?"

Idris had a long conversation. He swallowed hard and started to repeat the story back to me.

"They say their son is a good man, a good man. He was taken from the village and conscripted into the army a few months ago. They think that someone has accused him of supporting the Somali National Movement (SNM), but they're not entirely sure about this. Then he disappeared for many days and now he's dead."

"OK Idris. Ask if they know anything else?"

"They say they do not, but they have not been allowed to see the body. They think he has been tortured; it's what happens to people here."

"Why are they telling me this? What are they expecting?"

"They want justice, Dr John. They don't trust the system here. They want you to be involved."

This was indeed a great burden of responsibility. I thanked them for coming to see me, and I said I would think this through. I needed to talk to the team as this could affect all of us. As I stood up to leave, the mother grabbed my hand. She could hardly speak through the tears, and she looked at me with pleading eyes.

"Idris, can you translate?"

"She says what would you do if her son was your friend? They've been told you are also a good man, fair and truthful. Please help her."

Cathy and Gina were busy. I sat outside for a few moments to take in the morning air. Abdi came to sit down next to me. "Dr John, have you ever wondered what your nickname is?"

"Do I have a nickname?" I queried, wondering why he was asking me this right now. I had more important issues to think about.

"Of course. Many of us have nicknames. I am called Abdi Aposto, there is Aaden TB, Axmed Theatre and Axmed Lab. Some names are kind, and some are descriptive. For you some names are perhaps seen to be a little unkind, such as One-eyed Hussein, but it's in our culture."

"Well, I guess so, but I hadn't given it much thought, Abdi."

"Do you want to know your nickname?" enquired Abdi.

"Well, I'm a bit preoccupied at the minute Abdi, but perhaps it might lighten the moment."

"You are the Governor," declared Abdi, proudly.

"Is that a good or bad nickname? Surely, I am nothing like the Governor. The population around here don't like those in authority very much, as they're often from the South."

"It is a good thing. The Governor they mean is the old British

189

Governor. Many of us old folks remember him well. He was a great man, very fair, no corruption or bribes, honest, truthful. He stood up for ordinary people."

"Gosh," I said, a little surprised. "I suppose that is an honour."

"An honour, yes, an honour indeed. You didn't get out of prison for no reason, you know. People here do respect you."

I looked at Abdi. My secret was out.

"Do you think I didn't know? The whole town knows about the argument with Dr Omar. A small number are aware that it was Dr Omar who accused you of being a spy, and they know what happened to you in Hargeisa. How do you think the Major was informed?" he said. I sat thinking, but I wasn't quite sure what to say next. Abdi looked right into my eyes with a soul-searching stare, and he placed one hand on my right shoulder. "Perhaps now is one of those times you live up to your nickname." As always, he was right. I had to do the right thing.

Hours later, I was standing in the theatre room with Dr Muktar. Abdi was there to take the notes. Dr Muktar started with an external inspection of the body. The face was heavily bruised and swollen around the nose, left eye, and earlobe. There were marks around the wrists, suggesting that they'd been tightly bound, probably with rope. The right ankle was broken, and both ankles had similar marks to the wrists, suggesting they had also been bound. The soles of the feet were bruised and swollen, suggesting they had been beaten.

"Any conclusions, thus far?" I asked.

"My conclusion is that we have not yet found the cause of death," replied Dr Muktar.

"True, but what about all the pathology we've just described?"

"We are here to find the cause of death. What we've seen is

not necessarily the cause, or has even contributed to the cause," said Dr Muktar, emphatically.

"Yes, but they are still important findings. Surely, we have enough evidence to at least say this man has been beaten and probably tortured?"

"Dr John, we have to be very careful not to jump to any conclusions. Torture is a very inflammatory word. May I continue please?"

He opened the abdomen. The abdominal wall seemed bruised beneath the skin. There was blood in the abdominal cavity but no obvious source of bleeding. He continued and opened the chest wall. There was evidence of broken ribs on the left-hand side. Inside the chest, the left lung had collapsed under the weight of a large blood clot, and there was blood around the heart.

Dr Muktar stopped. "I think there is no need to go any further."

"No further, so what are you thinking?"

"That this man had a chest infection, a severe chest infection," replied Dr Muktar.

"What! I don't understand."

"I would like to finish," said Dr Muktar, "a severe chest infection that has caused internal bleeding in the chest cavity, leading to death."

I stood up from my seat, completely stunned by this conclusion. What had happened to fairness and honesty? Dr Muktar pulled off his rubber gloves, and asked Abdi to get Axmed Theatre to tidy up. He sat down at the desk in the corner to complete his report.

I was mesmerised by what I had witnessed. "Abdi, before you go, I need to say something." Abdi stood poised with his keys in one hand, whilst holding the door handle with the other. I turned to Dr Muktar. "If you are asking me to sign this report, I will not be able to do this," I said emphatically.

"You don't have to sign it. I just need to document that you were a witness," remarked Dr Muktar.

"I might have been a witness, but I don't want my name in the report," I insisted.

Dr Muktar looked at me with a glare. "We might be good work colleagues, but I do not want to end up like this man. It is fine for people like you with your principles. You could resign tomorrow and go back home. My world is different." He pointed to the dead body. "Take a look. This is my world."

Eventually, we came to a compromise, and Abdi left the room, seemingly very happy with my suggestion.

Later that day, a military representative came to collect the report. It was Major Yussuf. "I would like to read it first," he said, opening the report. He slowly scanned the pages, and then found the summary at the end. In both Somali and English, it read as follows:

"This soldier died of pulmonary and cardiac bleeding. It is possible this was secondary to a severe chest infection. However, the body also had signs of severe bruising and swelling of the face, wrists, ankles, and soles of the feet. The right ankle, and some ribs on the left, were broken. There was also bruising to the chest wall. The abdominal wall was also bruised with bleeding inside the abdominal cavity. These injuries could only have been caused by multiple trauma, suggesting he was severely beaten."

Major Yussuf looked up from the report. His face showed no emotion.

"Are you sure this is your final report?" he asked. "I see both your names are mentioned."

Dr Muktar looked at me across the room. He was visibly sweating. "Yes," he said. "It is the final report."

"Are these the conclusions of both of you?" enquired Major Yussuf further.

"Yes," said Dr Muktar, swallowing hard and glancing in my direction.

"Very well, I will take this report away with me. Thank you for your help." With that he marched out of the room.

This was going to be a real test for my relationship with the Major.

A week later, Abdi invited me into Dr Muktar's office.

"We have just heard from the family of the patient who had the PM," said Abdi. "The case will not go to court. They have been offered compensation, which they have accepted, so all is settled. The family are happy."

"Settled for how much?" I asked, with genuine interest.

"That is confidential," responded Dr Muktar.

"What about the Major, is he happy?"

"Very," replied Abdi. "It was not the army that did this, it was the secret police."

Was this good news, or bad news? I wondered. I wasn't sure. I just hoped the Major stayed around, and he wasn't transferred to another part of the country.

24.

NEW STAFF

It was Christmas. Gina had finally given up smoking, so was not sure what to put on her New Year's resolution list. Cathy, meanwhile, still sneaked the odd cigarette, behind the back of the house. What we thought would be a social visit by Brad became a review, and potential extension of contracts.

Brad reached for what he thought was a packet of Cathy's roll-up tobacco on the table. He helped himself to a handful, rolled himself a cigarette, and started to smoke. He took the cigarette out for a moment and looked at it.

"This tastes a little old," he commented, tapping the end of the cigarette in an ashtray.

"That's because it's a packet of raw tea leaves," smiled Cathy.

Brad was focused on the contract discussions. He didn't seem to hear what Cathy had said. He coughed, and then carried on smoking his cigarette. The contract discussions between Brad, Gina and Cathy continued for some time. They were not going well from Brad's perspective. Brad reached for the packet of roll-up tobacco once more, but I slid the packet away across the table, so he reached for his whisky.

After great deliberation, both Gina and Cathy decided it was time to go home. Both were missing their family and friends. Brad wasn't happy losing both at the same time, so negotiated a phased withdrawal. Gina would leave in early February and Cathy between March and May.

The gun turrets then turned to me. Brad did not want to lose the whole team. He was lucky. I was now enjoying the job more than before. The recent positive attitude of the town elders, and the arrival of Dr Muktar, was making a difference. In my head, the 'completer-finisher' in my nature held up its hand shouting 'me, me'. Before I knew it, I'd accepted an extension to my contract, and in a moment of weakness, I agreed to a further twelve months. Realising my rash decision, I asked for a review after six months, just in case the situation changed for the worse. Brad thankfully agreed.

"How am I ever going to explain this to my family in a letter?" I said to Brad.

"No need. You've been here just over a year now, so we're going to send you home for almost three weeks at the end of January. We can arrange for the office in London to pass your flight details to your parents, and they can meet you at the airport." Brad stopped, and with a glint in his eye continued. "I'm going to share something quite confidential with you. When you come back you need to be on best behaviour. I think you're going to have a visit from the President of Save the Children Fund, Princess Anne."

"Does this mean we get another toilet?" I asked with a grin.

Brad had agreed that I should take the quicker flight home via Djibouti. I had to change planes and airports in Paris. When I arrived in London, my suitcase did not. I was reassured that it would be found and brought to my home in the UK. It arrived only three days before I was due to return. I was a little envious, as it had been on holiday to the Seychelles without me, courtesy of Air France.

The time at home passed quickly, and soon I found myself back at Heathrow Airport. My parents stood proudly near the departure gate. I thought they would be sad to see me go, but they were quite cheerful under the circumstances. I suppose they could see I was in much better shape mentally, compared to my departure more than twelve months before.

"Have you packed your smart trousers and shirt?" enquired my mother.

"Yes, Mum."

"Did you pack a tie?"

"I don't need a tie; I've told you already."

"Are you sure? You need to look the part for when, you know, for when you have the visit."

I had received a written brief from the London office. Princess Anne was to visit in early March. The brief listed acceptable clothing, along with expected behaviour and etiquette. It indicated I was not to wear t-shirt or jeans, and that smart trousers and a smart shirt were preferred. I had neither of these in Somalia, so I had bought some, along with smarter shoes, from the UK. A tie had not been mentioned.

"You should never presume," said my mother, as she pressed a tie into my hand. "Just squeeze it into your suitcase, but don't screw it up mind."

It was easier just to take it. I opened my brown plastic suitcase, and I carefully placed the tie into the zip compartment of the lid.

"Make sure you send us a photo. I want to see you in your tie with Princess Anne," she said, just loudly enough for other waiting passengers to hear.

"Mum, shush, please." I realised my parent's cheerfulness had more to do with their excitement about the Princess Anne visit than my personal welfare.

It was time to go through the departure gate. My mother's excitement was still in full flow, as she kissed me goodbye. My father had been standing back, allowing my mother to do all the talking. Then, in his more reserved manner, he held out his hand to shake mine. He held it a little tighter, and for longer than usual.

"Goodbye son, do your best in your job, but more importantly look after yourself."

I could see a small tear welling up in his left eye. He took a deep breath, attempting to compose himself. "Well, my dear, let's leave him to go in peace." He took my mother's arm, and squeezed her right hand, whilst with the other hand he ushered me to go. I could feel for my father. He wasn't usually emotional, but he was struggling. So, I decided I should pass through the gates. I turned for one quick wave, and then I disappeared round a corner.

It seemed a strange return to Somalia. Whilst passing through Hargeisa, I met Jerry. While I was away, he had finally managed to repair the large generator, which supplied the whole town of Borama. Great news. But he followed this up with the news that he was leaving that week and returning to the UK. His work was done. Today would be the last time I would see him. This was a mega-surprise. What was I to do without his sense of humour?

When I arrived back at the house in Borama, Gina was standing packed and ready to go, or should I say raring to go. She was to travel back in the Land Rover that had brought me. I had not expected her to be leaving so soon.

"She's been packed and ready all week," declared Cathy.

Gina stood impatiently in the hallway. "I'm not good at saying goodbye," she said, anxiously. "It's been great working with you both. I think we've all learned a lot." She looked at me and smiled. "For example, I thought you were a complete dick when you first arrived. But I learned you weren't that bad after all, for a man."

She wiped a small tear from her eyes and sniffled. She gave us both a big hug, and then went back to Cathy. "You're just such a wonderful person, take care of yourself you hear."

She walked down the house steps, and I carried her bags. Once in the Land Rover, she wound down the window. "There is life after Borama, I'm told. See you on the other side." The vehicle set off at speed, as she had to get to Hargeisa before nightfall.

One week later, Jo, our new Paediatric nurse, arrived. She had been working at a top London teaching hospital and this was her first posting abroad. Jo was tall, with flowing red hair, a very fair complexion, and flashing blue eyes. She arrived wearing Ray Ban sunglasses and expensive jeans, blouse, and shoes.

While there was still daylight, we decided to have a quick tour of the hospital compound. The children's ward had a number of goats parading around. Jo looked more than surprised. Then two feral cats jumped through a window, raced across the ward, took food from a sleeping patient, and scuttled out of the door.

"Oh, my gosh," said Jo.

"I often have to start my ward round by sorting the 'animal visiting time,' and clearing the livestock first," I said casually. I waved my arms, and I was able to quickly shoo most of the goats out the door. One larger, more stubborn, goat remained. I sneaked up behind, grabbed the horns, and wrestled it outside.

"Do I have to do this every day?" asked Jo anxiously.

"All in a day's work," I said calmly, "all in a day's work."

Following the ward round, we went back to the house, where we had another brief tour.

"Where's the toilet again?" asked Jo, pushing her sunglasses to the top of her head.

"I'll show you," smiled Cathy. "We were saving that till last. Quite an attraction around here you know." She threw open the door to the toilet. "Welcome to Princess Anne's Throne." Jo looked puzzled but went inside, and Cathy returned, leaving Jo in the toilet.

We sat waiting in the dining room. Jo eventually returned looking a little miserable.

"Is there a problem?" I asked. Jo shook her head gently from side to side, and then pointed to the top of her head.

"Do you have a headache? I guess it's been a long day for you?" enquired Cathy.

Jo shook her head again. "I haven't seen a pit latrine before. I was inquisitive, so I shone the torch down the latrine to see inside."

I then noticed her sunglasses were no longer on her head. I looked at Cathy.

"Don't worry," replied Cathy, trying to keep a straight face, "we can explore the local market for sunglasses tomorrow."

From that day forth, Jo was always introduced as the person who lost her expensive Ray Bans to the cosmic black hole of Princess Anne's toilet. So, we wouldn't forget this sad occasion, we placed a commemorative plaque on the toilet wall. It read: 'Here lies poor Ray Ban who tragically fell in the line of duty February 1988'.

Later that month, Ali Interpreter became a father. He had

mostly been a qat-free zone for a few weeks, coming to work regularly, and on time. Becoming a father had been a turning point in his life. However, the weight of responsibility for his new son was beginning to show. The crying at night, which all new mothers and fathers can relate to, was a new phenomenon for him. He was turning up for work extremely blurry-eyed. Only half listening to the patients telling their medical story, his translations were delivered in a mere handful of words. Ali was always briefer than Idris, but we now noticed a big difference. In one clinic, he even fell asleep on the examination couch, whilst we were in the middle of interviewing a patient sitting in a chair nearby. Feeling sorry for him, we agreed he could come to work a little later in the mornings. Was relaxing our discipline to be a mistake? Only time would tell.

Towards the end of the month, we were all listening to the BBC World Service one evening. It was to be the most significant news we had heard for months, as it was announced that a new peace agreement had been reached between Somalia and Ethiopia. This would lead to a calmer situation along the border. We thought this was truly fantastic news for everyone.

Hearing this good news Jo sat down, and tucked into her poppy seed bread, or at least what she thought was poppy seed bread. We decided to let her enjoy herself, as she was still to have her weevil moment of discovery.

25.

A ROYAL VISIT

It was March and the evening before the arrival of Princess Anne. The team decided to have a rehearsal. Cathy had been the only team member present in January, when a royal inspection team had made a short reconnaissance visit.

"So, remember," said Cathy, "when Princess Anne arrives in the afternoon, we are to be ready in a line outside the house. When she gets out of the vehicle, we wait for one of her team to speak first. Got it?"

"Got it," said Jo.

"When you first greet her, you say 'Welcome your Royal Highness'. Do not attempt to shake her hand. Got it?"

"Got it," said Jo.

"Do you say it with a curtsy?" I asked.

"Oh, good point," said Cathy now less confident. "I can't remember that."

"Do I curtsy, or bow?" I asked.

"Now you're being silly. Are you taking this seriously or not?"

"Seriously, very seriously," I replied with a straight face.

"After the welcome, we go into the house. Having already spoken to her outside the house, when you speak to her again, we address her as Ma'am," continued Cathy.

"Why's that?" asked Jo.

"I don't know, we just do. Then we all sit in the dining room, OK?"

"OK, sounds good to me," replied Jo.

"After sunset, the first time you see Princess Anne, we welcome her with 'Good evening your Royal Highness,' and then after that we address her as Ma'am again. Got it?"

"Absolutely," confirmed Jo.

Cathy looked at me. "Have you cleared your room out yet?"

"Not quite but almost. I've left my posters up to keep it more homely, and to hide the plaster falling off the wall. As requested, ma'am!" I gave a military salute. My bedroom was to be the boudoir for Princess Anne, during her stay. Her inspection team, who had decided it was the safest room, had reserved it.

"Jo, have you arranged for the food?" enquired Cathy.

"Yes Ma'am," said Jo.

We were told that Princess Anne would be on a particularly strict diet involving pre-packaged food. This was to keep her healthy during her tour in Africa. We presumed this meant especially her bowels. Although the house had a Princess Anne toilet, clearly everyone hoped she didn't need to use it too often.

"We are all invited to the Somali Governor's dinner in the evening. After that Princess Anne will retire early, and we can all relax," declared Cathy.

"Very efficient," I remarked.

Cathy glanced at me. "In the morning, Princess Anne will do her morning exercise routine in your bedroom, and then appear for breakfast. The first time you meet her you say?" Cathy paused for our reply.

"Eh up love, did you sleep OK?" suggested Jo.

"I give up, now you're both acting silly. You say 'Good morning your Royal Highness,' and then after that it is 'Ma'am' again." She turned to read another page of her briefing. "After breakfast we will walk to the hospital, and then tour the compound. We will then return, have lunch, and she will leave for Hargeisa to catch her plane," concluded Cathy. Feeling suitably briefed, and buzzing with information, I went to bed. Tomorrow was going to be busy.

The next morning, we were sorting any last-minute issues. I went out in the Land Rover to ensure the hospital preparations were underway. There was a real buzz of excitement. At the entrance to the town, the children from a local school had made a colourful arched sign. It read 'Welcum Princes Annie', which personally I thought was great and quite endearing.

The hospital was spotless. All the staff were present, even those off duty. I hoped this didn't make the place look over staffed. Everyone turned up in white uniforms. I had hardly ever seen staff in uniform, so this was looking very impressive. Abdi was even sporting a new hat, a flat cap, for the occasion.

Outside the hospital, there was a growing crowd of people, all with varying levels of disability, and, in some cases, severe deformity.

"Why are all the people outside the hospital this morning?" I asked Abdi.

"Some are local people. Others are from out of town. I think they're hoping that Princess Anne will notice them and take some of them back to Britain for treatment." I wasn't expecting this but decided I should move on and complete a quick ward round to ensure the patients were not forgotten.

After lunch, the excitement levels were even higher. All arrangements were in place, but the staff were bustling around double and triple-checking everything.

Deeqa was especially anxious that the food was just perfect, and the Princess Anne toilet was kept spotless for the anticipated re-acquaintance with its namesake. We did not have a precise arrival time, so we knew there would be little prior warning before Princess Anne arrived at the house. We had to be alert. In response, we decided to sit outside the house in our smart outfits.

Then, Abdi arrived. "Everything is OK, but there's been a change of plan, or at least I think so. There have been concerns about security along the border, so it seems Princess Anne is now flying here. The problem is that the old runway outside the town is fully overgrown."

"Old runway?" I asked puzzled. I was not aware of any runway.

"There's an old runway from when the British had forces stationed here. But it hasn't been used for ages, so large crowds of people have gone out there to chop down the bushes," Abdi declared proudly.

"Why do we think she is flying?"

"The police have been listening on the radio. They overheard someone saying, 'the bird has flown' in English."

"Abdi, perhaps I'm wrong, but I'm not sure she's flying. Those words are just an expression meaning someone has left to go somewhere else. I cannot see they would fly to an old, and possibly dangerous, airstrip."

Abdi shrugged his shoulders. "Well, it's too late now, the townsfolk have already gone there. I just hope she's not greeted by a half empty town."

We all continued to stand in the sun, waiting. To be truthful, it was becoming a little boring and hot. Jama decided to entertain everyone by stomping around the compound showing us different military marches he had learned in the army. The quick march, the slow march, the... Suddenly, after swivelling around a few times, he must have become dizzy. He staggered slightly, and disappeared down into the mechanics pit, which was situated just to one side of the guardhouse.

I darted across, worried he might have seriously hurt himself. He was lying at the bottom of the pit. I hurriedly went down the steps. He smiled. A little dazed but other than the shock of falling he seemed OK. I slowly helped him up the steps, and out of the dirty greasy pit.

At this moment, the two other guards opened the gates to the compound. In a flurry, a convoy of three vehicles drove inside. The doors of the middle vehicle opened, and out stepped 'Princes Annie'. The Princess had been driven here after all.

I was still in the middle of escorting Jama to his chair, as Princess Anne walked towards me. In the heat of the moment, all the briefing paper, my rehearsal, and everything about behaviour and etiquette went completely out of the window. I stood to attention, while still clutching onto Jama. I held out my hand and said "Hi." Realising my blunder, I then tried to retrieve the situation. "Err sorry, I mean, welcome your Royal Highness."

Princess Anne said, "Hello, nice to meet you", shook my greasy hand, and then went to meet all the team.

205

Meanwhile, I escorted Jama to his seat.

Princess Anne and her entourage disappeared into the house. I washed my hands as quickly as possible, and I followed them inside. Deeqa appeared anxious, but the food and drink had already been proudly laid on the dining room table.

Everyone was seated and in deep conversation. There was one vacant seat in the whole room. It was the seat next to Princess Anne, who was sitting in the corner of the room quietly observing everyone. Jo nodded to me to sit down. I suddenly got the jitters. This had not been part of the rehearsal.

I couldn't let my mother down. I tentatively walked across the floor, and I sat in the empty chair.

"You must be John?" asked Princess Anne. I realised I had not even introduced myself.

"Yes, that's me," I replied, all coy.

"I've heard all about the wonderful work you are doing here in the hospital. I have of course been here before and it will be very interesting to look around." She paused. "But you must excuse me, it has been a long journey. If I am correct, you have rather a nice toilet here. Can you show me the way?"

On her return, I apologised for my poor welcome, and explained what had happened with Jama. All seemed to be forgiven, as Princess Anne talked about the hospital. She was very well briefed, and she seemed to be fully aware of how difficult it was to work in Somalia. The time went quickly, and Princess Anne proved to be extremely easy to talk to.

Before long, it was time to prepare for the Governor's dinner. Princess Anne disappeared into my bedroom with her Lady-in-Waiting, and later reappeared in an elegant dress with coiffured hair for the evening. We were almost ready to leave the house, when Abdi arrived. "Everything is OK, but I'm afraid one of your Hargeisa team, Abdirahman, has been arrested by the NSS."

"Arrested for what?" demanded Brad, who was accompanying the Princess.

"Arrested for carrying subversive material," replied Abdi.

It seemed Princess Anne, or one of her team, was carrying a selection of magazines to read during the trip. A copy of 'Good Housekeeping' magazine had been given to Abdirahman.

This was bizarre. How a copy of 'Good Housekeeping' could be subversive material was beyond me. This was no radical newspaper. To arrest someone for carrying that was bad enough, but in front of Royal visitors was a huge gaffe.

When this was explained to Princess Anne, it brought the realities of working in Somalia into sharp focus.

"Well," said Princess Anne, "simply outrageous." She pulled out the pins holding her hair, shook her head, and let all her hair fall down. She kicked off her shoes, and angrily slumped into a chair in the dining room. "Someone can tell the Governor that I'm going nowhere until the poor man is released."

Within forty minutes, this had the desired effect, and Abdirahman arrived at the house holding his magazine. He gently held it out and placed it on the dining table. "I think this needs to go back to Princess Anne," he said quietly.

The evening was now on. The dinner went smoothly, and it included dancing and speeches. Sadly, with all the unexpected activity, I forgot to take my mother's tie. Would I ever be forgiven?

The following morning, we walked from the house to the hospital. I was not prepared for the entourage, that now included the world's press and TV film crews, charging alongside. I wasn't entirely sure where so many of them had been staying overnight, as there were very few hotels in the town. Cameras were clicking, and microphones were waved in our faces. Although the media were there primarily to follow the Princess, it was clear they also wanted to take the opportunity to understand what it was like working in such a secretive country.

We had been briefed not to give interviews, as this might undermine our project.

This proved to be a non-issue. Every time a reporter came too close to any member of the team, our chaperones of Somali secret policeman would walk in between us, glare at the reporter, and wave them away. The excited crowd at the hospital was enormous. The cheering was almost deafening. Lining the way were even more people with severe disabilities, who were being physically thrust into the path of the Princess by their carers.

Waiting proudly on the veranda were Dr Muktar and Abdi. The TV crews were still filming our every step, as we walked around the compound.

"If only Jerry was here to show off his buildings," Cathy whispered. This was true. Jerry had given us the building infrastructure to work in, and he had made this all possible.

"Yes, but hopefully not actually demonstrate his latrines," I added with a smile.

We had previously selected a mixture of patients with both typical and more unusual problems to introduce to Princess Anne. The Somali nursing staff were clearly enjoying themselves. At one point, Princess Anne walked back to see a volunteer nurse changing a dressing.

"What is their problem?" she enquired, looking at the patient. I explained they had a nasty snakebite.

"And what is being put on the wound?" she asked further.

Before I could answer, the volunteer nurse said, "This is Dr John's papaya dressing." The Princess looked at me intrigued.

"It works, honestly," I said with pride.

It all passed so quickly. So much preparation for such a short visit. Then suddenly it was over. The Princess and the media were gone in a cloud of Somali dust, rattling their way back to Hargeisa. For the staff and the town, who had been absolutely thrilled by the Royal visit, it had definitely been worth it. But for all of us, it was now a return to reality. Would I ever see the hospital so clean again? Would I ever see the staff so smart in their uniforms again? Would Abdi ever get another new hat?

Not long after the Royal visit, a new midwife, Sally, arrived. This was in preparation for Cathy's departure. At least this time a handover was going to be possible. Although I was going to really miss Cathy, Sally seemed very easy-going as a person, and she was picking things up from Cathy very quickly.

Sally had a medium build, dark wavy hair, and an olive complexion. She also had an artistic flare, and within a very short time she added great pictures to our guidelines and posters. We had all recently been invited to take part in teaching sessions for community health workers, including RHU staff at the refugee camps. So, this artwork proved to be very useful.

Later in April, Asha was to be married, and it was finally her big day. In truth, I should say big week, as the festivities went on for several days. We were all invited. I was told the men would sit in their own room, chewing qat all night. This was not exactly my idea of fun, and I knew that there would be tremendous peer pressure to join in. In addition, I didn't really know many of the male guests.

Cathy must have shared my concerns with Asha, as on the actual night I was invited into the women's room. A large group of women were already sitting inside, giggling as I entered.

"What's happening?" I asked. I wasn't sure what was expected of me.

"You're an honorary woman for the night," declared a delighted Asha, as she waved me further into the room. I wasn't sure if the elders would approve of all this. So, I was a little hesitant. I didn't want another episode like the one involving Safiya. But all the women, including the older ones present, ushered me in and told me to sit down.

I sat with them for the whole night. There was singing, dancing, and loads of ululating. I couldn't sing or ululate, but I could dance, much to everyone's amusement. We had also taken a tape recorder, and, as a present for Asha, we recorded all the celebrations.

It was then time for Cathy to leave. She stood in the corridor of the house with her bags packed.

"You've still got your blue flip-flops on," I told her.

"True. I've worn them for so long I can't get my shoes on. My feet are too flat and spread out."

"Are you all packed?"

"Yes, I think so. I don't have too many things left. I've given most of them away." She paused. "Well, this is goodbye I guess, at least for now?"

I gave her a big hug. "You will write, yes?" She nodded.

The Somali team were waiting outside. They all had a soft spot for Cathy, and they had turned out in force. They had been really taken by her dedication and sometimes selfless acts of kindness. Cathy slunk in the Land Rover, blew her nose, and wound down the window. She tried to say a few more words but was now too emotional. Instead, she simply raised her hand, and pretended to give us a royal wave as she set off.

With both Gina and now Cathy having gone, it left me feeling a little melancholy. We had been through so much together, in such a short time. But there was now a new team, and I was the 'old man' of the team. I had to look forward, not backwards. I thought it was time to reflect on and summarise what we had achieved in Borama. I made a list to discuss with Brad, as our project review was to be held in the near future:

- Jo and Sally had settled in very quickly. Life was good.
- The main hospital was functioning.
- Although there was the odd incident, very few drugs and only a little food was being pilfered. The 'Man with the Keys' was most effective.
- The volunteer nurses programme was a great success, and in its second phase.
- We were involved in teaching. This was both in and outside the hospital.
- With minimal input, the TB hospital was running well, and there was a significant reduction in the number of patients absconding.
- Water, fuel, and food for the hospital came in irregularly from the town, but the army would often help out.
- The new hospital generator meant no power shortages, especially at night.
- Dr Muktar was now using the ambulance as an ambulance, and indeed Dr Muktar himself was a star.

- The lab had made a huge difference to patient diagnosis and follow up.
- Axmed Lab was still Mr Enthusiasm. In a way, he had become my personal mentor, and he regularly came to the house to talk about life and the universe. We discussed all sorts of local cultural issues, and how best to approach them in the hospital.
- The treatment guidelines enabled the nursing staff to cope with many common ailments. We had also introduced them to the local pharmacies hoping this would lead to more responsible dispensing.
- As a team, we were happy and worked well together. With new team members, there was renewed enthusiasm.
- The town and the elders now finally seemed to appreciate what we were trying to achieve, and they were supportive of us being there.
- 'Dr John's papaya dressing' was very popular, successful, and readily available, even when medical supplies were low.
- Ali interpreter was almost qat free, and he had become a responsible father.
- Jerry's latrines were fully functioning.
- Deeqa had a more extensive culinary repertoire.
- Princess Anne's toilet had become a major pilgrimage attraction for ex-pats.

We had achieved all these things. But obviously much still relied on the SCF team being present. So, the next phase was to ensure this was all sustainable in our absence, or we could never hand the hospital over. But over to whom? I pondered.

This question bugged me. There seemed to be little regular input from the Somali Ministry of Health. I couldn't see them running the show from Mogadishu. The RHU was relatively well run. But this was due to UN funding, and that was the reason they were well staffed, unlike government hospitals, such as Borama.

In contrast, Borama Hospital functioned because of input from a number of sources. SCF, the Ministry of Health, the town's people and elders, volunteer nurses, the army, and the Finnish WHO TB programme all had a part to play. Importantly, without Abdi Aposto, 'The Man with the Keys', I wasn't sure the hospital would run at all.

I had also received beds and other items donated from organisations in Hargeisa. I had even sent patients to Chinese surgeons in Hargeisa, and to military doctors and dentists in Djibouti. But if any of the above stepped down, the whole show would falter. Would we ever be able to hand this enterprise over to a single entity? I wasn't convinced. However, for now, I wanted the team to bask in the glory of our achievements.

It's funny how life, and things, can change. No one could have predicted what was now in store for us. In the next few weeks, our world would turn on its head.

26.

BATTLE FOR HARGEISA

Brad announced he had a new post in Nairobi. He would be leaving Somalia but would visit from time to time. Teams would of course still meet him, as they passed through Nairobi. I was pleased for him, as he deserved it. Though for a man who didn't like flying, his new post would require even more of it, not less.

The whole team from Borama set off for Brad's farewell party in Hargeisa. We were expecting to stay for one or two nights. The party was held on the night of Friday the 27th May. It went well with many people attending from a variety of NGOs.

After breakfast on Saturday the 28th May, we said our goodbyes to Brad, and we readied ourselves to head back to Borama. We tried to leave Hargeisa, but, on the road to Borama, we were turned back by the army checkpoint. We were informed that the road was closed today, and we couldn't travel. Occasionally, there were still security issues along the border. So, this was not entirely out of the ordinary. However, as there was now a new peace treaty with Ethiopia, this seemed more surprising. The army checkpoints were not always completely open about any live security issues, so being given no explanation was not unusual. We decided to return to the SCF house in Hargeisa.

Brad was unable to take his flight to Mogadishu, as the airport was also closed. Again, no explanation was given. So, he also returned to the SCF house in Hargeisa. The next day, Sunday the 29th May, we were given the same information. Something was not right, but we had no idea what.

On Monday the 30th May, we heard gunshots in the street. SCF team members, although staying in close proximity to each other, were distributed between several houses. Each house had a compound with high walls, and solid metal gates. From the kitchen window of our house, I could just see over the top of the compound wall, and down the small street outside.

Brad was running in a zig-zag path from the house a few doors away. He unlocked our compound gates, and then locked them again, after entering. I went to the front door to let him into the house.

"Not good," he said, "really not good."

"What's happening Brad? We all heard the gunshots," enquired Jo, looking alarmed.

"There's a full-blown SNM invasion from over the border," declared Brad. "This might be over very quickly one way or another, but I'm not really sure at this stage. I suggest we secure ourselves and prepare for the worst."

I wasn't sure whether Brad had experienced this sort of thing before, or he was just well briefed, but he whirred into action. We were so pleased someone knew what to do. He made us all move out from any room with windows. All beds and their mattresses were taken into the windowless central corridor of the house.

All doors were closed. Some spare mattresses were placed on the floor under the beds and others, along with any furniture, were used as barricades over and around the beds. "These are your safe havens. Any worries, and you dive straight inside these, you hear?" Everyone nodded.

Next, Brad searched for things to barricade the front door. We were told to bring buckets of water into the house from the underground tank outside. As much food as possible was packed in boxes in the corridor. "No lights," said Brad. "No looking out the windows, except the kitchen window, and only if absolutely necessary. From there, you can see if anyone is at the gate and down the road. You will all stay in this house." He paused. "Right OK. I'm going to get all the other staff, with their food and water, to move into two other houses. One is just next door, and the other is two houses away, on the opposite side of the passageway."

We were all going about our tasks when Brad spoke again. "One more thing: anyone got any games?" he asked, looking around at everyone.

"Games?" said Jo, confused.

"Yes, cards, dominoes, anything like that."

"Yes," answered Sally. "Why?"

"It might be a long day, or even several days, so it will be something to keep your minds occupied. I'll be back later. Once I've sorted the others."

I went to the kitchen window to see which houses he was going to. I wanted to be sure that I fully understood where the others were going to be staying. I could see him darting across the passageway, hugging the walls that lined the road to keep out of sight. Then he disappeared into one of the other compounds.

There was gunfire all day. Sometimes close, sometimes further away. We lay under the beds and mattresses the whole time, only getting out when it was quiet to get a drink or go to the toilet.

Night fell, and I had finally fallen asleep, when there was an almighty explosion. It was probably a few roads away, but the earth shook. This was followed by another, and then another, each seemingly louder and closer than the last. The earth shook continuously for thirty to forty minutes. Then, as suddenly as the explosions started, they stopped. We were left with the sounds of sporadic gunfire.

After a few hours, there was a lull in the fighting. I could hear Brad quietly knocking on the front door of the house. I unlocked it and let him in.

"Close the door," he whispered. He'd been running, and he was a little out of breath. "I'm just checking you're all OK."

"We're fine, I guess. How close is the fighting?" I asked in a hushed voice.

"Probably only a few streets away, not really sure. But there have been a few stray artillery shells that were too close for comfort."

We sat on the kitchen floor, talking softly. The gunfire started again in the distance. Through the window we could see tracer bullets, lighting up the night sky.

"OK," said Brad. "I'm heading back to check on the others. We didn't manage to move into fewer houses before, so I need to arrange that now."

"Do you need any help?" I asked.

"Absolutely not, you must stay safe here," insisted Brad. With that, he slipped quietly out of the door and into the darkness. Through the night, there was sporadic gunfire, but it was quiet enough to try and get some sleep.

On Tuesday the 31st May, at first light, I was already awake. I crawled into the kitchen to get more food and water. There were noises in the road outside. I peeped over the window ledge, and I could see a handful of uniformed armed men in the street. I had no idea if they were SNM or the army. I'd been told it was difficult to tell, as their uniforms were almost identical.

I watched, as they gradually sneaked two to three hundred metres further down our road, towards the main road at the very end. They disappeared around a corner. I sat down on the floor, and then decided to go back to the corridor with the food. I was taken by surprise, as loud machine gun fire erupted nearby. I dropped the food, but rapidly picked it up, and crept along the floor back into the safety of the corridor.

The machine gun fire, along with occasional artillery fire, continued all morning. We lay nervously playing cards, under the beds. With each explosion we would glance at each other and then try to focus on the game. It's amazing how competitive some people can be, even under these circumstances.

"How come you've played that card?" quizzed Jo.

"Which card?" said Sally.

"That one, the diamond. You said you didn't have any last time; that's cheating."

"Sorry, I'm a bit anxious. I didn't notice it before," answered Sally apologetically.

"Unbelievable," snorted Jo.

Before Jo could continue, there was a huge explosion, which must have been only two or three houses away. You could hear glass in one of our windows shatter across the bedroom floor. Thank goodness the doors were all closed. Things were getting much worse and too close. This blast was followed by an escalation in both machine gun and artillery fire. Jo and Sally gripped each other's hands, and curled up further under their bed. The noise continued for an hour or so, before it became quieter again.

"I'm desperate for a wee," said Jo. "Really desperate." There was an air of expectation in her tone of voice.

"Would you like me to go with you?" I asked. "I won't peep." She nodded. "Oh, I thought you'd never ask."

"Are you sure you can't wait longer?"

"Can we just go, or I'm going to burst here on the mattress."

We crawled along the floor and finally into the toilet. I sat looking the other way, whilst Jo relieved herself. At that exact moment, the guns ceased firing.

"Perhaps I should go for a wee more often," quipped Jo.

There was gentle knocking on the front door that sounded like Brad. Then he burst in with four to five other people. "Sorry guys, the shells were getting too close. We've had to move now, before they came any closer." The new people in the house were a mixture of SCF Hargeisa and UN staff. Each one was holding a few items of belongings, a box of food, and a water bottle.

Brad however had managed to salvage for himself a packet of cigarettes and a small bottle of whisky. "Wasn't sure there'd be enough rations here, so we brought a mixture of things. I don't think we can risk going backwards and forwards between places anymore."

We sat quietly in the corridor eating, drinking, and playing cards. The silence was broken by the noise of aircraft flying overhead. Then there was a faint whistling noise in the air, followed by the largest explosion we had heard so far. "Bloody hell," shouted Brad. "They're dropping bombs, everyone under the beds." I found myself under the same bed as Brad. "Time to pray. If one hits us, these mattresses are not going to save us," he whispered.

One of the UN staff, named Hussein, was lying under the next bed. He looked very anxious. "I really don't like this. The UN has only recently had reports that the Somali government has been given nerve gas by the Libyans. I just hope they're not stupid, or desperate, enough to use it." This was just what I didn't want to hear.

In the early hours of Wednesday the 1st June, we could hear what sounded like tanks, or armoured cars, trundling down the main road. Then they turned into our side street. This was followed by the sound of falling masonry.

"They've probably driven through a compound wall nearby," explained Hussein. There was shouting, then rounds of machine-gun fire, as a gun battle ensued.

After a few minutes, the vehicles then trundled on, and you could hear the same process happening a little further away. It appeared they were working their way along the road and clearing out the houses. "I don't think the SNM have armoured vehicles," said Hussein. "Sounds as though the army are using tanks to break into compounds that they suspect are supporting the SNM and shooting anyone inside." Artillery, planes, tanks, what was next?

As dawn approached, there was a further lull in the fighting. At first light, there was a loud banging on our compound metal gates. We sat rigid and ignored it. The banging continued. Then someone shouted in English, "Open the door". We crept into the kitchen, and we peeped over the window ledge. Just above the compound wall, we could see the top of a camouflage painted pick-up truck. It had a large, mounted machine gun at the back.

There was a Somali man in battledress controlling the gun, but it was pointing back down the road, not at the house. He seemed to be on the lookout for any surprise attack. We couldn't quite see who was actually knocking on the gate.

Brad decided he and Hussein should go out to the gates, and then speak with whoever it was. He asked everyone to stay inside. As they walked to the gate, I peeped around the edge of the front door. Brad unlocked the gate, and slowly opened it just enough to peer outside. I could see another man in battledress holding an AK47, which he was waving, and pointing through the gate. Brad responded by uneasily opening one gate door a little wider.

In the street, there were four men. A driver, two men in the back of the pick-up truck, and the man at the gate who seemed to be in charge. All were in battledress uniforms, but none were wearing any helmets or hats. It was unclear whom they represented.

"Is this an NGO house?" asked the man holding the AK47. He spoke reasonable English.

"Yes," replied Brad warily.

"Which one?" asked the man.

"Save the Children Fund," replied Brad.

"So, you have a doctor?" queried the man.

"Yes," said Brad, even more suspicious of what they wanted. At this point, I walked out of the house to join Brad and Hussein. I wanted to hear what they were saying.

Brad saw me approaching. I think he was actually horrified that I had left the house. "Come here quickly," he said, motioning at me to stand by his side.

"Are you the doctor?" quizzed the man, pointing a finger at me.

"I am a doctor. Why do you need a doctor?" I asked.

"We need surgeons. There are none at the hospital. None have come to the hospital. We are looking all over the town for all the surgeons."

"I am not a surgeon," I replied. "I am not a surgeon."

"But you are a doctor?"

"Yes, a doctor, a children's doctor and for women, but not a surgical doctor. I don't do surgical operations."

"You must still come," insisted the man.

"If I do, I cannot operate. I am not a surgeon. I do not see the point in going to the hospital, if you want surgeons. It's not what I do."

The man stood thinking. He now looked annoyed, and we weren't sure what he was about to do next. Somalis sometimes love a proverb. "You can lead a horse, or a camel, to water," I said calmly, "but you cannot make it drink. Just like with me: you can take me, even force me, to go to the hospital, but you cannot make me operate. I'm not a surgeon. I would not know what to do."

I could see Brad's hand twitching by his side. Sweat was beginning to pour down his forehead. It reminded me of when we first sat in the plane together. Until this point, Hussein had been standing very calm and quiet. He finally decided to speak. "He's right. You'd be taking someone who would be dangerous. He might do more harm than good to anyone who is badly wounded. Better you find a real surgeon."

Eventually, the armed man lowered his AK47 and pointed it at the floor. He ambled back to the jeep, despondently. He climbed into the passenger seat, banged hard on the dashboard, and waved for the driver to set off. They sped off down the side street towards the main road. As they turned to the left, there was a loud explosion, followed by gunfire. The jeep had probably been attacked and blown up.

Brad turned and glared at me. He was very upset. "You do realise you could have got us all killed by talking to him like that?"

I stared back blankly, not knowing what to think, it had all happened so quickly.

"At first, I was going to throttle you for being such an idiot," continued Brad in his rant. He then suddenly looked really relieved. "But you know what, I'm glad you said what you did. You, or any of us, could have been in that jeep."

"You probably saved the day," hinted Hussein. "I guess there is a very fine line between being an idiot and being brave." He gave me an enormous slap on the back, and he waved us all back in the house. I stood for a moment, looked at the sky, and heaved a sigh of relief. I felt glad to be alive.

During a lull in the fighting, Brad and Hussein decided to go to the other SCF house, which had a radio. A few hours later Brad returned, and he wanted to hold a team meeting. "First," said Brad, "I think you're all holding up really well under the circumstances. We can, and we will, make it through this. I do have some news from the UN office. It seems the SNM have launched a major assault on Hargeisa. Just like this morning, with the men at the gate, we don't always know who we're dealing with outside. The government has moved heavy artillery and tanks into the town, and of course we heard the planes recently. So, the prediction is the government will do whatever it takes to regain control of the town."

Sally looked straight at Brad. "That doesn't exactly sound like good news for us, does it?"

"Of course, we could get caught up in the middle," continued Brad. "The UN is trying to evacuate us. There is a US warship off the coast on standby. The British have planes in Nairobi, and the French in Djibouti."

Jo anxiously looked around the team, and then she focused on Brad. "So, what's stopping them?"

"The problem at the moment is that the government will not let us out. The UN thinks they want to try and keep all this quiet. They don't want the outside world to know what's happening here, and they are trying to avoid international attention."

"So, what now?" asked Sally.

"We have no choice but to sit tight," instructed Brad, glancing directly at me. "We have to wait for more news."

"Any news about Borama?" I asked.

"No, but all the news we have suggests the fighting is just around Hargeisa," replied Hussein. "For now, we need to focus on keeping safe here."

The fighting continued on Thursday the 2nd June. There was a gun battle in the road outside our house. We lay under the beds for most of the day. An artillery shell landed in one of the neighbours' houses, blasting out more of the windows in our house.

At one point, I thought it was quiet. I crept to the toilet, and then I went to the kitchen to get more food and water. I could hear shouting in the road. I peered over the window ledge. Four to five houses further down the road, I could see two Somali men in civilian clothes being dragged from their house. They were made to kneel down in the street with their hands behind their heads.

There were three armed men in uniforms standing over them shouting. One of the armed men had an AK47. He was shouting at his colleagues, whilst pointing to the two men kneeling on the floor. One of his colleagues had a rifle slung over his shoulder, but he was also holding a pistol in his right hand. He looked very nervous as he raised his right hand out and pointed the pistol at the heads of the two kneeling civilians. He hesitated, and his hand was shaking. He was obviously having difficulty carrying out his orders, while the man with the AK47 shouted instructions even more loudly. Eventually, the third man, who had been impatiently waiting, snatched the pistol. He put both hands on the gun and shot both civilians in the head. Their bodies slumped to the ground.

I have no idea what happened next. I was so stunned that I sank down onto the floor beneath the window ledge, trembling. I'd almost grown used to the bombs, the shaking ground, the tracers in the sky, and the gunfire. But seeing two men shot in the head so close was unbelievably shocking. Terrifyingly, I could hear the process being repeated, presumably at the next house down the road. I decided not to share any of this with the team.

I sat on the floor trying to compose myself, and then started to creep back towards the corridor. I had only managed two or three metres, when there was another loud explosion. I hit the floor and stayed completely flat, as I heard more glass shattering, but didn't know where. After a few seconds, I got up and scurried back under my bed. I stayed there for hours.

27.

EVACUATION

The morning of Friday the 3rd June seemed unusually quiet. Brad appeared at the house with Hussein. He had news. "OK folks. The evacuation is on." There were cheers from some of the team before he continued. "The instructions are as follows. You are absolutely not allowed any bags or belongings. Just you and what you are wearing. Have you all got that? Your watch is OK but strictly no cameras. The government will not want any photo evidence to get out. Is that clear?" Everyone nodded.

Brad continued. "We need a list of everyone here. You have exactly one hour to get ready. People will be collected in waves to get to the airport. The vehicles will mostly have UN logos, but not all. Each vehicle will need something white tied to the aerial, or to hang out of a window. So, find something quick. Good luck and see you later."

"Sorry," I said. "When you mentioned a list of people, what about all the Somali staff?"

Hussein shuffled his feet uneasily. "I'm sad to say that we're not allowed to evacuate any Somali staff. The government will not budge on that point."

"I find that very difficult to accept," I insisted.

Hussein was looking exhausted, and he had probably been up all night negotiating. He was in no mood to continue the conversation. "May I remind you," he said sternly, "we are lucky the government are allowing us out at this point. The UN has decided on everyone's behalf to accept the chance to evacuate you. Get ready, you have fifty-five minutes left."

"I know it's hard, but there's really no other option for us," said Brad.

Two hours later, a small convoy of UN vehicles arrived outside the house. I gave our list of names to Hussein, as we were herded into each car.

"Do you have anything white?" he asked. This was something we had been struggling to find.

Sally coyly handed him two pairs of her knickers. "It was the only thing we had," she said.

"Except they're not quite so white after this ordeal," sniggered Jo, trying to lighten the moment.

The knickers were ripped, tied together, and attached to the aerial at the front of the vehicle. We were then instructed to sit along the middle bench seat.

At the prospect of leaving, Jo was buzzing with excitement. She leaned over to Sally. "Wait until I see your mother. I can't believe it. You've only been in the country five minutes, and you're being chauffer driven through the streets of Hargeisa with your knickers on full show to everyone?" Sally attempted a fake smile but didn't see this remark as remotely humorous.

The vehicle pulled away slowly, and carefully travelled down the side street, towards the main road. As we turned the corner, I recognised the burnt-out wreckage of the jeep that had called at our house, looking for the surgeons. There were body parts of the soldiers lying around the vehicle and on the ground. We were so lucky not to have been riding with them. This grim reality stifled Jo's momentary period of elation.

We stopped outside another house. Here an English family rushed to get inside. There were two adults, and two children about eight to ten years of age. I had met them a few months earlier. The father was helping to train local carpenters. This included teaching them to make wooden legs for people who had lost limbs after treading on land mines. The mother, who was a teacher, had been schooling their children at home.

"Are you OK?" I asked, but then felt stupid. How could anyone feel OK in this situation?

"I'll tell you later," said the father. The children appeared deeply troubled, and in a state of shock.

With two more people, the vehicle was full, and we headed in the direction of the airport. The scenes in the streets were shocking. Houses were partly flattened by artillery, tanks, or bombs. We passed scores of dead bodies, lying on the pavements, and weaved around bodies lying in the roads. Some were uniformed, while others were in civilian clothing. There were tanks and armoured cars parked at many junctions. I didn't see any civilians walking around, just military personnel. The only civilians were dead ones.

At one junction, a bulldozer was making a pile of dead bodies, stacking them on the roadside against a wall.

"Don't look directly at all this, please. We don't want to draw attention," instructed the driver.

I looked behind me. The weeping children sat hugging their mum and dad. The parents held their hands over their eyes to shield them from such terrible scenes.

"Truth is they've seen worse," commented the father. "Our

back garden wall was used by a firing squad over the past few days. I'm not sure they will ever recover from this." I had nothing to say in reply.

Jo and Sally sat completely still for the whole journey. Their heads didn't turn, but their eyes stared around, trying to take in this macabre world.

We were stopped by a military checkpoint.

"What's happening?" I asked the driver quietly.

"Not sure," he replied, "but I'm not arguing with the man holding a gun."

I looked across to the other side of the road. There was a mutilated dead body on the floor, and a wild dog was gnawing at one of the limbs. The soldier at the checkpoint seemed oblivious.

We waited a few more minutes. Then two more vehicles with UN logos pulled up behind us, and the soldier waved us on. Our small convoy weaved its way through the remaining streets, and around any debris or dead body in the way, and then started the incline towards Hargeisa Airport.

The tarmac runway at the airport was lined with Russian-made MiG fighter jets. Some appeared to be readying for take-off. There were also three small light aircraft of varying sizes. I was no expert, but they appeared to be able to carry between eight to twelve passengers each, at the very most. Our vehicles pulled up about fifty metres away, and we were all waved out.

Hussein was waiting outside. "When we get to the planes you will find there are no seats inside. Don't be alarmed. They have been removed so that we can get more people in. As you get into the plane, give me your name and organisation, so I can tick you off the list. Remember, no belongings, or bags. Once inside, the pilots will tell you what to do."

We were hurriedly taken in single file to the planes and divided into three groups. At this point, I was split from Jo and Sally. I tried to protest to keep us all together, but the Somali military were not interested. They started to frisk each person before boarding. I relaxed when I noticed Jo and Sally were with other SCF staff from Hargeisa.

I was waved into the largest of the three planes. Once inside, we were made to sit on the floor with our legs tightly bent to allow as many people as possible to get in. More passengers were ushered inside, and they sat with their legs over the top of others. We were packed like sardines in a tin. The two pilots sat in the front, plainly visible to us all. One was black and the other white. They were having a whispered conversation.

In all the confusion, I wasn't counting precisely, but this small light aircraft must have had twenty passengers or more. The door to the aircraft was closed by one of the pilots, and the handle was turned to lock it. He clambered over the top of everyone to get back to his seat. Meanwhile, the other pilot started the engines, and the twin propellers began to turn. We quickly began to taxi down the tarmac.

Suddenly, the pilot put down the throttle, and we accelerated down the runway. We continued for a long time, much longer than when I had previously travelled to Djibouti. I was beginning to wonder if we had too many people to actually take off.

We were at the end of the runway, when we finally, and gently, lifted up into the air. The plane seemed to be struggling, and it dipped down slightly. The pilot pushed the throttle down further, and the plane gradually started to gain height. However, within a very short time we suddenly lost altitude, and started to dive towards the rooftops of Hargeisa.

They say your life passes before your eyes in such moments. I guess that happened to me, but I was distracted from this by the passenger sitting next to me. He had grabbed my arm out of fear. His grip was so tight it was beginning to hurt. I looked round at him. He was so scared that he started to urinate in his trousers. He sat rigid, looking straight ahead. Behind me, another passenger was vomiting profusely. Fortunately, I was just out of range. Other passengers were not so lucky.

The plane carried on diving. I genuinely thought 'this is the end, this is it', when suddenly the plane was pulled out of the dive, and we raced over the rooftops of the houses below. We were as close to them as you could possibly be, and I almost felt I could touch them. We carried on flying at this low level, until we left the town behind. Then, as if by magic, the plane soared gracefully into the bright, blue sunlit sky.

The co-pilot looked back at the passengers. He gave a toothy grin and thumbs-up sign. I'm not sure if he was expecting applause at this point, but there was none. Everyone sat in stony silence. There was little conversation for the rest of the flight. I think most passengers were still recovering from having just contemplated their own demise. The only noise was the roar of the engines.

I have no idea how long the whole journey lasted. I didn't know where we were going or how long it would take. I was just glad when it ended. We landed on a small dirt strip in the middle of a desert. I presumed it was still Somalia. But most importantly I was alive.

The door opened, and a white man waved us out. Having sat for some time in my crouched position, it was a little difficult to stand up at first. My friend with the wet trousers remained seated on the floor.

"We can get out now," I indicated to him.

He was still in a sort of trance.

The engines were beginning to die down, but they were still very noisy.

"We can get out now," I shouted loudly. I offered my hand and helped him up.

I stood on the dusty ground in the oppressive heat. "Welcome to Garowe," said the white man with an Italian accent. I had heard there was an Italian construction team, who were building roads in the middle of Somalia. So perhaps this was their camp. At this time, there was no fighting taking place this far south. We were marched away from the plane and into a workers' cafeteria area. Sitting in the shade, sipping cold drinks, were Jo and Sally. Their plane had taken off and arrived before mine.

One of the pilots from my plane walked up to our table and sat beside me. "You OK?" he asked, in a South African accent.

"I am now," I remarked.

"Sorry about the bumpy ride," he added. "There was a gun battle going on at the end of the runway, which I was trying to avoid. In these places, anyone with a gun can have a pop at you. It's always best to scoot over the rooftops. You've come and gone, before they know it," he commented casually.

"It would have been nice to know that before we set off," I suggested.

"I realise that," he replied, "but some of you might not have got in. I'm a mercenary pilot from South Africa. I've done this sort of thing before." He finished his drink, said goodbye, and set off for the next evacuation flight.

The planes went back and forth to evacuate more people, until around one hundred and sixty of us were taken out to

Garowe. Brad and Hussein arrived on the last flight out. They proceeded to tell us the full story. An Italian businessman owned the planes. He was the only person the Somali government would trust, and that they would allow in to evacuate us. Brad continued with the tale for some time. I was heavily distracted by someone who sat on the next table with a large bowl of ice cream.

"Excuse me. Where on earth did you get that?" I asked.

"There, over there, mate," he said, pointing to the other side of the cafeteria. "These Italians know how to live. They even have their own ice cream machine." Brad was still talking, when I returned with my own bowl. Two bowls later, you could say I was chilled out.

The next task was to ferry everyone down to Mogadishu. Some left on Saturday the 4th June. But it was a longer flight, and it was getting late. We couldn't all get out on the same day. I was very happy to wait my turn and sample the ice cream machine a few more times.

I arrived in Mogadishu on Sunday the 5th June, and went to the SCF main office, which was overflowing with staff from the North. Now out of the danger zone, my thoughts turned to more practical issues. I only had the clothes I was wearing, which I almost needed to peel off at this stage. More importantly, I had no passport, as it was still in Borama, along with all my other belongings. I was also really worried about everyone in Borama, although the information given to us suggested there had been no fighting there yet.

Brad held a team meeting. "At this stage, we have no idea whether any of you will be able to return to work in the north. What we can say is that it will take time for this situation to settle and return to normal. I think we can safely assume that all your belongings and passports will have been stolen. So, priority number one is for everyone to go to the Embassy tomorrow morning to get a new passport." This was sound advice, which we followed, and obtained our new passports complete with renewed visas.

On Monday the 6th June, anyone who had been evacuated from the North was placed under house arrest. We were told that everyone was to be expelled the next day on a single Somalia Airlines flight and flown to Nairobi. The conspiracy theorists reacted with accusations of the Somali government wanting everyone on one plane, so the engines could stall, or they could shoot the plane down. This would get rid of all the witnesses to the atrocities. Eventually, a Kenyan Airways flight was chartered for Wednesday the 8th June, and anxieties abated.

As we queued to board the plane, an Officer at the departure desk took all our passports. He skimmed through them, and with great gusto he stamped really hard on the page with our Somali visa. When he handed them back, it read 'ANNULLATO' ('Annulled' in English). No mistaking that you are no longer welcome.

At Nairobi airport, the world's press was waiting for us to land. We had been briefed to refuse all interviews, as anything we might say could jeopardise the safety of any Somali or ex-pat staff still in Somalia.

In a comfortable Nairobi hotel, I sat eating steak and chips followed by strawberries and cream. It made me think. This country is just next door and yet worlds apart. You would never know what we had just seen or been through. Was anyone here, other than the press, even concerned?

SCF put us on gardening leave to recover from the ordeal.

We waited in Nairobi for news, any news. There was very little other than the rumours that the whole population of Hargeisa had fled to the surrounding countryside. No one was allowed to travel north, and so no one had the remotest idea what was really happening.

I eventually became bored waiting. So, at Brad's suggestion, I bought tickets and travelled to see other SCF teams in Kenya, Uganda, and Zanzibar. I thought it would be educational to see if there was anything I could learn from what they were doing. I was still hoping I would be able to return to Borama.

I visited Zanzibar first. Shortly after my arrival, the local team suggested that I relax, and go down to the nearby beach. The coastline was fantastic: the waves were lapping on the sand and the beach was deserted other than a few small empty fishing boats. I was so exhausted I fell fast asleep.

I awoke later in the bright sunshine, unaware of how long I had slept. As I began to focus, I saw an old fisherman mending his nets. He was sitting a few metres away. He smiled. I noticed he had several front teeth missing.

I looked around me. To my horror, I realised my belongings had gone. All I had was the shorts I was wearing. No other clothes, no shoes, no bag, nothing. I had only just acquired all these after leaving Mogadishu. Fortunately, my passport was back at the SCF house. With no shoes, I walked carefully back to the SCF office. As I passed the old fisherman, he smiled again. He pointed to a small boat heading out to sea. I could see one of the men was wearing my T-shirt. At this point, it felt as if the world really didn't love me anymore.

On returning to Nairobi, I arranged a ride on an SCF truck heading to Uganda. The world for the SCF team there was far more peaceful. The country had just been through a violent civil war and now had a new President. One of the main SCF projects was rehoming child soldiers who had been taken from their families and made to fight in the war. The children had seen some terrible events, and they were often quite traumatised. It was simply amazing to see parents' faces as their children were handed back to them.

I also visited the main hospital in Kampala. I sat in the HIV/AIDs clinic all day. At that time, the prevalence of HIV was rising exponentially in the country. There was one Ugandan doctor, and one receptionist. I couldn't count the number of patients that were waiting to be seen. It was to become one of the most emotional things I have ever done. Most of the patients were waiting to be seen for the first time. They would be told whether they had HIV or not. The vast majority were positive. The doctor was simply amazing. He sat with every patient, giving them the time that they needed to absorb the news he had just delivered to them. The clinic significantly ran over time. The receptionist went home, and the doctor continued by himself with my support.

I remember one particular patient. She was a woman in her thirties. She was very thin, and she had all the signs of advanced AIDs. Her small two-year-old child sat next to her, playing with a small rag doll. Her husband, his two girlfriends, her mother, and her brother had all died of AIDs. The patient asked what she could do; was there anything positive to live for? All day, the doctor had desperately tried to find something positive for each patient to cling on to, some glimmer of hope. With this patient, he struggled.

There was a long pause, and then he looked at the girl. "If you feel you have nothing else to live for, then think again. There's someone sitting to your right. She needs you. She needs you every day. I encourage you to think of her first."

At that moment, the girl held out her arms and asked her mother for a hug. The mother picked up her daughter, thanked the doctor, and walked out of the clinic.

"I don't know how you do it. Is it like this every day?" I asked.

"Yes. Every day. I've been doing this for months. It's emotionally draining, but I guess someone has to do it. I sit here every day, and I have to deliver hundreds of death sentences."

He then proceeded to berate the hospital managers. He told me that for many months they had been debating the size of the car park, and yet could not find the time to discuss more important issues, such as the resources for his HIV clinic. Apparently, he had recently been reprimanded. In his frustration, he had commented that the catastrophic number of HIV deaths would mean the size of the car park would soon be irrelevant, as there would be no one left to drive any cars. Fortunately, he was too valuable to the hospital, and they had retained his post.

After my travels, I went back to Nairobi. Putting my beach experience aside, I realised that the SCF staff in these other countries had their own issues with their projects. However, they had quite a civilised existence. They had no daily danger and lots of local community support for their work. None had anything like our experience in Somalia over the past eighteen months. My original briefing had been correct. Borama was the toughest posting that SCF had on offer.

I was really disappointed that I couldn't get back to Borama. I had no idea what had happened to all our Somali friends and work colleagues or to the hospital itself. After several weeks of waiting, I eventually decided to return home. The office in London had informed my parents that we were safe and were resting in Kenya. I had also spoken to my father briefly on the phone. News of what had happened in Somalia was trickling onto the international stage, but the full scale of what we had seen was still not reported in the media. I had decided to shelter my parents from the full story, until I could tell them face-to-face.

My father came alone to meet me at the airport in London. With his usual reserve, he shook my hand to welcome me home. No fatherly hug or tears of joy. Instead, with no time to lose, we marched straight to the car park to minimise his parking fee. As he was unlocking the car door, there was a loud bang. It was only a car engine backfiring in the car park, but, with my recent experiences, my instant reaction was to drop face down on the ground for safety.

My father, having been in the army when younger, immediately realised something wasn't right. He started asking me more challenging questions about what had actually been happening in Somalia. So, on the journey home I shared the whole story. He sat, and without interruption, listened, while driving. My story was still not finished, as we pulled up at my parents' home.

I was about to get out of the car, when my father held my arm and stopped me.

"I can see you need to tell your story. But not right now. Not a word to your mother. I'm not sure she's ready for all this. Let's go in smiling, with only stories about Princess Anne."

On entering the house, I was not prepared to see my mother in a wheelchair. This had not been mentioned in any letters. I had been sheltering them from the realities of my work. But they had been doing the same with what was happening at home. She was asleep with my sister by her side. "Nothing too serious, just bad rheumatoid arthritis," said my father. "She can't walk at the moment. Let's get your things to your room."

My father pulled a file from a drawer, and he placed it on the bed in my room.

"A little bit of light reading for you. But don't let your mother see it," he said casually. He left the room, and I opened it to look at the contents. He had been keeping a secret file of newspaper clippings about Somalia. The UK newspapers had been publishing accounts of what was happening in the north of Somalia in some detail.

I read with interest a number of articles:

- Accounts of scorched earth policies by the Somali government, who had destroyed villages and water supplies to make areas uninhabitable along the Ethiopian border.
- Confiscation of money from bank accounts, and driving licences, along with vehicles in Hargeisa.
- Incursions by the SNM from Ethiopia into Somalia at night.
- Recent fighting in Hargeisa, and the evacuation of ex-pat staff.
- Pictures with mass graves being found.
- I then read an article about ethnic cleansing of the Isaaq clan in Hargeisa, led by a General Bashir. This was the very man I had shaken hands with at the hospital in Borama, and whose pet cheetah had startled me in his residence. He might have even been responsible for my release from prison.

I reflected on all the rumours and stories that had been half shared with us during our time in Borama. We had been protected and sheltered by the staff and local people. Perhaps they had thought this was in our best interests, but no doubt it was also theirs. They didn't want to scare us away. My father had been more aware than I had realised. My stories in the car had only confirmed with more detail what he had already suspected.

Settling in back home was not easy, after all my adventures. Importantly, my mother was improving, and she had started walking around more easily. But I was tired of staying in someone's spare room. I had been advised by a friend to buy a house, as this would 'nail one foot to the floor of reality'. However, my first task was to get a job.

I went for an initial interview at a large hospital. I sat in front of the panel, answering their questions. One member of the panel lowered his glasses to the end of his nose, and he peered across the table at me. "I see your CV says that you have been working in Somalia. Where in India is that?" I decided that perhaps this post was not for me. Instead, within a few days, I had obtained a locum post in a nearby general practice.

A number of weeks later, it was the end of October, and I arrived home one day from work. "Papers are through on your new house," said my father, from behind his newspaper. "Also, there's a message for you," he continued, putting down his newspaper. "Someone called Brad. He says he's in London, and he wants to speak with you urgently. He's left his home phone number for you to call him tonight, if possible." With that, my father picked up his paper, and carried on reading.

I wasn't sure what the phone call was about, but I wondered if it was news from Somalia. I called Brad but only reached an answer machine with a voice I didn't recognise. I hoped I had left my message on the right number. I was dozing on the sofa, late that night, when the phone rang. "It's Brad," said my father. "Perhaps you should take it upstairs."

Forty-five minutes later, I put the phone down. Brad wanted me to go back to Somalia, to Borama. The UN and a small number of NGOs were attempting to start humanitarian work, after the fighting. It would be safe, or at least safe in Borama. However, the town was completely surrounded by fighting and mayhem. They needed someone who knew the good guys and the bad guys, as a completely new team would be going in. The main selling point for me was that they didn't know what had happened to many of the SCF staff, and I might be able to find out. However, it was certain that some of them would be in prison.

Unsafe maybe, but this really pulled on my heartstrings. If there was a chance to help any of the local staff in Borama, then I thought I should take it. I had a restless night, thinking this fully through. It would be a hard sell, the hardest of sells, to my family and friends.

28.

NOVEMBER 1988 –
BACK TO BORAMA

I just wanted to get on the plane and go. Standing in the airport departures area, I repeatedly checked my watch, but this wasn't going to alter the fact that my flight was delayed by an hour. Waiting was giving me too much time to think, and I might change my mind.

My father waved from a distance, as he returned from parking the car. He walked hurriedly towards me, my mother struggling to keep up. They both gave me a long hug.

"I'm not going to say too much," declared my father. "You seem to be determined about this, and I don't want any more upsetting conversations before you go. I want to wave you off with a smile, and I will."

My mother looked at me with sorrow in her eyes. "Remember we love you very much, and whatever happens we're very proud of you. Come back safely, take no risks now," she choked, wiping a tear from her eye, and gave me a kiss on the cheek.

Neither of them had noticed my flight was delayed. My father gave me another hug. He wasn't usually the hugging type of person. For him, two in one day was a world record and almost as many as he'd ever given me during my entire life.

What was I to say? I couldn't afford to be hesitant. "Keep an eye on my new house, and remind my sister no pets allowed, whilst she's house-sitting," I said. "Don't forget the bank manager has sorted the special insurance for the mortgage, and he has another copy of my will." I paused. "Give everyone my love, and I promise to write when I can."

"Yes, yes, I know all that," replied my father. "Now you need to go, before your mother cries again. We'll just wait here, whilst you go through." With that, I picked up my suitcase, and passport in hand I took a deep breath, and passed through the departure gate.

I knew my parents were thinking the worst. It might be the last time they see me for quite a while, and in their eyes possibly ever. They lingered, making the most of these last few seconds. I stopped and turned to give my final wave. I then went around a corner and disappeared from their sight.

That was it. I was on my way. In the passport queue, I took out a tissue, wiped my eyes, and blew my nose. I'd had many goodbyes with my family in the past, but this one was by far the worst. Why was I doing this again? I had to keep reminding myself. I'd been reassured it would be safe to return, and I wanted to try and complete what I had started. I had friends out there, and I simply needed to help them. But I was going back into a war zone in Somalia, and anything could happen.

Stepping off the plane in Mogadishu, I was hit by the familiar oppressive heat and humidity. On entering the main airport, I collected my suitcase and joined the usual long queue, where my belongings would no doubt be rigorously checked. I offered my passport for inspection. A tall Somali officer dressed in his blue

243

uniform peered over his sunglasses, and he stared me up and down. He then turned his attention to my passport. It seemed to take forever, as he leafed through all the pages. I remained calm and casually looked about me.

The Officer waved to another colleague to come over. He held my passport open on the page with the large '*Anullato*' stamp across my old visa. They had a brief conversation, and I was ushered into a side room. I started to perspire a little more than usual, and I could feel my pulse step up a gear.

The First Officer spoke to me sternly in Somali. I shrugged my shoulders, pretending not to understand a word. He gestured for me to unlock my suitcase, which I politely opened to display the contents. The Officer grabbed my belongings, and he placed them all over the counter top until the case was completely empty. For some reason, the main item of interest seemed to be my khaki bush hat. I began to wonder if they thought it had some military significance.

The Second Officer was still going through my passport with a very stern face. He had found my new visa, which was stamped on another page. He flicked backwards and forwards checking the visas and dates. He looked up and murmured something to his colleague. At this point, I was not sure if I would actually be allowed in the country. I began to worry that, worse still, if they realised that I had previously been thrown out, I might get arrested.

"You have been here before?" asked the Second Officer in English. "What is your business here?"

"I'm a doctor, and have been asked to work in the north," I replied. "Err, with the UN," I added, with a degree of authority. Only partly true, but I thought it would help.

He picked up my khaki bush hat. "What's this?"

I thought that was pretty obvious. Dare I say it is a sandwich box, a pencil case, or something equally silly? Best not as the humour will be wasted. "A sun hat, my skin burns easily," I replied.

The Second Officer gestured for me to repack and close my case. He kept my hat in his hand. "This stays with me," he insisted.

I quickly packed my case. After a brief body search, I was taken back into the main airport, where my passport was stamped, and I walked through the gates into arrivals. A great welcome back, but I was seriously relieved, and lucky they only took my hat.

SCF staff met me outside, and they took me to the Mogadishu office. The team seemed in relatively good spirits. At this stage, the fighting had only been in the North, so all was peaceful in the capital. I enjoyed an evening meal of meat and rice, and then catching up on gossip. I went to bed early, tried not to think of my comfortable bed at home, and drifted off to sleep.

Flying north was now easier than before, and the next day I was put on a Dornier Twin Prop for a direct flight to Borama. The old RAF airstrip, from World War II, had been reopened. The plane was full. The other passengers were mostly UN staff, who now had a significant presence in Borama.

The flight touched down at the town of Garowe for one hour. I reflected on the last time I was there. An enterprising local man sat on the tarmac in his Toyota pick-up truck. He was waiting for the plane doors to open. He herded as many passengers as possible to his truck. He took everyone a short distance to his hotel and teashop, whilst the plane was refuelled. He then went back for another carload. A captive audience and great business, I thought. Interesting how some people can make money out of any situation.

Some passengers told me that the return journey was even longer as the flight actually stayed overnight in Garowe. I wasn't sure why they would need to stay overnight. My suspicion was that the pilot was the brother of the hotel and teashop owner. Even more business.

On arrival in Borama, a number of vehicles were lined up on the edge of the airstrip to greet the passengers. Amongst them was a Land Rover with the SCF logo and the familiar face of Mahdi Driver sitting at the steering wheel. He jumped out of the car and gave me an excited wave. "Good to have you back," he declared. My suitcase was loaded, and we set off.

As we journeyed into Borama, I noticed that it was absolutely teeming with people and vehicles. The population had exploded in a very short time. Mahdi explained it had become a semi-safe haven for both locals and refugees, and that most families were hosting displaced people. Many had nothing, and hundreds were sleeping in the streets. Mahdi also warned me that the SCF house had been used as a brothel during my absence. Women had been allowed to take anything they wanted as payment. He was not sure what I would find inside.

Eventually, we arrived at the compound of the SCF house. Outside at least it still looked the same. Many of the previous local team were waiting on the steps of the house, as a welcoming party. They looked so happy and excited, as the vehicle burst through the gates. As we drew to a halt, they surrounded the car, and could hardly wait to greet me. This was exactly why I had come back. These people were almost like family, and, in many ways, this was also my home.

I looked round the group and noted a few familiar faces were missing, including Idris. This was no surprise, but still upsetting. Finding out where they were, and whether they were alive and safe, was to be one of my first tasks. I wondered what it would be like trying to work without Idris. He was my right-hand man.

I thanked Mahdi Driver for the lift, and I stepped out of the vehicle. All the staff formed a line, from the Land Rover to the door of the house. I walked down the line, shaking everyone's hands. It was as if royalty had returned. I presumed my suitcase was somewhere in the crowd, and it would find its own way.

I came to the end of the line and climbed the steps up to the house. Jama stood on the threshold of the door. He had the biggest of grins, and he gave me a vigorous military-style salute. I noticed that he was wearing my favourite shoes and shirt that I had left behind with all my other belongings. At least he'd had them, rather than someone else. I saluted back and shook his hand. It was great to see the old guy safe.

The house was cool, shaded, tranquil, and perfect for a rest after all my travels. I walked into the main living room to sit down. I was taken by surprise by a loud 'Hooray,' as inside there were more people hiding to greet me. Before I could respond, I had a tap on my right shoulder. Standing behind me with a big toothy smile was Idris. He was alive. I was so excited that I just forgot everyone else, and, with joy, I gave him the most enormous hug.

Now I had landed, I needed to get to work, and, as they would say in Somalia, 'by the Will of Allah', I was determined to deliver.

The staff, anticipating my arrival, had thoroughly cleaned the house. Other than some missing furniture, it now looked pretty much as we had left it. I went into the toilet. Princess Anne's throne was gleaming.

Idris's face looked somewhat gaunt. I discovered that, without any reason or explanation, he had been released from prison the previous day. As we all sat at the dining table, I noticed he was rather slumped in his chair. Deeqa entered with a large bowl of spaghetti bolognese. "I thought you'd have missed your favourite dish," she said with a smile, and gently placed it in the middle of the table.

It was obvious Idris had not eaten properly for some time. He was normally a slow eater. His plate was emptied in super-quick time with no conversation.

"Do you mind if I have more?" he asked politely, whilst wiping tomato sauce from around his lips. I pushed the bowl across the table towards him.

"Idris, you eat as much as you want."

Each time I attempted to ask how all the staff were, they looked around the table at each other, and avoided my questions by changing the subject. Everyone was so polite, asking where I'd been, how my family were, and when had I arrived in Mogadishu. I decided a more specific question was needed. There was one particular person missing who would normally be the first through the door at the mention of a party or food.

"Where is Ali Interpreter?" I asked innocently. There was a palpable silence around the table. "Idris, do you know?"

"I genuinely have no idea, Dr John," he replied, between mouthfuls of food.

Axmed Lab, who had sat politely, and unusually quiet, at the end of the table, could not contain himself any longer. "Ali, along with others, is probably in one of the detention centres. There are many people who have gone missing."

"Detention centres?" I quizzed.

"Yes, Dr John, or prisons you could call them. There are a few spread around the town."

"And where are they exactly?"

"As you can imagine, they're not exactly well signposted," said Axmed. "Each one is not very large. They are basically converted buildings and compounds. The giveaway sign is that they've had much higher walls and gates built around them."

"So, who runs these centres?"

"The NSS with the help of the army," replied Axmed. He was beginning to shuffle around in his seat, and he was getting more nervous answering my questions.

"Anyway, we've been here long enough. We will leave you to rest in peace. Idris, let's take you home." He held out his hand to help Idris, who stood up shakily from his chair.

Idris wiped a small tear from his eye.

"Dr John, I am so glad you are back. I am ready to start work tomorrow," he announced. He was so devoted to his work, but he really looked as though he needed a rest, and a few days' decent food.

"I think you need time to recover. Tomorrow, I'm meeting the head of the RHU. Why don't you take it easy, and I will call on you later?" I suggested.

Axmed took Idris's right arm and helped him down the corridor.

Shortly after lunch, a large Toyota Landcruiser arrived outside the house. Out stepped a bald, well-dressed Somali man, probably in his mid-fifties, with a paler, Arab-like complexion. I went to the front door to greet him. "Hello, I'm Hassan Saddiq," he announced, whilst giving me a firm handshake. "I am the head of the RHU here in the North."

With no time to waste, he invited me to his vehicle for a tour around the area to orientate myself. I had been informed in

London that I was to be employed as an RHU Medical Officer. The fighting had displaced many people, and thousands had wandered from a variety of areas to the safety of Borama. They had set up a new unofficial refugee camp called Dhammug, which the RHU were attempting to support. The camp sat on the outskirts of Borama.

The RHU itself had lost many staff, amidst all the mayhem. So SCF were to send a larger contingent of staff to backfill and help run this camp. I had been informed that, although we would be living in Borama, we would not be working in Borama Hospital. When I asked why, the answer was 'all will be clear when you get there'.

"First, let's have a little drive around Borama," suggested Hassan, whilst waving to his driver to set off. "I think you will notice a lot of change." The number of people milling around in the streets was simply unbelievable. Hassan sat calmly looking out of the window. "Although the local population has not at this point been involved in any fighting like Hargeisa, the town is effectively on the edge of a war zone to the south and east," he announced. "With the Ethiopian border to the west, the only safe route out is north to Djibouti, but with a small risk of being ambushed." This was more or less what I had expected to hear. Hassan continued. "Your movements will be restricted to the town, and from here to the Dhammug. This is for your safety."

As our vehicle contained a white person, this had been noted. A large crowd began to gather and surround us. We crept slowly forwards, as a group of men started to jeer, and bang intimidatingly on the doors of the Toyota. Hassan lowered his window, and he shouted angrily in Somali. The crowd instantly stopped banging, and reluctantly walked away. "Some people are desperate at the moment," said Hassan. "We have to take care. Borama is not as you remember it."

He was right. It had shifted from being a small relatively peaceful town, nestled near the mountains, to a bustling thoroughfare of displaced people, with buses, trucks, and military hardware trundling through the streets. Most of the population, including refugees, had received no access to decent healthcare since May 1988.

We stopped outside the hospital. On the veranda was the small, willowy figure of Abdi Aposto, sitting in the shade. He jumped to his feet, and, rushing with excitement, he almost tripped down the steps towards our vehicle. "Dr John, Dr John, everything is OK. You are back, welcome back, I knew one day you would come." He looked around and shouted to other staff to join him, including Aaden TB.

We went on a short tour of the hospital. Normally there were four wards, each containing twenty-six beds with space for a few extra in emergencies. The beds themselves had gone. Now there were only old mattresses or blankets strewn around wherever there was space on the floor.

I counted over two hundred patients. Most were men from the military. Only six were civilians, four women and two children. There were very few qualified nurses and only a handful of the SCF volunteer nurses. The busiest room seemed to be the operating theatre. Here Axmed Theatre and two male nurses were doing their best to patch up wounded soldiers.

The pharmacy had barely any supplies. The lab amazingly still had equipment and reagents inside. I discovered Axmed Lab was still working voluntarily part time, and he would come to the hospital at Abdi's request.

As I passed through the final ward, there was a volunteer nurse preparing 'Dr John's papaya dressing' for a patient with a deep wound. Ali noticed me looking.

"Some things have not changed," said Abdi, smiling at the nurse. "But, as you can see, the hospital is not as you left it." Abdi looked quite thoughtful, at this point. "When do you start?" he enquired.

I was pondering how I should reply, how to explain I was not here to work at the hospital. This was still clearly Abdi's hospital, and without him who knows how much worse it would be.

"He's not here to work at the hospital," declared Hassan, looking at Abdi's now saddened face. "He's going to work in Dhammug. But there is a rumour that another NGO might come to help with the hospital," he hinted.

"I understand," said Abdi, looking dejected. "But we will see you sometimes?"

"I'm sure you will, Abdi, I'm sure you will. By the way where is Dr Muktar?" I asked.

The conversation stopped. Abdi looked furtively at the staff around him.

"Let us say the hospital doesn't have a doctor at the moment," replied Hassan.

Hassan indicated that we needed to leave. "Not sure how safe it is working in the hospital now," said Hassan in a hushed voice, as we walked back to the vehicle.

"Why is that?"

Hassan stared me in the eye. "In this crazy world where we find ourselves, looking after the military could be seen as choosing sides. Here it's best to be seen as neutral. As for Dr Muktar, he is, how would you say, a little detained at the moment."

29.

WELCOME TO DHAMMUG

It was a short drive to Dhammug. The road was full of people and vehicles heading in both directions between Borama and the camp. Hassan asked the driver to stop for a moment. The camp lay before us. It stretched in all directions, as far as you could see. The domes of the aqals were spread like a giant egg box, over the hills and countryside. The area covered was larger than the town. There was hardly a tree or bush left anywhere. Everything had been cut down to help build the camp and provide fuel for fires.

We proceeded along the road. The dwellings varied tremendously. Some were well-built and completely covered with traditional matting or other weatherproof materials. Others were far more rudimentary, just a few sticks covered with cardboard, offcuts of tin sheeting, and even old plastic shopping bags. Their owners had obviously gathered whatever they could find. But they offered little shelter from the elements.

"Remember," said Hassan, "as camp Medical Officer, you are one of the most important and influential people in the camp. Do not forget to use this when necessary. It's not like Borama

Hospital, where you worked with the Somali doctor. Here you are in charge. You are the doctor, and you are my deputy, here."

"How many people are here?" I asked.

"We don't know precisely, around fifty to sixty thousand refugees. It grows rapidly by the day. Sometime soon, we will need to do a headcount. But for today that's enough, and you need to rest. You'll have a busy day tomorrow. As for me, I have other camps to review, but I will pass by soon to see how you are."

That evening, after eating, I went to sit with the guards around their fire. Jama was proudly wearing my old walking shoes and socks, strutting around as if he was back in the army. Despite their circumstances, they seemed in cheerful spirits, and delighted to see me back in the house.

"I have something for you," announced Jama, reaching down to the floor.

"It's OK, Jama, I don't want my shoes back," I informed him.

"Your shoes are most comfortable." He smiled. "I have something far more important." He picked up a plastic bag and handed it to me. "I just knew you'd come back. I've kept a few things from the house safe, before others could take them," he announced with pride.

Inside was my camera. I had presumed this would have been stolen, or at least swapped for money or food. The plastic bag contained another small brown bag at the bottom. Inside were rolls of used film. These were really irreplaceable. They had captured much of my time in Somalia, and they were much more important to me than my other belongings. I was really touched by this gesture. It was probably the best return home present I could have been given.

It was time for bed. I thanked Jama for my camera, and I walked with my torch to the shelter, which contained the generator at the end of the compound. I switched it off and all was silent. The stars were glimmering in the clear night sky. At least some things don't change.

Holding my torch, I slowly walked back in the dark. The cat was asleep on the steps. It opened one eye, as the beam from the torch flashed past. I nearly jumped out of my skin, as suddenly loud machine gun fire rang through the air, close to the house. This was followed by rowdy noises, as if someone was having a party and firing guns to celebrate. I hastened into the house and went to bed. I was happy to be back. But back to what exactly, I wasn't sure.

There was a mumbling noise, which became a general rambling. Someone was talking in Somali, and then English, but not making any sense. At first, I thought I was dreaming. I opened one eye, and tried to focus in the early morning light, which was coming through my thin curtains. Then, I noticed a man sitting in the chair in the corner of my bedroom. He was Somali, but with a lighter complexion and wavy hair. He seemed reasonably well-dressed in a clean patterned shirt, and sarong with leather sandals. More worryingly, on his belt he had a large traditional knife in a sheath, which he was pulling out with his right hand. He looked up at the ceiling and shouted something in Somali. He then continued in English, "What am I doing here?"

"Hello," I said calmly in Somali, whilst slowly sitting up in bed. "Do I know you?" I added.

He looked at me, and then continued to talk to himself, as if I wasn't there. "Where am I, where is this place?" he murmured, as he looked around the room. His eyes started flitting between the window, the curtains, the ceiling, and then the four walls. He started muttering in Somali again. I was not completely sure, but he appeared to have a mental health problem.

"Hello," I repeated gently in Somali. "What's your name?" There was no answer.

"Do you speak English, you speak English, yes?" I asked.

This time he looked at me directly, as if seeing me properly for the first time.

"I'm lost," he said. "Where is this place?"

"This is my house. Where is your house?" I asked in English.

"In Abu Dhabi, I live in Abu Dhabi," he replied. He was surely confused.

"This is my house, and it's in Borama. Do you know Borama?"

His eyes darted around the room more rapidly. His right hand was beginning to twitch around the handle of his knife, which he had now drawn from its sheath. "Who are you, why are you here?" he demanded, as he became more agitated.

My pulse was racing, but I needed to keep my composure. "I live here in Borama," I said calmly.

"Borama. Why am I in Borama?" He then started mumbling in more Somali.

"I mean you no harm. I'm a doctor, and I work here in Borama."

"You're a doctor?" he said appearing less agitated. "Are you here to take me home?"

"I can try if you will let me. Shall we try to take you home?"

"Yes, I want to go home to Hargeisa, to go home."

"OK, let's go home then," I said, as I gently eased myself out of the bed, and lowered my feet quietly onto the cold tiled floor.

I looked at my bedroom door to ensure there was nothing in the way, should I need to make a hasty exit.

"What is your name?"

"Sharif, my name is Sharif."

"OK, Sharif. I don't think you will need your knife to go home, do you? Why not put it back in the sheath."

"My knife?" he said looking down, surprised to see a knife in his hand. He suddenly dropped the knife, and it landed with a clang on the tiles.

"Sharif, shall we go home now, you want to go home?"

"Yes, I want to go home to Hargeisa, to my sister."

I held out my hand, and I helped him from the chair, while I gently nudged the knife with my foot under the bed, and out of sight. My heart finally stopped beating so fast.

Outside the guards were waking up, except for One-eyed Hussein, who was already patrolling the compound.

"Sharif, do you like Land Rovers?" I asked.

"Yes, yes, I like Land Rovers," he replied. He was now far less anxious, as I sat him inside the Land Rover and closed the door.

I walked over to Jama. "How did this man get into the house this morning?"

Jama sat rubbing his hands over the dying embers in the charcoal burner. "What man?" said Jama with a yawn. I pointed to the vehicle.

"No idea," replied Jama unhelpfully. He obviously didn't realise what an experience I had just been through. He continued, with the other guards, to warm his hands.

"Perhaps you can ask the others if they know anything?"

Jama obliged, and then gave me an answer. "Hussein says the man arrived this morning speaking English, and he asked to go

257

in the house. He thought it was someone you knew, and let him in."

"Thank you Jama, very useful." But not exactly reassuring, I thought.

"He wants to go home, Jama. Do you know where he might live?"

"Dr John, the town is now full of people. I don't know."

Who could I find to help at this early hour of the morning? I pondered. Of course, Abdi Aposto, he was always in the hospital at the crack of dawn.

I drove calmly to the hospital, whilst speaking gently to Sharif, who was now talking about Abu Dhabi again. My saviour Abdi was walking along the veranda. I parked, and I explained what had happened in my house. "Since the fighting, Dr John, quite a few people escaped from the mental health hospital in Hargeisa. Maybe he's one of them," suggested Abdi, as he approached the vehicle. Abdi then had a short conversation with Sharif. "I think he might have a sister in the town," suggested Abdi, waving me back into the vehicle.

We drove into the town and pulled up outside a small new house made of concrete breezeblocks. Abdi went to the house, and he spoke to a woman who was standing outside. Seeing Sharif in the car, she started to smile and walked with Abdi to the vehicle. "This is Sharif's sister," said Abdi. "She will take over from here. He went missing last night." Sharif then happily went into the house with his sister and Abdi.

I waited in the vehicle for Abdi to return. The street was becoming busier, and some people walking past began to stare, which made me feel uncomfortable. Eventually, Abdi came out of the house, and climbed back inside the Land Rover.

"I hope Sharif will be OK," I commented.

"Everything is OK. Now there we have a story," declared Abdi. "It seems Sharif works in Abu Dhabi. He came back to see relatives in Hargeisa, and to give them some money. But he was caught up in all the fighting. Quite a few of his relatives were killed, and he has taken it very badly."

This was now beginning to explain Sharif's tale.

"His sister isn't sure, but she wonders if he has been on mental health medication in Abu Dhabi that has now run out. So are his problems due to that, or is it the fighting?"

"Or is it both, Abdi? We will probably never know."

"One of many sad stories at the moment," added Abdi.

"What are you carrying?" I asked.

"Breakfast, a present from his sister."

We took a short drive out of Borama, carrying our breakfast. Abdi asked me to stop, and suggested we climb a small hill. At the top, we sat on a rock, and admired the view in the early morning light. You could see both the town and the refugee camp stretching into the distance. Abdi appeared to be deep in thought.

"What are you thinking?"

"As a child I used to sit here, on this exact spot, with my father." He sighed. "At one time, this was a forest with animals, can you believe it. In my lifetime, it has all gone. Look at it now. I can only see one tree, there, on that hill over there." I was shocked, and I wasn't sure the land would ever recover.

Over breakfast, and with no one else to overhear our conversation, I decided to ask Abdi a few questions.

"Where is Dr Muktar?"

He looked at me in disbelief. "You mean you don't already know?"

"I have my suspicions, but I needed to ask."

"Like most other people from Hargeisa, he was rounded up by the NSS. Unfortunately, he's in one of the detention centres, but I don't know which one. Some centres are allowed visitors and others not. I haven't seen him, or heard any news, since he was taken."

After talking further, it appeared the NSS, or the army, could take anyone for no reason. Those from Hargeisa were especially at risk. Anyone in the population with a grudge, and especially those with any influence, could accuse another person of anything. This could lead to them being locked away.

I was getting late for work. I took Abdi back to the hospital, collected Mahdi Driver, and headed into the camp. Mahdi Driver stopped the Land Rover to speak to someone on the road, who then opened the door, and climbed inside.

"This is Jabriil. He's the senior RHU nurse in the camp," said Mahdi, introducing my fellow passenger.

"Hello," said Jabriil. "I speak English, but not so good," he said apologetically, whilst shaking my hand.

On the outskirts of the camp, I could see mounds of stones. They were in lines on a distant hillside. Jabriil noticed my gaze. "It's a burial zone, a cemetery," he declared. Then, turning, he pointed to another area on the opposite side of the camp. Here, although far away, you could see a few people crouched near the ground. "No latrines, so that's the defaecation zone for the camp. Except the camp is big, and it's too far for some, so they might not use it. This is more common in the night, which causes hygiene problems."

As we went further into the camp, I noticed that many men were walking in the same direction. They all had an AK47 slung over their shoulder.

"Local militia," declared Mahdi. "I think they have training today, with practice for marching and shooting."

"The people here are neutral, when it comes to all the fighting," Jabriil informed me proudly. "They have to be able to defend themselves, if things get worse."

I hadn't anticipated that the refugees would be armed.

Finally, we stopped and climbed out of the Land Rover. I was discovering that Jabriil's English was actually very good, and he was to become my 'go to' person in the camp for advice. After a short walk, we stopped outside a small tarpaulin two-man ridge tent.

"This is your clinic," indicated Jabriil.

"My clinic?" I asked, surprised.

"Yes, for now. We don't have any proper facilities yet. But now you're here, we can start sorting the buildings soon."

"Where do I sit?" I asked.

"Here," announced Jabriil. He placed a rock in the shade of the tent entrance. It was just large enough to sit on.

With the rock in position, it sent a signal to nearby refugees. They immediately started walking across, and they sat forming a line on the ground nearby. For the rest of the day, I sat on one rock, and Jabriil on another. By the end of our mammoth session, we had seen over two hundred patients. This was to be the norm over the next few weeks.

For many of these people, there had been no access to healthcare since May 1988. Fleas, scabies, chronic diarrhoea, chest infections, malnutrition including scurvy, TB, and malaria were all common problems. Importantly, there was a case of measles. In most western countries this was something not seen as too serious. Here in Africa, compounded by malnutrition, this caused great alarm. It was a potential death sentence for small children.

"Vaccines are coming," reassured Jabriil. "They are late, but they are coming." I just hoped they would arrive soon. Measles is very infectious.

That evening, under the cover of darkness, I was asked to meet with Abdi at the hospital. He quietly led me to one of the latrines, handed me a torch, and invited me to enter.

"What do you see, Dr John?"

"Abdi, the last time we did this, it was to convince me to build more latrines. If this is what you want—"

Before I could finish my sentence, I stopped. I was completely surprised by what I could see. Floating on the surface of all the fluid in the pit latrine were hundreds of glass vials of medication, gleaming in the light of the torch.

"Vaccines, Dr John. You are looking at vaccines."

"But who would do such a thing?" I asked.

"Some people are desperate, some just greedy. They take and sell, or swap, what they can. Vaccines are not worth anything. But syringes, cold chain boxes, fuel in the vehicle, well they're worth something. I found them earlier today, but they could have been dumped here anytime in the last few days."

I remembered Jabriil's comment that the vaccines were late. The next day, I had to inform the RHU nurses and get a message to Hassan Saddiq. We needed another batch of vaccines as soon as possible, if we were to stem the number of measles cases.

The following day, I explored Dhammug on foot with Jabriil. The weather was getting colder at night, and during the day the clouds had begun to settle over the hills and mountaintops. The majority of aqals were not weatherproof, and most refugees only had what they were wearing or had been able to carry.

Jabriil didn't seem to be moved emotionally by all the sights that day. Presumably, he had seen it all before.

"Tents for the refugees, tents for feeding stations, observation ward, clinic stations, and storage tents," I suggested.

Jabriil gave me an earnest look. "There are no tents available. Maybe we could get plastic sheets and blankets, for now?"

As our shopping list grew, we arrived at the main road passing through the camp, and we began to walk back to the vehicles.

"You don't seem too phased by all this, Jabriil," I remarked.

"Remember, Dr John, I might be an RHU nurse, but I'm also a refugee myself. I live here, these are my people, and I will do what I can for them. But what you see is all quite normal at the moment. Supplies are very low."

Despite the circumstances, and all the poverty, some industrious members of the refugee community were doing well for themselves. We passed a number of temporary shops along the road. A tailor was sitting under empty plastic food sacks that he had draped over wooden sticks. He sat pedalling his Singer sewing machine backwards and forwards. He was mending an enormous pile of clothes. How he could remember which clothes belonged to who was unclear.

Only a few metres away sat a very large tent. The RHU staff couldn't get tents, so how did this one get here? Some of the tailor's customers were entering. I decided to take a look. Inside, there was a TV and a Video Cassette Recorder (VCR) machine. The tent was packed with people watching an Indian movie. For a small price, this tent offered a little bit of escapism from the world outside, including for those waiting for their clothes to be repaired.

Later in the clinic, we had another case of measles. There was also an elderly woman with a very large irregular lump in the groin. It was about the size of a grapefruit. Her foot was wrapped in an old cloth. She was a nomad, and she had heard there was a white doctor in the camp. She had travelled to see if they could treat the lump at the top of her leg.

I was hoping to see an infection that I could possibly treat. However, when I peeled away the cloth, I could see that she had a large melanoma (skin cancer) on her foot. It had been there for months, and it had obviously spread up to the lymph nodes at the top of her leg and possibly even further. At this stage of the disease, there was nothing I could do in the camp. Idris explained the situation to the patient and her husband. They received this sad news without any emotion; there seemed to be an acceptance of their fate. They thanked us, said it was the 'Will of Allah,' and left to travel back to their village.

30.

NOISES IN THE NIGHT

Over the following days in December, there was an expansion of UN and SCF ex-pat staff. An administrator called Josh arrived, accompanied by Brad. This was good news, as I would be released to do more medical work, and Josh could sort all the logistics. He carried a suitcase, in one hand, and a small stereo, in the other. He was six feet tall, with a big build, short straight blonde hair, and a pale complexion.

"Great to meet you," he said, enthusiastically shaking my hand. He was softly spoken with an impeccable Oxford English accent. Before unpacking his bags, he was straight into his job, touring the camp with Brad and listing everything needed with Jabriil.

That evening, with building and supply requirements all itemised, Josh and Brad sat happily at the dining table, sharing a small bottle of whisky. Josh was listening to his favourite Spanish classical guitar music on a cassette tape. "There will be additional nursing staff arriving from the UK soon," announced Brad. "So, we've decided in order to accommodate them we're going to rent another house. The one next door in fact. I would really like you and Josh to move in there." He looked at Josh and then me. "The nurses are all female. I'd like them to feel safe. This house is in better shape. Are you happy?" he enquired. We both nodded in agreement.

"One more thing," said Brad. "We need to temporarily accommodate the new Dutch NGO team, until they sort themselves a house. Probably only for a week or so."

"Their role being what?" asked Josh.

Brad peered over his glasses in my direction. "To run John's beloved Borama Hospital." This was something I had to get used to.

Over the following week, the UN set up a large truck compound to distribute food wherever needed. The Dutch team leader was a temporary resident with us, and managed to procure accommodation in time for the arrival of the full team. Oxfam installed water collection points around the camp. These were huge water containers that were to be refilled by water tankers. Hassan Saddiq also arranged for a new batch of vaccines to arrive as a priority.

The original intention was for Josh to contract a local builder to construct the camp facilities. However, there are always some people who want to profit by preying on the misfortunes of others. The builder, sensing a large pay cheque from an NGO, held out for a fee almost five times the going rate. Josh reacted by bringing everything from outside and sourcing building materials from Djibouti. These were mostly concrete, wood, and tin sheeting. This caused a degree of tension, not only with the builder, but also with some related town elders. Josh however was a no-nonsense type of person. Not only did he ignore their complaints, but he also contracted refugees, who had previously worked as builders, to construct the camp facilities. I liked his style. Amazingly, he also acquired large tents for an observation and an obstetric ward.

Some large plastic sheets and blankets arrived for distribution. We had 50,000 to 60,000 refugees, but only 2,000 plastic sheets and 4,000 blankets. These were stored in a secure fenced compound in the camp. However, due to the desperate nature of some people's circumstances, their arrival almost caused a riot. Distributing them fairly, and to the most needy, was not going to be easy. The secure compound needed armed militia guards to protect it.

After discussion with Jabriil and camp elders, the proposed solution was to divide the camp into small zones. Each zone would have a set number of aqals and a nominated link person. This would not only be useful for distributing the sheets and blankets, but also for identifying malnourished women and children, those needing vaccinations, and anyone who was really ill.

To police this distribution, we had to walk from zone to zone with armed militia guards. The link person in each zone had generally acted in a fair manner. However, some zones were poorer, needing more sheets and blankets than others. In some, the link person had clearly identified their family and friends above others. So occasionally we had to override their selection. The armed guards were very necessary to achieve all this. We were glad we had listened to Jabriil's advice. When I went to medical school, I never dreamt that, as a doctor, one day the biggest contribution I would make to people's health would be to hand out plastic sheets and blankets under armed guard. By the end of the day, we felt a great sense of achievement.

Back at the house, to my surprise and delight, I was informed that a new SCF nurse had arrived. I eagerly bounded up the steps and into the house. Sitting at the dining room table, complete with new Ray Bans, was Jo. Despite her recent experiences in Somalia, she had agreed to return. It was great to have at least one familiar face in the team.

All my belongings had been moved to the neighbouring house. The wall of the compound had been partly removed to allow us to walk freely between them. The gap was close to the guardhouse. The three musketeers, Jama, Malik, and Hussein, now had the task of looking after both houses. My new room was quite large. It had a camp bed, mosquito net, and chair. It was situated next to the shower room, or should I say bucket-and-cup washroom. The toilet, of course, was a standard pit latrine. By moving house, I had lost the proximity to, and luxury of, Princess Anne's toilet. The view from my window was not picturesque. No plants, no trees, just a dirt strip and a neighbour's wall which was several metres high and made of concrete breezeblocks. The wall stretched both to the right and to the left.

I lay in bed under my mosquito net. It had been a long day, and I quickly went to sleep. But I was abruptly woken by a high-pitched scream in the middle of the night. I got up and looked out of the window, but I could see nothing.

I walked outside into the central courtyard of my new house, and I shone my torch around. There was nothing to be seen in the courtyard. I approached the guardhouse. Jama, and the others, were dozing around their charcoal burner.

"The noise Jama, what's going on?" I asked, in a hushed voice.

"One of the nearby houses is a new detention centre," stated Jama, pulling his blanket further up, and over his shoulders, to keep warm. I then realised the noises were coming from over the wall outside my bedroom. With hindsight, perhaps I should have guessed it was a detention centre by the height of the walls. However, a number of neighbouring houses in that direction had high walls, and sound travels more easily at night. It was difficult to be certain of the exact source of the noises.

I made my way back through the courtyard to return to my bedroom, and nearly bumped into Josh in the dark.

"Can you hear the noise, can you hear that?" exclaimed Josh, seemingly perturbed.

"Apparently, we have a detention centre as our neighbour," I replied.

"But it's awful, what on earth is going on?"

"Josh, you're on the other side of the courtyard, imagine what it's like in my room."

Josh followed me into my room. "Good God, man, it sounds as though they're beating up the prisoners."

"Yes, but I don't know what's worse, that, or the cynical laughter of the guards." I recalled my story of the post-mortem victim and his injuries to Josh. I wondered if the inmates next door were suffering the same fate.

In the morning, having hardly slept, I entered the dining room in the other house for breakfast.

"Boy, you don't look so good," quipped Jo. "Almost as bad as Josh. What were you both up to last night?"

"Don't ask. I'll explain another day. What's for breakfast?" I muttered.

That day, I decided to discuss the detention centre confidentially with local staff. Idris recounted his experience. Although not subjected to any beatings or torture himself, he gave graphic detail of what the NSS, or army personnel, had done to others in his centre. Beatings were frequent and quite random, but those from Hargeisa would be beaten more. Torture included being hung from your wrists behind your back, whilst being beaten. This could also include tying your feet behind your back to your wrists. Some people were even placed into the underground water tanks. Most could not swim. The lid would be put back in place, and the NSS officers and soldiers would bet to see which person lasted the longest in the water.

This made me even more determined to see if I could get people released. I wasn't sure how to do this, so I had discussions with UN staff. They said they would see what they could do. But they could not make any promises.

During the day, I was faced with relentless lines of very sick people, often accompanied by crying and screaming children. At night, I was kept awake by frequent screaming, shouting, and pleas from those being beaten for their tormentors to stop. Josh and I went back to see the UN staff again, a few days later. Although they hinted that they would try to see what they could do, we were reminded that NGOs, and the UN, were lucky to be allowed to work in Borama. Too many complaints, and we may well be thrown out with dire consequences for those most in need.

Each morning, Josh and I would arrive late for breakfast. We'd discuss what we had heard during the night in some detail. Before long, these nightly occurrences were so frequent that it was no longer news. Our tolerance levels were raised, and it became almost the norm. Our morning conversations became much shorter.

"Did you hear the screams last night?"

"Yes. What's for breakfast?"

Something had to be done. I arranged to see Abdi for a confidential discussion and advice.

I arrived after dark at the hospital. Abdi was waiting for me on the veranda.

"Dr John, everything is OK?"

I explained that I wanted to talk about missing people and detention centres. Initially, he seemed reluctant but then agreed. He stated that the majority of people in the detention centres had recently come from Hargeisa due to the fighting. However, there were others from Hargeisa who had lived in Borama for some time, but, due to the government's general mistrust of anyone from Hargeisa, they had also been detained.

Idris, being from Ethiopia, had also been detained. Following the announcement of my imminent arrival, he had been released, possibly as a good will gesture, as he was known to be my interpreter. However, Abdi warned me to be extremely careful when getting involved in any discussions about detainees. This was a very sensitive issue, especially with the NSS.

"Who organised the release of Idris?" I asked.

"Not exactly sure, but, if I was to guess, then I imagine it was probably Major Yussuf," hinted Abdi. "But he has been temporarily posted to another part of the country. Can I suggest that if he returns, I let you know immediately?"

I just hoped this would happen soon.

A few days later, whilst returning home from the camp, I noticed a line of vehicles parked along the outside of another NGO compound. On top of each vehicle were groups of boys. As we drove closer, I realised they were peeping furtively over the top of the compound wall and giggling amongst themselves. I wondered what was so interesting that it had created such a gathering. I asked Mahdi Driver to pull up at the end of the line, close to the wall. As we stepped out of the Land Rover, our arrival was noticed by some of the boys. They quickly jumped down from the vehicles, and they ran into the town laughing.

I clambered onto the rooftop of the SCF Land Rover, hotly followed by Mahdi. We both looked over the wall. To my amazement two of the staff were sunbathing partly clothed on the veranda of their house. I couldn't believe it, such cultural insensitivity in a Muslim country. Mahdi was transfixed. I was just trying to think how to explain this, when he turned to me.

"Is this what you do at home, perhaps with even less clothes?" he asked politely.

"Sometimes privately, but not usually at the front of your house," I replied, somewhat embarrassed. "There are beaches, where some people sunbathe with even fewer clothes, in some European countries." I stopped there. I didn't want to venture into explaining naturist beaches and camps.

"Exposed almost like the lady in the Kodak advert," said Mahdi, smiling.

Kodak advert? Where had I seen a Kodak advert? Of course, in the town, there was a Kodak advert on a cardboard placard, outside a pharmacy shop. It had a white woman, dressed in only a bikini, holding a roll of film. These adverts were normal in Europe. I had seen it, but I had thought nothing of it at the time. But now it made me think. What impression did this give to local people?

I decided to pay a visit to the NGO team. We had an interesting conversation, where I tried to alert them to cultural differences. Initially, they responded with comments that including: 'our compound is private', 'they shouldn't be looking', and 'what we do inside our compound is our business'. I was not impressed. At best, they would become more popular than the Borama outdoor cinema. At worst, their safety, and that of other white female NGO staff, could not be guaranteed, if they gave the wrong impression. Amazingly they had not thought about this. I discussed this further with the head of the team later that day, and I left with a promise that as a team they would reconsider this. Thankfully, I never saw any crowds peeping over the wall again.

The newly built feeding centre, complete with tin roof, was gleaming in the bright sunlight. Standing outside was Jabriil. He had a very large grin. "The vaccines have arrived," he declared with great delight. By this point, there had been almost forty cases of measles in the camp. We now had to pull out all the stops to get every child vaccinated.

"Vaccinating everyone will not be that easy," he hinted. "As a family, if you don't know where your next bowl of rice is coming from, vaccinations aren't necessarily high on your list," he continued. I obviously hadn't thought this through. "Better we work through the link person in each zone. They can encourage all the mothers to attend, and we can distribute food at the same time," suggested Jabriil. Here we definitely had a man who had done this sort of thing before.

Each team was made up of RHU and SCF nurses with their interpreters. Children were screened for their height, weight, and vaccination history. They were assessed for state of malnutrition, given their vaccination, and then directed either to collect food

273

from the ration tent, or to attend the feeding centre. Those who were sick went to the clinics for assessment. We saw hundreds each day, by working through each zone. Within a short time, we had covered the camp. It was all amazingly efficient. As new children arrived daily, and of course some immunisations required more than one dose, the exercise had to be repeated every so often.

In the middle of all this, a Toyota Landcruiser arrived with Hassan Saddiq. He had brought two patients for me to see from outlying refugee camps. The first was a teenage boy. When he took off his hat, I could see he had a chronic infected bleeding sore on his head. It had been there for months, and it had gradually spread to cover one half of his scalp, from which he had mostly lost his hair. He had been given many treatments, but none had been effective. I presumed he had a fungal infection, but I had never seen anything as severe as this before.

The second was a teenage girl. Her face was covered by her headscarf, which was lowered by her mother to reveal a horrific sight. She had a chronic infection. It was so severe that it had eaten away her whole left cheek. You could see right through to the back of her throat. Her teeth on that side had been lost, as the infection had spread to her gums, and it was now starting to involve the side of her tongue. I looked at her mother, who was sitting by her side. The girl could hardly speak, and she had great difficulty swallowing.

"Idris, ask how long she's had this."

Idris had a short conversation with the mother. "Many months. But the main reason she has brought her daughter here is that with this face she won't be able to get married."

I had seen pictures of something very similar called 'Cancrum

Oris' in old medical textbooks, when I was a student. The poor girl was in a terrible state. I found a space in the Observation ward to start treatment.

Both these cases were eventual success stories. After many weeks, both infections cleared up. With anti-fungal medication, and Dr John's papaya dressing, the boy's skin began to grow back. The infection in the girl's face was hugely improved, but her face was already so destroyed that her disfigurement remained. We convinced a truck driver to give her, and her mother, a free ride to Djibouti. Armed with a letter to see the French military's plastic surgeon, they sat on top of the truck, gripping on to whatever they could find. As the truck set off, for the first time, the girl raised her right arm to wave, and she attempted a faint smile. That was all we needed to reward our efforts.

31.

THE MAJOR RETURNS

"Dr John, good morning to you. I have come to seek your help." I was surprised to find Axmed Lab sitting on the steps of the house. It was seven in the morning, and he didn't want to miss us before we left for the camp. "I cannot carry on working voluntarily at the hospital. I need to earn money for my family. I need a job. Do you need any interpreters?" He was surely aware that Jo had arrived and more nurses were to follow. He would be a great asset to the team, so I led him straight into the house to meet Josh. This was a better start to the day.

After a busy day on the camp, I strolled to the hospital around dusk. I had received an intriguing message, saying that Abdi wanted to see me confidentially, as the Major had returned to Borama. The screams at night had been getting worse not better. I was not sure I could take it anymore. The return of the Major was hopefully welcome news.

There was no usual welcome from Abdi, as I stepped up onto the veranda. He remained silent and just kept looking all around, whilst fumbling with his keys. After quietly opening the door, he covertly ushered me into the hospital office, and locked the door behind us. Inside, in the dim light of an oil lamp, the Major sat at the table, waiting. As usual, he was smartly dressed in his uniform.

"Major Yussuf, it's very good to see you back in Borama." I shook his hand.

"I'm very pleased to be back; to me, in many ways, this is my home." This was an interesting comment, since although he was not from Borama, he had always seemed to care about the town.

"I see you have also returned, Dr John. Abdi reassured me you would come back at some point."

I replied to say I was also pleased to be back, and I explained that I'd been contracted to work with the RHU in the camp and not the hospital.

The Major looked slightly disappointed. "Well, the refugees are in desperate need of medical care," he admitted.

"How is your wife by the way?" I asked.

"She is well, very well, thank you. But enough of pleasantries." He placed his arms on the desk and looked over the table at me. "What is the main reason for this meeting, Dr John? I'm a busy man."

"It is a delicate matter. One that others have encouraged me not to raise." I was feeling a little anxious, and there was a slight tremor in my hands.

I continued. "I am aware that my interpreter, Idris, was kept in a detention centre." I paused for a few seconds to gauge his reaction. There was none.

"I'm not sure if you were involved, but Idris was released just prior to my arrival. Having worked with Idris for so long I had developed a bond, almost a dependency on him as my interpreter.

He understands what I am going to say often before I say it. It is very good that we are able to work together again. It's also very important for me to see him safe. I'm sure you can understand?"

The Major nodded his head, but otherwise sat without moving. He was giving away nothing with his body language. I continued. "There are other SCF, and hospital staff, who are still missing. I'm not sure what has happened to them. It's possible they are also being held in detention centres."

At this point, the Major turned his head and glowered at Abdi, while uttering a few words in Somali. He then looked back at me. I was not sure whether to continue, but I decided this might be my only chance to make a difference. "For SCF and the hospital to function as well as possible, we really need all the existing trained staff to be able to return to their work as soon as possible."

The Major rocked back in his chair, and he crossed his arms defensively. He was not happy. "This is not entirely within my power," he declared forcefully. "Abdi, why have you organised this meeting?"

I interjected. "Abdi only reluctantly arranged this meeting at my request," I said attempting to defend him.

The Major was clearly agitated. "You understand this is a very delicate matter, even for me to raise."

"I appreciate that. I really do, and I don't want to affect your own position here or Abdi's." The conversation was not going well. I decided to alter my tactics.

"You have been posted away for a while, and now you are back. I need to tell you a story if you will listen?" The Major nodded positively, so I continued. "Often at night I am woken, and I hear noises from a neighbouring house, sometimes terrible noises. These are noises of great pain and suffering. Noises of pleas to stop." I paused, and I looked more intently at the Major. "Detention centres for security are one thing. But those noises are another."

The Major looked thoughtful. "Why do you share this story with me?"

"I would never forgive myself if I did nothing, if I didn't ask the one person I thought could help, the one person I thought was better than all this."

The Major's face softened. "Every night you say, noises every night?"

"Not every night, but most nights, usually late at night."

The Major sat quietly ruminating, and he looked down at his hands on his lap. Slowly he raised his head.

"For the SCF staff I will see what I can do, but I make no promises."

"What about all the others?" I pleaded.

"Sometimes as a soldier you have to take orders. Sometimes those orders are not what you want to hear. But you must, as a soldier, you must obey." His face became quite sorrowful. "Releasing all is a step too far. I cannot ask for this. But the noises, you are right, we should all be better than that." He stood tall from his seat. "I need a few days," he said, as he held out his right hand to shake mine.

Abdi took out his keys and unlocked the door. The Major turned, walked quietly out of the office, and drove away into the darkness. Later that night, as the screams continued, I dragged my mattress across the courtyard and into Josh's bedroom, where I tried to sleep with my head under my pillow.

More SCF staff arrived from the UK. The team now had six nurses.

This was a great bonus, and it reduced our excessive workload. The SCF nurses were deployed to the feeding centres, the ongoing vaccination and screening programmes, and the health clinics, which included obstetric care.

After one morning's work, I walked into the town with Idris. It was simply bursting with people. Men were sitting in small new teashops on virtually every street corner. Most had no work and nothing to do. I felt uncomfortable, as so many eyes watched us walk along the street.

Eventually, we reached a small square where a teacher was taking a class of children, which included both boys and girls. This was unusual, as many schools were not functioning. They were all sitting under the shade of a giant eucalyptus tree, which was gently swaying in the breeze. The children were arranged in a semi-circle facing the teacher. Suddenly, two children jumped from the rocks on which they were sitting, and ran over to us, excitedly shouting. They grabbed our hands, and led us back to the teacher, who stopped the class, and introduced us to all the children.

I said hello in Somali, and gave them a wave, whilst turning to Idris. "This is like a special occasion, everyone is so excited, why?"

"You don't remember them, Dr John? These were once your patients."

The truth was I did not. I had seen so many children it was difficult to remember them all.

"These two children were burnt in a fire in the town last year, and they're telling all their friends."

The teacher took my hand, and gave me a firm and excited handshake, whilst enthusiastically waving his other arm in the air.

"He remembers the fire well," said Idris. "He says they were most fortunate that you, and the nurses, were in the hospital that day." I nodded and continued to shake his hand, as he seemed very reluctant to let it go.

"Idris, before my hand drops off, tell him we have to go. But he has to carry on with his very important work here with the children. It's brilliant to see the children at school."

In this entirely mad world, there were still people trying to get on with life as usual, to do their job, and help their community.

Further inside the town, we passed close to the main market square. A number of pick-up trucks rattled past and stopped. They were all loaded high with fresh qat leaves.

"My God, I've never seen so much, Idris!"

"It's like this most days. The qat comes from Ethiopia," explained Idris. "The trucks get loaded up, and somehow make it over the border. Fresh, cheap, and there is money to be made."

"Idris, for so much to get here like this, it has to be very organised. Getting all this over the border under the noses of the NSS and army, they have to know or—"

I was stopped in mid-sentence. "Or be involved," said Idris quietly.

Large groups of men surrounded each pick-up truck to unload it. Once finished, they set off in different directions, each clutching bundles of qat. I noticed that even the Donkey Man, who previously had delivered water, was loading up qat into packs on the backs of his donkeys.

In a nearby shop, I could see boxes of whisky on the floor. As Somalia was a dry country, with alcohol banned, I was so surprised that I pointed to the shop.

"Idris, would you look at—"

Idris interrupted me sharply. "Please don't point; make it look as though you meant something else quickly," he instructed.

I moved my finger slowly into the air, and I started talking about a passing bird.

"We need to move on, you didn't see anything OK?" Idris pulled my arm to lead me away. "Please don't look, but the NSS are watching over the road."

I noticed a smartly dressed man, with a patterned shirt and sunglasses, leaning up against a wall close to the shop.

Once we were out of earshot, I couldn't resist asking Idris about the boxes of whisky.

"I have no idea where the boxes are from, but I presume Djibouti," replied Idris.

"And the NSS obviously know?"

"I think that much is clear," he confirmed.

"But qat, whisky and guns, they're not a good mix, Idris. Not a good mix at all." This deeply concerned me. "Idris, the town is doomed if this carries on," I said.

At the time, I didn't know how prophetic my words were. This experience, and seeing more armed men milling around the streets, was quite unsettling. As we walked away, I could hear the odd gunshot into the air. It was beginning to have a 'Wild West' feeling about the place.

Over the coming weeks, we saw more people moving into the camp. Some were from villages along the Ethiopian border. Most of these were women and children. Many had burns and gunshot wounds, as their villages had been attacked. Their menfolk were missing with some having been killed and others conscripted into the army. There had been talk of the government creating a sort of 'no man's land' along the Ethiopian border to prevent SNM activity, even in early 1988. Newspaper articles, I had read back in the UK, supported this. These casualties suggested the process of creating a 'no man's land' was still continuing.

Everyone in the camp cooked on open fires inside their aqal, so fires and burns were a constant problem. One day, whipped by high winds, a terrible fire rapidly spread between neighbouring aqals. Fortunately, most people were not inside or managed to escape. However, one mother and child became trapped and were not so lucky.

I had seen the mother, and her small baby boy, twice before in the clinic. On both occasions, she had brought her baby with a severe chest infection. After the second episode, I had decided to visit her at her home. She was amongst the poorest of the refugees. The few sticks making her aqal were mostly covered with small pieces of cardboard. The lining of the aqal was completely black with charcoal dust from the open fire.

There were very few belongings inside. The mother only had one change of clothes, and she had a small thin threadbare blanket with large holes. There was one very old, darkened metal cooking pot, and one dirty plastic water container.

The thick smoke from her open fire made us all cough as we entered. It was clear why her baby had such a bad chest. Regardless of how many antibiotics were given, he was not going to get better breathing in this thick smoke.

We moved them both into the Observation Tent for treatment. Once fully recovered, we gave the mother a spare blanket and a plastic sheet for her aqal. But not long after returning home her aqal had caught fire, and within minutes it had spread to other

283

dwellings. The fire was very intense. Most refugees only had very small plastic water containers for their aqals. So, their desperate attempts to throw whatever water they had onto the flames were futile. They stood helpless as the mother and baby perished inside.

I was rushed to the scene by a small group of refugees to see if I could help. By the time I had arrived, a large crowd surrounded the aqal, and the flames had been extinguished. The dwelling had completely burnt down but was still smouldering. Inside the burnt remains of the aqal, the charred and blistered bodies lay on the ground. You could see the mother had lain over her baby, trying to protect him. This was a sad day for all.

In addition to this, it had generally been a difficult day for the healthcare staff in Dhammug. The measles outbreak had been halted, following the vaccination campaign, but levels of malnutrition were still high, despite the work of the feeding centres. A number of small children in the feeding centre had died that morning.

Feeling drained by the events of the day, the team arrived late at the SCF house. Unusually, Abdi was sitting outside of the house. He could hardly wait for the vehicle to stop, as he launched himself down the steps.

"Everything is OK, Dr John. Good news, great news," he declared, whilst taking off his hat and placing it over his heart. In all this time, I had never seen Abdi without his hat. I could see his hair was thinning on top.

"All the SCF and hospital staff are free. They came out of the detention centres today."

I bent down slightly, and I put my arms around him to give him a hug. "Abdi, what would we do without you," I said gleefully.

"And us without you, Dr John."

"Where are they? We need to celebrate. Can we see them, Abdi?"

"All in good time. Not too much attention you understand. There are some in the town who might not agree with this."

"And you say all of them?"

"I think so. We will know more by tomorrow. But there is one person we must see tonight," decreed Abdi.

That evening, I stood by the bedside of Ali Interpreter. He opened one eye and nodded gently to acknowledge our presence. Although now free, he did not look well. He had no obvious signs of being beaten, but he was very thin and looked anaemic. He lay in bed coughing with beads of sweat pouring down his brow. After a brief examination, it was clear he had a severe chest infection, probably pneumonia. I just hoped he had not caught TB.

His wife sat in the corner of the room, almost in disbelief that he was at home. She was holding their baby boy, Muuse, who was now one year old. They both looked well, considering what they had been through.

Ali opened both eyes, and he took a sip of water. "You're back," he spluttered, almost inhaling the water.

He held out his hand, which I took, and gave it a gentle squeeze. "It's you that is back, back, and a free man."

"You came back for my 'payback' of course," he said, trying to muster a cheeky grin. "How can I ever thank you?"

"By getting well as quickly as possible. We need you back at work. And no more qat!" I instructed, waving my finger.

Following the release of the SCF and hospital staff, the screams at night from the neighbouring detention centre coincidentally stopped. I will never know if the staff were released due to my meeting with the Major, or whether this would have happened anyway. Equally, we didn't know if it was just our neighbouring detention centre that had taken action to stop the beatings, or if it had stopped in other detention centres too. It was impossible to tell.

From that night on, I slept more peacefully. However, there were some nights, I would still wake up dreaming of the noises. This prolonged experience had affected me more than I realised.

32.

MALARIA, MENINGITIS, AND MILITIA

"They've taken the tortoise," exclaimed Jama, as I walked through the gate of the SCF compound.

"Who? Where?" I asked.

"Men with guns, this afternoon."

"Probably to kill it for meat," suggested Jo. "Not sure why they would want to take it otherwise." She shrugged her shoulders. "Things are getting desperate, if they need to steal the tortoise."

Axmed Lab stood by her side, listening. He was thoroughly enjoying his role as her interpreter. I had to admit he was doing a truly fantastic job. With his previous training and knowledge, Jo would often need to say very little before he would launch into questions for the patients. He still preferred his nickname of Axmed Lab, even though I guess he was now Axmed Interpreter.

As before, he was also enjoying being a mentor to the team concerning anything to do with local culture, and religion. He was now training to become a Sheikh, and often came to the house dressed in his white Sheikh robes. Our evenings were made more enjoyable with his injections of infectious positivity.

"I don't think so," he said with an air of authority. "Eating tortoise is prohibited in the Koran," he concluded. After a brief pause, he continued. "But I too have no idea why they would steal a tortoise."

The only pet left was the cat, which was sitting on the steps of the house. He still followed me around the compound, but he seemed to miss his short early morning walks part way to the hospital. Now, I only travelled to work by Land Rover. It was too far to walk to the camp regularly. The cat would follow me down the steps to escort me to the vehicle, and then follow the vehicle to the gate as we drove out of the compound. He would then return the short distance to his favourite spot on the steps and lie in the morning sun.

There was a storage tent in the compound, and today the cat had discovered a mother mongoose with her babies. They were all tightly packed together, behind large storage boxes.

"What do we do now?" asked Jo, looking at Josh.

"Empty the boxes, as we need the contents, and put them back, I presume. Try not to disturb them," suggested Josh.

"Handy to have a resident mongoose, I guess. If there are any snakes it can catch them, and eat them," commented Jo.

"Also prohibited in the Koran," added Axmed Lab with a slight smile.

We walked into the house to eat, while Axmed Lab continued talking. What a surprise.

There was a sudden burst of machine gun fire from somewhere nearby.

"My God, what's happening?" shouted Jo.

Axmed Lab looked at his watch. "That was the execution," he declared.

"An execution?" I said with surprise. "Why?"

"It was due this afternoon. There has been a rape of a young girl in the town," informed Axmed. "The authorities wanted to make an example. They cannot allow the town to become lawless, and the family of the girl agreed."

Having seen the hordes of men wandering around the town, and the influx of qat and whisky, this should not have been a surprise. It sent a shudder through the nurses in the team, and it was a moment of truth for our NGO colleagues.

The rains eventually arrived in April. Monthly supply trips with the SCF truck to Djibouti and back would now be far more difficult. This included our mail delivery and contact with the outside world. With the rains came the flies and the mosquitos, and with the mosquitos came malaria.

The defaecation zone in the camp was a constant haze of flies. During the rains, even more refugees did not use the zone, especially at night, and they would deposit their waste closer to where people lived. The conditions in some parts of the camp were therefore very unpleasant for all.

Amongst our malaria patients were ex-pats working for the UN, and even the local Governor. Gina would have been particularly delighted, as I had to see the Governor on a home visit. He had asked personally for me to see him, and it didn't seem reasonable to expect him to come and join the dusty line in the refugee camp.

In the camp, there were several cases of cerebral malaria, with patients presenting in a delirious state with fever or even unconscious. To make matters worse, there was also an outbreak of meningitis. As patients presented with similar symptoms, it was often difficult to be clinically sure whether they had cerebral malaria or meningitis. The treatments however were very different. Initially, we decided to offer both treatments where necessary, but our medical supplies were getting low. Axmed Lab came into his element, as we decided to set up a small, temporary diagnostic lab on-site in the camp.

The situation worsened so much that Hassan Saddiq visited the camp to advise. The result was 'drastic measures for drastic situations'. There had been forty or more cases of meningitis. All the patients, and their relatives, were placed in a fenced quarantine site. However, this did not stop people wandering in and out. The RHU responded by placing armed militia guards around the site. Most patients came from a small number of zones in the camp. All residents in the affected zones were given prophylactic antibiotics to try and stop the spread of the disease. This was eventually successful.

During the outbreak, I was dragged urgently from my clinic by one of the RHU nurses to see a patient. There was a very aggressive man armed with a machete. He had already wounded one of the militia guards. The man was now cornered against the quarantine fence by a semi-circle of armed militiamen. Their guns were all poised, ready to shoot.

I looked at Jabriil, who was talking with the patient's wife.

"Ask if her husband has any previous mental illness," I instructed.

"He has not," replied the wife. "Please don't shoot him," she pleaded.

"Has he been unwell recently?"

"Yes, he has had a fever," reported the wife.

"Has he complained of a stiff neck, or about bright lights? Jabriil, come on, ask her quickly, before this situation gets any worse."

"Yes. This morning he woke with a headache," replied the wife, who was now beginning to cry with fear.

The man was getting more distraught. He had started to walk away from the fence, waving his machete in the air at the militia, who walked slowly backwards to keep their distance, whilst maintaining their aim. I wondered if this was malaria, or meningitis, affecting his mental status.

"Shall we shoot?" asked one member of the militia.

"Jabriil, please tell the militia not to shoot unless they have to. We need to make him calm. Can we get the machete from his hand, and hold him to the floor, so we can sedate him?"

Jabriil explained to the staff, and then ran off to find the medication.

I pushed my way through the circle of militiamen, and, with Idris, started to talk calmly to the patient. He was quite delirious, with sweat pouring down his face. I thought he was going to charge at us, but seeing a white man seemed momentarily to confuse him. He walked around in a circle, and lowered his machete, whilst looking over his shoulder at Idris and me. Two militiamen jumped on the patient from behind, forced the machete from his hand, and held him, kicking and screaming, on the ground.

Jabriil sprang into action, and he injected the patient. Now sedated, we took him to the quarantine tent. His blood test later proved to be positive for malaria. Under constant sedation and treatment, he amazingly made a full recovery. Once recovered, this mild-mannered father of four could not remember any of the events, and he was horrified to hear what he had done. I was more horrified that we had nearly shot him.

There were intermittent rifle shots in the camp most days. The number of armed refugees was slowly increasing. Any celebration, no matter how minor, seemed to be an excuse to let off a few bullet rounds in the air. In the clinic one day was a small girl around nine years old, who was accompanied by her father. He was pressing a bloodstained cloth over her shoulder. She had a bullet entry wound on the top of her shoulder but no exit wound. The bullet was lodged near the top of her shoulder blade. Whilst examining the girl, Idris asked the father how this had happened. The father mimicked holding a gun being fired in the air whilst cheering. One of these bullets had obviously descended and lodged in his daughter, whilst she was innocently playing outside their aqal.

I needed to talk to the elders in the camp to see if they could stop this unruly behaviour. I had been walking with Idris for a few minutes, when I heard a 'zinging' noise right by my left ear.

I looked at Idris. "Was that a bullet?"

"I think so, Dr John," replied Idris, looking a little shocked.

This was too close for comfort. "Was it meant for me?"

"Meant for you? Not in the camp. I can't see anyone would do that deliberately."

People like Idris were so loyal and protective. I truly believed that if they knew a bullet was heading my way, they would stand in front of me to protect me. His words were reassuring, but the episode was still unsettling.

Later, I sat in a large aqal and explained my concerns. Jamaal, one of the lead elders, seemed to agree, and indicated he would call a meeting to try and stop the reckless shooting in public areas. I stood up from my seat, and Jamaal waved to a guard standing outside. The guard entered, and after a brief conversation, Jamaal gestured for him to hand me his AK47.

Idris looked at me. "Jamaal asks if you would like your own AK47?"

"My own? I don't think so. Please explain I don't want to buy it, thank you!"

"Jamaal says it is a gift, the guard has others."

"A gift?" It was always more difficult refusing a gift. "Please tell him he is very generous. But I'm not sure it's sensible, or safe for me to accept."

Jamaal shrugged his shoulders, and he sent the guard back outside.

"Dr John," said Idris. "Jamaal says this world will get worse. You may regret your decision today. If you ever need any help, you only need to ask."

"Tell him thank you, he is very kind. I will."

Back at the SCF house, we had visitors. Brad and Hassan Saddiq were waiting in the dining room. Brad sat next to a full ashtray, and a small but unopened bottle of whisky. His serious face implied he had bad news for the team.

"Late yesterday, some of the Dutch team were kidnapped in their vehicle."

"Our understanding is that they were taken over the border, and later released in Ethiopia," added Hassan Saddiq. "Obviously, the vehicle was the main prize."

"I presume everything is OK here?" enquired Brad.

The team all looked around at each other, and they nodded reassuringly.

"Good," said Brad. "I think you are much safer working in the camp. As the hospital is primarily used by the military, this is just the sort of reason why we didn't want to return to work there."

"The UN staff are starting to get nervous," commented

Hassan Saddiq. "Following some sort of celebration in the town, a few gunshots were fired."

I interrupted. "But that happens all the time."

"Yes, but these must have been close to the UN compound. They panicked and called on the radio, inferring they might need to be evacuated. So, we, and others, have been asked to assess the situation."

"We are fine here, really," remarked Josh, who was sitting listening to his tape of Spanish classical guitar music.

"We just want to get on with our jobs," said Jo.

"I can see that," replied Brad. "The Dutch team are naturally more rattled by this. The taken staff will not be coming back or replaced. The remaining members of their team are seriously considering their position. They may leave."

"Which will put more pressure on your SCF team," said Hassan Saddiq.

"Changing the subject, I was due to visit, anyway," said Brad, in a more positive tone. "Your contracts are coming up for review. Not exactly the best timing I know. But I need to offer extensions to you all for three to six months. We need to ensure the smooth running of the camp."

Following the news about the Dutch team, this caused a lively debate. The SCF team were all committed and hardworking, but for some this was their first time overseas. Josh and I were a little surprised by the discussions. I don't think either of us had a full grip on the strength of feeling in the team. Jo and I both knew what we were missing compared with our earlier time in Somalia. We were having no picnics in Amuud, no visits to see friends, no walks in the countryside or mountains, and no breaks in Djibouti. The work was also far more relentless. But it was extremely rewarding. I suppose I had also become a little desensitised to the levels of danger. The 'completer-finisher' in me once again held up its hand. My mission was only partly accomplished. Although SCF and hospital staff were out of prison, they were not yet safe.

The only takers for the contract extension were Josh, Jo, and me. The rest of the team were much more unsettled by the local situation, and they wanted to go home at the end of their contracts. They would all be leaving in June and July.

I could see Brad was disappointed. "Relief work is full of three-to-six-month contracts," he commented. He then looked at Jo and me. "I was lucky with you and the team in Borama Hospital. It was more stable then. You had time to settle in the town, get to know each other, and things were looking good. This situation is all quite heartbreaking."

Most of the team went to bed. For the first time, I joined Brad in a glass of whisky. Hassan lit a cigarette. "Can I congratulate you?"

"For what?" I asked, turning to Hassan and spluttering as I tried to swallow the shot of whisky.

"On getting the staff released. Even I couldn't have achieved that. How did you do it? Whom did you talk to?"

I felt uneasy, and I was unsure what to say. How did he know that I might be responsible for their release? Although he was from the South, I presumed Hassan was a good man, a friend, and an ally. But I was beginning to question many things that were happening around me. My inner circle of trust was becoming very small. You could never be completely sure who knew who, who was related to who and their underlying politics.

"I have my contacts," I smiled, giving nothing away. "Useful contacts."

Towards the end of the month, it seemed the majority of men in the town, and the camp, were armed. The qat trade was booming. Soldiers at checkpoints often had retracted eyelids and green teeth, not only from the night before, but were still chewing qat on duty in the mornings. This made navigating military checkpoints more anxiety-provoking. In the camp, following our hard work in the feeding centres, the levels of malnutrition seemed to be reducing. But the size of the cemetery was steadily growing.

It had been a particularly emotional day for the team. We'd had two difficult cases. The first was a mother who had been in obstructed labour for over a day, when she arrived at our clinic. Her foetus was lying in a difficult position. Both mother and baby were struggling. The mother had three other young children to look after, and she had lost her husband. After a very difficult time, including manipulation of the foetus and using forceps, we delivered a dead baby. Always upsetting. Mother survived, but she had lost a lot of blood.

The second case was another pregnant woman, who had originally presented a few days previously. Following a very long labour, the mother was unable to deliver her placenta after the birth of her baby. She was bleeding badly, and this required me to manually remove the placenta. After this, she developed a severe infection, and, despite our best efforts, she had also died that morning.

To add insult to injury, during a late morning ward round in the hospital observation tent, a gale with a whirlwind hit the tent, and ripped it from the ground. The tent was thrown in the air, and it landed broken several metres away on its side. It all happened so quickly that the patients had no time to move. All the mothers and children were still sitting in rows on the floor. They all looked at each other with blank faces, and then gazed into the blue sky over them. Fortunately, not one person was injured, and they all burst into hysterical laughter.

Later that day, just before dusk, Idris took the team to the teashop for a deserved drink. We were quite a large group, so it was unusual for half of the customers to be white. We had been sitting for a few moments, when I overheard a conversation in a nearby group of young men. I didn't understand everything, but I had heard enough to know they were being rude about 'white people'.

It had been a difficult day, I was tired, and perhaps my guard was lowered.

"I heard that," I said angrily in Somali. They instantly stopped talking, and looked a little embarrassed, as they sat quietly sipping their tea.

"Time to go," said Idris, putting down his glass.

"But I haven't finished my tea," exclaimed Jo.

Idris was in no mood to listen, and he ushered us through the exit into the street. I noticed a figure standing just outside the doorway in the familiar patterned shirt and sunglasses. Idris was quietly unhappy with me. "Today you know too much Somali," he declared. "You know how the authorities do not like ex-pats understanding everything. Today you have shown the NSS officer you understand too much. You have to be more careful."

I realised he was talking sense. I now felt quite guilty for reacting as I did.

"Things are changing, Dr John," hinted Axmed Lab. "One annoyed person could mean a stray bullet comes your way."

This comment stopped me in my tracks. I'd somehow thought

I had some protective halo surrounding me, keeping me safe, but obviously not.

The following day, we were travelling from the camp back to the house. I noticed a long line of trucks. They had cargoes covered with tarpaulin sheets. Trucks normally carried a few people on top for a small fee. But today there were many more trucks with crowds of people already on top, and countless more waiting to board. Some trucks were already beginning to lean to one side.

"What's happening?" I asked Idris.

"The exodus has started," commented Idris.

"The trickle will become a flood," added Axmed Lab. "People are getting worried. Those that can get to Djibouti, or anywhere safe, will probably do so."

"These travellers include ex-pat Somalis from Middle Eastern countries. They have returned to collect any relative physically able and willing to travel," added Idris.

The route north to Djibouti was still relatively safe, with no reports of attacks or land mines. These unbelievable scenes were to become an almost daily occurrence. Those travelling included unaccompanied children. I wondered how safe this was, and what fate awaited them. One truck had just arrived from Djibouti, and it was reloading to return. Two waiting passengers turned, and they walked towards us. It was the girl we had treated with Cancrum Oris and her mother.

"The mother has come to thank you," declared Idris. "She can now eat and speak much better." The mother peeled back the headscarf to reveal her daughter's face. Both mother and daughter smiled with joy. I was amazed. Although still somewhat disfigured, and recovering from surgery, the plastic surgeons had done an amazing job. I was really pleased for her.

"Why has she returned, when everyone else is leaving?"

"They came back to collect her two other sisters from the camp. They return to Djibouti later today."

"Idris, tell them both it's great to see her looking so well. I am so pleased for her. They need to take care, and I hope they have a safe journey. Good luck in Djibouti, or wherever they are finally heading." They waved as they strolled back to the waiting truck. It was success stories like this that kept me resilient.

33.

EXODUS

It was the festival of Eid-al-Fitr in May, something for everyone to look forward to. Since their release from prison, I had been unable to visit any of the SCF or hospital staff. I had been advised that it might attract unwanted attention to them, and their safety must come first. Therefore, unlike the previous year, there was no large SCF party. This was deemed inappropriate. Instead, we were invited to Ali Interpreter's house.

He had mostly recovered from his ordeal, and he had been back at work with the SCF nurses for a few weeks. Following his experience, he had been quieter than usual, but he came to work each day and had gradually become stronger. His cheeky grin had returned, even if his cheeks still looked a little hollow. Despite its increasing availability, he had remained a qat-free zone.

He sat proudly with his son, Muuse Ali, on his knee. "I would like to make an announcement," he declared standing up theatrically from his cushion on the floor. He was holding his son with one arm, and his glass of Pepsi in the other hand. "I have decided that my son's nickname will be Muuse John in honour of Dr John." He looked around the room, and he started to raise his glass.

"A great honour I'm sure," I said, somewhat surprised.

"But is it wise to have a Christian name," enquired Axmed Lab with raised eyebrows.

"It is only his nickname. If someone can be called Lab, Theatre, TB or Aposto, why not John?" questioned Ali.

"If Dr John was still here, and known to the people in the town, then they may understand. In twenty years, the world will have changed," suggested Idris.

"And so can his nickname, if he wishes," declared Ali. "Anyway, I have made up my mind."

With that all the glasses were raised, and the Pepsi gulped down. The deed was done.

However, within just a few days, the whole world of Borama was to change.

On the 11th of May 1989, most of the trucks in the UN compound were stolen overnight. On the 12th of May, all the remaining Dutch vehicles were stolen. More trucks than ever started to set off daily for Djibouti. SCF staff and some hospital staff released from detention centres, including Dr Muktar, decided it was especially insecure for them. As I walked past today's line of trucks, I noticed that waiting passengers included familiar faces. For their safety, I couldn't say goodbye, or even acknowledge their presence. They merged in with the huge crowds boarding the trucks to avoid NSS attention, and over forty-eight hours they disappeared from the town.

On the 17th of May, Hassan Saddiq arrived unexpectedly at our house, having been brought by one of our drivers. He had cuts and bruises to his head and face, and was looking a little shaken. I presumed he'd been involved in an accident, but discovered that armed men had ambushed him for his vehicle. He had then tried to object, and prevent them from doing this. Being a high profile, and well-respected, local figure, normally he would have been safe. The armed men had been chewing qat, and Hassan had smelt whisky on their breath. The new world order did not care who he was, and nothing would stop them taking his Toyota. For me, this was a really significant event. If Hassan Saddiq was not safe, then who was?

On the 18th of May, Ali Interpreter spoke to me confidentially, as we patrolled on foot around the camp. "I can't visit your house without being noticed," he muttered. "It is safer talking here." He looked quite anxious.

"Ali, are you OK? What's the problem?"

"I wanted to thank you for everything, Dr John. I love my job, but I have to think about what's best for my family." He peered around to ensure no one was watching or listening. "I just wanted to say goodbye, whilst I have the chance."

"Will you be arrested again? Are you going now?" I whispered. I didn't know what he meant.

"I can't say when, but one day something could happen, and I may not be able to get to work. You understand. Either way, it is important for me to say goodbye, we didn't get to do this last time. Just assume I am OK. I pray you, and all of the team, stay safe."

Early on the 20th of May, I was working in the camp. I had heard that thirteen refugees were killed near to Borama. Thus far, those clans living in the camp had lived peacefully alongside those from the town, and relationships were good. What had actually happened, and the reason for these killings, was not clear.

Ali Interpreter did not come to work that day, and I was

never to see him again. I received a message via Idris. To avoid any attention from the NSS, he and his family had left during the night.

"But I didn't think any trucks went overnight?" I asked Idris.

"He didn't leave by truck, Dr John."

"Then how, Idris?"

"With the Donkey Man," declared Idris.

"The Donkey Man?" I asked, even more puzzled.

"For a smaller fee than the trucks, he takes you over the border at night."

Of course, he was a businessman, and this was a natural transition. From delivering water, to then delivering qat. But once you knew where all the minefields were, you could move on, and make money by walking people over the border at night. I just hoped they had made it safely.

On the 23rd of May, there was a high-profile visit by the UN, and an officer arrived from SCF London. There was a day of inspections and discussions with their own ex-pat teams, and local dignitaries. The UN and SCF agreed that staff could stay, with the situation to be kept under constant review.

The inspection teams left us on the morning of the 24th of May to depart from the airstrip in Borama. They were transported safely to board their plane. After take-off, their vehicles headed back to Borama town. While the vehicles were still driving through the countryside, they were sprayed with machine gun fire. One driver was killed, and all the vehicles stolen.

We waited for the inevitable. Later that day, a radio message to the UN compound ordered all ex-pats to leave immediately. Once again, this evacuation was only to include ex-pats. No local staff were allowed to go. As a team we found this intolerable, but our hands were tied, and there was nothing we could do to alter this decision.

On the 25th of May, the majority of ex-pat staff, including most of the SCF nursing team, were evacuated to the airport under army escort. Josh, Jo, and I were to remain, along with a small number of UN staff. We would all be evacuated the following day. It was made clear by the UN and SCF London that we would not be returning in the foreseeable future, if ever.

I had twenty-four hours to try and complete my action list. I had things to do and people to see. That day, with the help of SCF and RHU staff, we emptied the house. We sorted a minimum amount of clothing and belongings to take out with us. Everything else was given to the local staff, including any money we had. We distributed most of the drugs to the camp medical store. This was now under armed militia guard to protect any remaining supplies. I kept a small box of essential drugs to take with me to see Abdi.

It was too unsafe to travel around the town, including to the hospital, by myself. I sent a message for Abdi to come to the house, and he arrived very soon after. "Before you say anything Abdi, let me say that at the moment everything is definitely not OK."

"You are right, Dr John. This is indeed a sad day. I have seen many things in my life, but this is probably the worst day for Borama."

I gave him the box of medication for the hospital. "Here Abdi, supplies are low, so I'm giving you what I can. Keep them safe for emergencies." He nodded.

He took off his hat, and for the first time, Abdi the man who had lived through and seen everything, began to weep. I put my arm around his shoulders.

"Abdi, what are you going to do?"

"I still have the hospital to look after. This is my home. In truth, Dr John, I have nowhere else to go. All my family here have died or are long gone."

I wanted to put him in my pocket and smuggle him out, but of course it was his beloved hospital that had kept him going all these years.

"The hospital will now need you more than ever. I think we should rename it, The Abdi Aposto Hospital Borama." He tried to raise a smile. With that he said goodbye, and with watery eyes, he walked out of the house. I presumed this was to be the last time I would ever see him. I went to the door. I gave a sigh, as I watched him descend the steps and go into the street for his short walk back to the hospital.

We travelled to the camp. I was very worried about all the staff. Idris was sitting calmly by my side in the Land Rover, looking at the scenery, as if nothing had changed. I wondered what was really going through is mind.

"What are you thinking, Idris?"

"That I will miss you all," he replied, without emotion.

"Idris, what are you going to do? Do you need any help? Do you need any money to get on one of the trucks?"

"I don't have any family in Djibouti, and Ethiopia is no longer my home. If I go back, I could get conscripted into the army and be on the front line in Eritrea. Little point. This is now my home, and there are others who need your money more than me. I will stay here, at least for now," he declared despondently.

So many people had helped me whilst in Borama, but Idris

was my protector. In practice, I could do little to help him. I felt completely helpless. He finally agreed to accept some money and clothing, once we were back at the SCF house.

There was a great commotion in the camp. A group of elders were waiting to meet with us, including Jamaal.

"Jamaal is asking if you are actually going," translated Idris.

"The answer is yes, tomorrow. But we have brought whatever supplies we have. They need to keep them secure," I instructed.

"He says you are their doctor and their nurses. What are they to do without you?"

"You will still have the RHU staff," I said, pointing to Jabriil and his team, who were standing nearby. "They are among the best."

What came next was a complete surprise.

"He wants you to come and live in the camp," declared Idris.

"Live in the camp?"

"Yes, live in the camp. He has thousands of armed men, and no one will dare to enter the camp to cause any problems. It will be very safe for you."

I noticed we were surrounded by dozens of armed militiamen. I wondered if they would be desperate enough to keep us in the camp against our will.

"Tell him I'm very sorry, but we have to leave."

Jamaal looked visibly dismayed.

"He says this is truly a sad day for us all."

I turned to Jabriil and his team. "Take care. It has been a real pleasure, and an honour to work with you all. You will be the health leads now. Use the stores wisely." I was going to miss the staff here. They were such a dedicated bunch, and a delight to work with. In the short term, I was sure they would carry on looking after their people. However, I wasn't sure how they would cope, when the food supplies and medicines ran out in a few weeks' time.

We headed back to the SCF house. Just outside the camp, I stopped the vehicle on the mound of a hill. I climbed out. I stood for one last lingering look into the distance, and over the camp. It was like a sea of aqals. What was to become of all these people? What was their future? I returned to the vehicle despondently, and I continued back to the house.

It had been a dusty day. I stood in the shower room, washed my face, and looked in the mirror. Walking around the camp, going up and down all the hills each day, at this altitude, had made my face look very weathered. Even so, physically, I was probably the fittest I had ever been.

As a team we had achieved so many things, including saving countless lives, safely delivering thousands of babies, and training dozens of health care workers. But there was always more to be done. At last, after two and a half years, the 'completer-finisher' in me had to realise that I wouldn't achieve all I'd wanted to do. As I had frequently told Cathy, you cannot save Somalia by yourself. Also, I had probably now used up most of my nine lives. I just hoped I had one more left to get out of the country safely. I had to accept it was finally time to go home.

The only items now remaining in the house were mattresses to sleep on the floor, and chairs to sit on while eating our last supper together. Jo was trying to stay calm reading a book, whilst Josh sat listening to his favourite Spanish classical guitar music for the last time. "Not sure anyone will really appreciate this type of music," he said, whilst tapping his hands and feet to the rhythm. "I'll find a space in my case. But I'm sure someone will love my stereo. But who to give it to?" He glanced at Idris and Axmed.

Jama appeared in the doorway, looking flustered. "Dr John, please come," he said, waving me to the door. "There are armed men at the gate."

Not knowing what lay ahead for us we followed Jama to the compound gate, which was still closed. In the dusk, standing outside the gate, was Jamaal with a small army of men. There were at least fifty in number.

"What's he saying?" I asked Idris who had fortunately joined us.

"He asks if you have changed your mind. He has come to escort you to the camp. It will be safer."

I really believed that this time we would be taken to the camp, whether we wanted to go or not.

"Tell Jamaal that we still have to leave tomorrow. As head of the militia, surely he understands. Those are our orders; our orders are to leave."

"He says even if you are only staying for one night, it will still be safer in the camp."

He could be right, and I was not entirely sure what to do. My main concern was that if we went to the camp this could send the wrong message, and it may be difficult to then leave tomorrow. I looked at Josh and Jo for help. It was clear they both wanted to stay in the house.

"Tell Jamaal our absence tonight could cause unnecessary alarm, should anyone call to check on us from the UN. Although we are taking a risk, I think it is best we stay here." Idris turned to Jamaal and explained.

"Jamaal says in which case the camp must come to the house."

I wasn't sure what he meant by this, as he swiftly gave orders to his men. About half of them peeled away, and they started to walk around the house.

"What is he doing?" I asked.

"They are forming an armed protective ring around the house," replied Idris.

Was this a good or bad idea? It might draw attention from the town.

"Please explain that we don't want any of his men to be put at risk or harmed by doing this. I realise that he wants to protect us, but perhaps it's better to take his men back to the camp."

"He says the town is much more dangerous than you think. SCF have looked after his people, now they must look after you. No one is going to be allowed to harm you. It is an honour to protect you tonight."

He was obviously determined that his men should stay, and he would not be swayed otherwise. Although I was worried, this commitment to our safety demonstrated such devotion. Idris decided to stay with us for our last night, and he slept in a spare room. Axmed Lab said a short goodbye, and he quickly disappeared into the dark night. The militiamen sat around the house all night, taking it in turns to stay awake. Jama and the boys could take the night off.

The circle of militiamen was still present, and they started to stir in the early morning light. I could hear quiet, padding footsteps down the hallway. I opened my eyes to see Jama standing in the doorway. He wanted everyone awake, so he and the other guards could move the mattresses and remaining furniture into the guardhouse.

Within a short time, the house was finally empty. I checked my watch. We had two hours before the agreed pick-up time by the UN, when Axmed Lab appeared in the doorway. All that was now left in the dining room were two large empty cardboard boxes. We turned them upside down to sit next to each other. I looked around the bare room. Slowly wafting between us was a light hanging from the ceiling, with an old Indian lampshade. It was a little worn and a little faded. It was the first time I had really looked at it, and I noted the intricate patterns made from the knotted beige string. It all made a sad departing scene.

I looked across at Axmed. "Thanks for coming, it means a lot."

"I came to greet you on your very first day in Borama, remember?" said Axmed.

"I do, I remember it very well, Axmed."

He tried to raise a smile. "Therefore it is only proper, and fitting, that I come to see you on your very last day here too."

We both sat staring sadly at the floor, not knowing what to say next. It was the first time I had seen Axmed short for words.

Eventually, he spoke. "Well, here we are, Dr John. I am trying to be positive, I really am. But today I feel very low. You are leaving us, and I wish you Godspeed. But for us here, I cannot think what is to become of us. I am so worried, so worried for everyone."

Idris walked into the room.

"Idris, you are coming with me, to live with me and my family," exclaimed Axmed. "Much safer than living by yourself."

"Very kind and most generous. If it doesn't work, we can always move to the camp. Jamaal has already offered sanctuary there," said Idris.

"And if that doesn't work?" I asked.

"That problem is for another day, Dr John, not now," said Axmed. "We must try to remain positive."

"That's great!" exclaimed Josh, entering the room. "I don't have to make my big decision, you can both share the stereo," and he handed it over to them.

We were joined by Jo, and all moved to sit on the steps of the house. The pet cat came to nestle by my side. He seemed to know something was not quite right today. Outside the house, Deeqa and the three guards were all waiting anxiously. Jabriil had also travelled out from the camp, and Jamaal was already standing with his men. I took out my camera, and I turned to Idris. "I know this isn't exactly the best of circumstances, but can I have a picture of everyone?" They all huddled up on the steps, and they tried their best to raise a smile. Even the cat stood to attention.

I walked across to Jama. I reached inside my bag, and I pulled out my short wave radio. "Here Jama, it's for you and the other guards." He looked at me, delighted.

"You can listen to the BBC Somali world service, but don't tell the NSS."

He scanned around to ensure no one was looking over the compound walls, and he sneaked into the guardhouse to hide his new present.

There was a tooting noise at the gate. The UN vehicle had arrived to take us to the airstrip, accompanied by two army vehicles. One-eyed Hussein opened the gates, and the vehicle entered. The line of militia guards reluctantly parted to let it through.

"I'm not great at goodbyes," I said as my eyes began to water. I scanned the team, who looked forlorn. "It has truly been a great honour to work with you all. My time here has been all the better for knowing and working with you. You have made this my home, and you are my family here. This is probably the last time we shall see each other. So, I hope and pray that you all stay safe, remain well, and importantly look after each other." I stopped. Emotionally, it was all too much. I couldn't say anymore.

Just as on my return six months previously, I departed the same way, by walking down the line, and shaking everyone's hands. Josh and Jo said their own goodbyes to everyone and joined me at the vehicle. As we were about to climb in, Jama walked to stand in front of us. He stood to attention, and he gave us his best military salute. I wiped a tear from my eye, and I saluted back. I turned, waved to all the team, and got into the vehicle, followed by Josh and Jo.

Jamaal and his men were reluctant to hand us over to the army escort, but eventually they parted, allowing us to pass through into the street and make our way to the airstrip. It was still relatively early in the morning. The road was quiet and the journey uneventful. A small Fokker twin prop, with about twelve seats, was sitting on the tarmac. There were two empty UN vehicles, waiting nearby. They had already delivered their passengers, who were waiting to board.

Standing by the plane was Major Yussuf with a handful of soldiers.

"Safe journey," he said to everyone, as they were being ushered into the plane.

I stood for a moment. "Thank you for everything Major," I said as I shook his hand. "A safe journey for you, your family and your country."

"Goodbye Governor, and Godspeed to you all," said the Major, as he gave me a military salute.

Once inside, we sat calmly in our seats. There was little conversation, as we waited for our departure. The plane took off promptly, and it soared into the blue sunlit sky. This was a very different evacuation to the previous one from Hargeisa.

I looked out of the window, as we circled once over Borama town, before heading to Garowe. Somewhere below in Borama was our house. The house was patiently waiting for a new owner, a new owner during a time of peace and stability. I wondered who and when that would be.

I could make out the hospital below. There was a small man wearing a hat standing on the veranda. He rushed into the hospital forecourt, took off his hat, and frantically waved it at the plane overhead. I waved back to 'The Man with the Keys', even though Abdi would not see me.

My mission was over. I had met some amazing people. Some extraordinary characters that had made this place feel like my home. Like the rest of the world, Somalia is full of ordinary people. Each of them, in their own ordinary way, is trying to do their best for their family and themselves, despite what goes on around them. But, just like the rest of the world, Somalia has some extra-ordinary people, who in their own unselfish way, despite encroaching adversity and the world collapsing around them, are also doing their best for their community. It is people like these who make this world a place worth living in. Some had left the horrors behind to try and find a new life. Others had stayed on with their people and their home, despite all the risks. Just like Abdi Aposto, I take off my hat and salute them all. I salute them, whatever happened to them, and wherever they are now.

AUTHOR'S NOTE

This section is not intended to be a full summary of recent Somali history.

On the 1st of July 1960, the former Italian and British Somalilands were unified to form a new independent Somalia republic. Following unification, many people in the north of the country thought they were not treated fairly. The government was dominated by people from the south, especially those from the clan of the president. In response to the perceived nepotism and subjugation of northern Somalia, the Somali National Movement (SNM) was formed in 1981 with an office in London.

In 1988, the Somali civil war first started in northern Somalia. It led to the eventual collapse of the Somali government with the President, Siad Barre, being ousted in 1991. UN peacekeepers were deployed in December 1992 but left in March 1995.

On the 18th May 1991, local authorities in North West Somalia, led by the Somali National Movement (SNM), unilaterally declared independence. The self-declared state of the Republic of Somaliland was formed with similar borders to those previously held by British Somaliland, with Hargeisa as the capital. Within this republic, Borama is the largest town of the Awdal region.

There has been no international recognition of independence for the Republic of Somaliland, and they are considered an autonomous region of Somalia.

As they strive to build their future, they continue to seek international recognition.

GLOSSARY

AK47	Assault rifle (Avtomat Kalashnikova 1947)
BBC	British Broadcasting Corporation
CV	Curriculum Vitae
FGM	Female Genital Mutilation/Female Circumcision
HTA	Help the Aged (NGO)
MSF	Médecins Sans Frontières (NGO)
NASA	National Aeronautics and Space Administration in USA
NGO	Non-Governmental Organisation
NSS	National Security Service (Somali Secret Police)
Oxfam	Oxford Committee for Famine Relief (NGO)
RHU	Refugee Health Unit (in Somalia)
RAF	Royal Air Force in UK
SCF	Save the Children Fund (NGO)
SNM	Somali National Movement
TB	Tuberculosis
TBA	Traditional Birth Attendant

UN	United Nations
UNHCR	United Nations High Commission for Refugees
UNICEF	United Nations Children's Fund
WHO	World Health Organisation

ACKNOWLEDGEMENTS

First and foremost, thank you to my wife and children for being there to motivate me and for supplying copious cups of tea while I was living in a darkened room writing my book.

To everyone at Troubador for their help and support in bringing my story to print.

To Jericho Writers, and especially Edward F, for supporting me and reviewing my manuscript.

To Rachel O, who helped me correct my use of grammar to make it 'betterer'!

To SCF, for offering me the post in Somalia and for being a great employer. Without this, I would not have had the opportunity of a lifetime.

To all my friends who supported me going to Somalia, writing all their letters while I was there and having the stamina to listen to all my stories on my return.

To my proud parents, who supported me over the years, but who are sadly not around any longer to read the book they encouraged me to write.

To the people of Borama, who provided most of the stories, looked after me, and kept me safe.

To Liverpool Medical School, who gave me a chance to be a doctor and develop an early interest in tropical health.

To the NHS, who trained me, employed me, and kept me safe during Covid so that I could finish my book.

But especially, I would like to thank all the local unsung heroes in Somalia, wherever they are now, who provided the inspiration for my book.

ABOUT THE AUTHOR AND LIFE
AFTER SOMALIA

I went to Liverpool Medical School and qualified in 1980. We were taught that being a doctor was not just a job, not just a profession, but it was a vocation. It required study, yes, but much more than that. It required hard work, dedication, and integrity. Like most naive young doctors of the day, I was to go out and 'save lives'. But I was not sure which specialty I would choose to 'save lives', or where I would live and work in the future. Should I be a surgeon, a general physician, another form of hospital consultant, or a general practitioner (GP)? What I did not anticipate is that at one point in my life the most important thing I would do to 'save lives' would be to distribute blankets and plastic sheets to thousands of the most needy.

After qualification, I worked as a hospital medical registrar in Jamaica and Australia from 1982-1984, and I then returned to the UK to complete my GP vocational training. Following this I went to work for SCF in Somalia from 1986-1989, where I had my blanket and plastic sheet moment.

My experience overseas in Jamaica, and East Africa, highlighted that the health of the population is not simply down to the health service and its staff. So, on my return to the UK, I decided to retrain as a consultant in public health medicine. My biggest dilemma was not seeing patients face to face anymore. I suffered withdrawal symptoms, and finally came to terms with this after six months. The instant rewards of seeing patients were replaced by more long-term work and goals. With my newly acquired public health knowledge and skills, I realised that if I were posted to Somalia again, I would have approached my post very differently.

I worked for the NHS in this new capacity from 1990-2018, in the East Midlands of England, before retiring. During these years, I retained my Somali passion for clinical guidelines. I trained many budding consultants, and I taught both undergraduates and postgraduates the principles of Public Health, including what to expect if they decided to work overseas. I also had the honour of being selected by the NHS to represent them at an NHS 60th Anniversary celebration held by the Queen at Buckingham Palace.

Sadly, I was never able to convince the powers that be about the benefits of 'Dr John's papaya dressing'. There was one exception, a grateful dermatologist, who successfully treated many long-term patients in his leg ulcer clinic, with the help of the local supermarket, who regularly supplied the papaya.

You may be wondering about some of the other characters in this book. Shortly after leaving Somalia, Cathy and Jo worked in refugee camps in Ethiopia, close to the Somali border, where they came across many SCF staff and others who were now refugees in that country. Cathy, Gina, Jo, and Sally also worked for SCF in other parts of the world, but they later settled in the UK, working for the NHS. Brad continued to work in East Africa. Some characters have now retired in the UK.

HOW TO LEAVE A REVIEW

Thank you so much for taking the time to read *Noises After Dark* and I hope you enjoyed it. If you have any time and wouldn't mind leaving a review so that more people can find and read my book, that would be greatly appreciated.

You can do this by leaving a review on the following link to the Troubador website (https://bit.ly/3U6DaaG).